D1766041

Egypt

WORLD BIBLIOGRAPHICAL SERIES

General Editors:
Robert G. Neville (Executive Editor)
John J. Horton   Ian Wallace
Hans H. Wellisch   Ralph Lee Woodward, Jr.

John J. Horton is Deputy Librarian of the University of Bradford and currently Chairman of its Academic Board of Studies in Social Sciences. He has maintained a longstanding interest in the discipline of area studies and its associated bibliographical problems, with special reference to European Studies. In particular he has published in the field of Icelandic and of Yugoslav studies, including the two relevant volumes in the World Bibliographical Series.

Ian Wallace is Professor of Modern Languages at Loughborough University of Technology. A graduate of Oxford in French and German, he also studied in Tübingen, Heidelberg and Lausanne before taking teaching posts at universities in the USA, Scotland and England. He specialises in East German affairs, especially literature and culture, on which he has published numerous articles and books. In 1979 he founded the journal *GDR Monitor*, which he continues to edit.

Hans H. Wellisch is Professor emeritus at the College of Library and Information Services, University of Maryland. He was President of the American Society of Indexers and was a member of the International Federation for Documentation. He is the author of numerous articles and several books on indexing and abstracting, and has published *The Conversion of Scripts* and *Indexing and Abstracting: an International Bibliography*. He also contributes frequently to *Journal of the American Society for Information Science, The Indexer* and other professional journals.

Ralph Lee Woodward, Jr. is Chairman of the Department of History at Tulane University, New Orleans, where he has been Professor of History since 1970. He is the author of *Central America, a Nation Divided*, 2nd ed. (1985), as well as several monographs and more than sixty scholarly articles on modern Latin America. He has also compiled volumes in the World Bibliographical Series on *Belize* (1980), *Nicaragua* (1983), and *El Salvador* (forthcoming). Dr. Woodward edited the Central American section of the *Research Guide to Central America and the Caribbean* (1985) and is currently editor of the Central American history section of the *Handbook of Latin American Studies*.

VOLUME 86

Egypt

Ragai N. Makar
Compiler

CLIO PRESS
OXFORD, ENGLAND · SANTA BARBARA, CALIFORNIA
DENVER, COLORADO

© Copyright 1988 by Clio Press Ltd.

All rights reserved. No part of this publication may be reproduced, stored in any retrieval system, or transmitted in any form or by any means, electronic, mechanical, photocopying or otherwise, without the prior permission in writing of the publishers.

British Library Cataloguing in Publication Data

Makar, Ragai N.
Egypt.—(World bibliographical series; v.86).
1. Egypt.—Bibliography
I. Title   II. Series
016.962   Z3651

ISBN 1–85109–039–8

Clio Press Ltd.,
55 St. Thomas' Street,
Oxford OX1 1JG, England.

ABC-Clio Information Services,
Riviera Campus, 2040 Alameda Padre Serra,
Santa Barbara, CA 93103, USA.

Designed by Bernard Crossland
Typeset by Columns Design and Production Services, Reading, England
Printed and bound in Great Britain by
Billing and Sons Ltd., Worcester

THE WORLD BIBLIOGRAPHICAL SERIES

This series, which is principally designed for the English speaker, will eventually cover every country in the world, each in a separate volume comprising annotated entries on works dealing with its history, geography, economy and politics; and with its people, their culture, customs, religion and social organization. Attention will also be paid to current living conditions – housing, education, newspapers, clothing, etc. – that are all too often ignored in standard bibliographies; and to those particular aspects relevant to individual countries. Each volume seeks to achieve, by use of careful selectivity and critical assessment of the literature, an expression of the country and an appreciation of its nature and national aspirations, to guide the reader towards an understanding of its importance. The keynote of the series is to provide, in a uniform format, an interpretation of each country that will express its culture, its place in the world, and the qualities and background that make it unique. The views expressed in individual volumes are not necessarily those of the publishers.

VOLUMES IN THE SERIES

*To my teachers
in Egypt and the United States,
with gratitude*

Contents

Contents

Contents

Introduction

Egypt, which is situated in the Northeast corner of Africa and in Southwest Asia, abuts the Mediterranean Sea in the North and has borders with Libya to the West, with Sudan to the South and with Israel to the Northeast. The great mass of the nation is situated in Africa; the Sinai peninsula is located in Asia and is separated from the rest of the country by the Suez Canal. Geographical factors, however, have always meant that Egypt does not offer an easy route between Asia and Africa. The country covers some 385,000 sq.m. of which barely 13,000 sq.m. are inhabited. Some 96% of its territory is desert. The narrow valley of the Nile runs through Egypt from south to north, fanning out into the Delta towards the Mediterranean. The dividing line between cultivation and desert is very abrupt, and on either side of the river valley the land is extremely arid except for the Mediterranean coastal fringes. A series of oases in the Western Desert permits agricultural settlement using underground water, but otherwise cultivation is possible only in the Nile Valley and Delta, and it is in these areas that 99% of Egyptians live. The seaports, Alexandria and Damietta, and the Canal towns, Suez, Ismailiya and Port Said are the other centres of habitation. Cairo, the capital, is much the largest city with an estimated population of some 7 million, and the area of Greater Cairo contains some 10-12 million inhabitants. Alexandria is the second city with a population of 2.3 million. The River Nile, the nation's lifeline, traverses Eastern Egypt for about 900 miles (1,450 kms.) and in the South Lake Nasser, a huge artificial lake impounded by the famous Aswan High Dam (built between 1960 and 1970) stretches for some 300 miles down into the Sudan. The dam is at the heart of a major, and enormously beneficial, irrigation and hydroelectric power project, although the lake did result in the total displacement of the Nubian communities living along the Nile valley above the Dam, who were re-settled in

Introduction

Upper Egypt, and the flooding of a number of important archaeological sites, including Abu Simbel. The building of the High Dam, which has had some adverse ecological effects in spite of its benefits, put a final end to the annual Nile inundation which, until the various irrigation schemes of the 20th century, had been a feature of Egyptian agricultural life for thousands of years.

Travel up and down the Nile has always been relatively convenient for those in control of the entire country, but until the advent of the aeroplane, to defend the Nile Valley from attack from any quarter has not required great military superiority. Throughout its history, Egypt has been concerned with events in the Sudan to its south, lying across the river on which its existence depends, and with the territories to its east. Egypt has at times dominated southern Syria, and at other times been conquered by rulers of this area, but has never been able to afford to ignore its neighbours in this direction. Relations with the Libyans, whose sparsely inhabited country is separated from the Nile by the expanse of the Western Desert, have, on the contrary, been largely a matter of routine, although the Fatimids established their rule over Egypt from a power base in North Africa.

The country's population totals about 50 millions representing an admixture of various peoples from Asia and Africa. Some 90% of the population is Muslim with Coptic Christians and others forming the remaining 10%. Islam is the state religion, and the Copts comprise much the largest religious minority. Arabic is the official and national language but English and French, as well as Nubian and Berber dialects, are also used; illiteracy remains high at about 60%. Despite an increase in industrialization in recent years, agriculture remains the most important economic activity employing some 40% of the labour force and producing nearly half of the nation's exports. The most significant cash crop is cotton and Egypt is one of the world's main cotton producers. The production of petroleum is the country's main industrial export and supports a growing refining industry. Other important industries include iron, steel, textiles, sugar, cement and armaments. The main sources of hard currency for Egypt are the Suez Canal, tourism, oil, expatriate labour and, more recently, arms exports. The high rate of population growth (approx. 2.7% per annum) places a strain upon Egypt's economic resources, and feeding the nation has been a major policy concern of all post-war governments.

The present constitution, which was approved by a referendum on 11 September 1971, and amended in 1980, declares that Egypt is an 'Arab Republic with a democratic socialist system of government'. It provides for an executive president nominated by the People's Assembly and confirmed by plebiscite for a six-year term. The president is supreme commander of the armed forces and also presides over the defence council. Moreover, the president appoints ministers to the cabinet (ministers are responsible to the president) and determines policy, which the cabinet implements. The unicameral legislature is the People's Assembly (458 members, 448 of which are elected and 10 appointed by the president). The constitution reserves 50% of the seats in the Assembly for workers and peasants and 31 seats for women. The Assembly sits for a five-year term but can be dissolved by the president. There is also a National Consultative Council (Shura Council) which has 210 members and which serves in an advisory role. In addition to the national Democratic Party, which holds the majority of seats, there are five legally established parties: the New Wafd Party; the Socialist Labour Party; the Nationalist Progressive Union Grouping; the Socialist Liberal Party; and the Umma Party. In addition, the constitution guarantees the independence of the judiciary (religious courts were abolished in 1956 and their functions transferred to the national court system) and freedom of the press, the latter somewhat cautiously exercised. At the local level the country is divided into twenty-five governorates, each headed by a governor appointed by the president; local councils, which have administrative functions, are responsible to the governor.

Egypt's long history as a nation may be said to begin early in the third millennium BC with the first unification of the country from the Mediterranean to the First Cataract – traditionally by a king "Menes" at the start of the 1st Dynasty. Although an oversimplification, the usual division of dynastic Egyptian history into three periods of greatness (the Old, Middle, and New Kingdoms) when art and architecture flourished, interspersed by "Intermediate" periods of disunity and hardship, is broadly justified. To set against this is the amazing continuity of ancient Egyptian culture, perhaps arising partly from the unique configuration of the Nile Valley. To speak, as many have, of an Egyptian "Empire" – even in the case of the New Kingdom – would be an exaggeration; nor should the later periods of dynastic history be seen simply as ones of decay and foreign control. Foreign peoples had frequently entered Egypt and become assimilated; the first truly foreign rule, and one widely resented at the time, was that of the First Persian Domination. The invasion of Alexander the Great in 332 BC liberated Egypt from the Second Persian Domination, and thrust the country into a major role in the Hellenistic world, a role maintained with diminishing success by the Ptolemaic kings of Greek descent.

Roman rule of Egypt was a period of unsympathetic control and exploitation. Alexandria's pre-eminence as a centre of scholarship and, later, theology, steadily declined, but late-Roman and early-Byzantine Egypt was the cradle of organized monasticism. In AD 640 the country was conquered by Muslim Arabs and became a province of the Caliphate. Egypt has remained part of the Islamic world ever since, its fortunes fluctuating in mediaeval times with the rise and fall of the various Islamic dynasties.

In 1517 Egypt was overwhelmed by the Ottoman Empire and it nominally remained under the rule of the Turks until 1914, although in 1798 it was invaded by Napoleon. This event is generally regarded as the starting point of modern Egyptian history, as it opened Egypt to Western influence and penetration. Napoleon was subsequently driven out by the British. Egypt became virtually independent with the accession of Muhammad Ali in 1805 and as a result of revolts against the Sultan in 1832 and 1839 it obtained the status of an autonomous hereditary principality. It was under Khedive Ismail Pasha that the Suez Canal was completed (1869) and thirteen years later Egypt was occupied by the British, who had shared dual control of the country with the French (1879-82). The British consolidated their authority between 1883 and 1907 when Evelyn Baring, Lord Cromer, was Consul General and *de facto* ruler. By 1904 France, Italy and Austria had all agreed not to prevent Britain from staying in Egypt indefinitely.

A British protectorate over Egypt was declared on 18 December 1914 and this lasted until 28 February 1922 when Sultan Ahmed Fuad was proclaimed King of Egypt and the country became independent, although issues of British military occupation and the Sudan were only settled by treaty in 1936, leaving the British military presence intact. Egypt was neutral in World War II but in September 1940 was invaded by the Italians who were driven out by the British in December 1940. In November 1941 the Germans invaded Egypt and in June-July 1942 they reached Al-Alamein where they were defeated by the British and the Allies in one of the most important battles of the war.

After World War II, Egypt clashed with the newly formed state of Israel (1948-49) and in July 1952, following a military coup d'état, King Farouk abdicated in favour of his infant son, who became King Ahmed Fuad II. However, in June 1953 the Revolutionary Council deposed the young king and a republic was established. Neguib faced increasing domestic opposition and in February 1954 resigned and Nasser took over full power the following November. There followed a period of tension. There were continuing troubles with Israel, particularly over Gaza, and Nasser began to contemplate trade agreements with communist countries. As a result, Great Britain and the United States withdrew offers of financial assistance for the building of the Aswan High Dam. In retaliation, Nasser nationalized the Suez Canal Company and appointed an Egyptian Suez Canal Authority to administer the waterway. By doing this Egypt precipitated a confrontation with Britain and France aided by Israel that led to the events of October-December 1956, better known in the West as the Suez War and in Egypt as the Tripartite Aggression.

Nasser's nationalization of the Suez Canal Company and expulsion of the British made him a national hero who had finally achieved Egypt's true independence by ridding it of foreign occupation. The failure of the invasion and withdrawal of foreign troops greatly enhanced his prestige in the whole Arab world. However, Nasser's championship of Arab nationalism under Egyptian leadership amid mounting tension with Israel finally led him to disaster in the Six-Day War of 1967, during which Israel invaded the Sinai for the second time and occupied the peninsula. In the Yom Kippur War of October 1973 Egypt attempted, unsuccessfully, to recapture the territory it had lost in 1967. However, Sinai was returned to Egypt in April 1982 as a consequence of the treaty which had been concluded in 1979 following the Camp David Accords between President Sadat (Nasser died of a heart attack in September 1970) and the Israeli leader, Menachem Begin, which had formally terminated a 31-year state of war between the two countries. President Sadat was assassinated on 6 October 1981 by a group of Muslim militants and was succeeded by his Vice-President, Husni Mubarak. In October 1987 the Egyptian people elected President Mubarak with a large majority for a second six-year term.

Egypt is by far the largest Arab country in terms of population (double the size of Morocco, the nearest rival) and by virtue of this, its geographical position, and its relatively advanced state of socio-economic development, has naturally occupied an important place in the post-war Arab world. From a position of leadership at the peak of Nasser's power, Egypt found itself almost totally isolated after signing the treaty with Israel. Only in the late 1980's, after much patient diplomacy, is it gradually restoring its links with the Arab world. As of 1988, Egypt has resumed diplomatic relations with most Arab countries but is yet to be fully rehabilitated.

The bibliography

Egypt's long and varied history, the richness of Ancient Egyptian civilization, and the modern nation's pivotal role in Middle Eastern affairs have all ensured that the country has attracted a great deal of interest and study. Accordingly, the literature is enormous, and the task of selecting the 1,022 items for inclusion in this bibliography was extremely difficult. In line with the general objectives of the *World Bibliographical Series*, most (95%) of the publications listed are in the English language. The bibliography aims to cover Egypt from the beginnings of its history to the present day, but the basis of the selection of material on the periods before the Arab conquest is deliberately more limited than that applied to the mediaeval and modern periods. For Ancient Egypt and Christian Egypt down to AD 640, apart from the standard works of reference and bibliographies, items have been chosen as being either of interest to the general reader, or of use for comparative work in the social sciences or the humanities. The hundreds of excavation reports, of museum catalogues, and of text-editions which form the backbone of any specialist library therefore do not feature here. There also exists a large periodical literature devoted to the earlier periods; this is generally of a detailed and technical nature, and no attempt has been made to represent it, or to list all the relevant journals. For the period since the Arab conquest, the choice of items of periodical literature has been wide-ranging but highly selective, and the most important periodicals are indicated in the relevant section. More space has been devoted to books and monographs. As far as I am aware, no up-to-date, multidisciplinary, selective, annotated bibliography of Egypt is currently available and I hope, therefore, that this volume will be a valuable reference tool for many groups of users who wish to gain an overall understanding of the country.

Acknowledgements

Although I am the compiler, this bibliography in fact represents a Marriott Library project. Indeed, many of the works selected were available in the University of Utah Marriott Library which houses some 2.25 million volumes and which has an excellent Middle East collection. It would have been impossible to compile the bibliography without the encouragement and support of Dean Roger K. Hanson, Director of the University of Utah Libraries, and Dr. Gregory C. Thompson, Assistant Director for Special Collections. I would like to thank both of them for their encouragement of research within the Library Faculty. I would also like to thank Dr. Lee L. Bean, Director of the University of Utah Middle East Center, for his support and personal interest in this project and a previous library project. I am also indebted to Professor Aziz S. Atiya, distinguished Professor of History at the University of Utah, for his helpful suggestions and to my wife, Professor Lois Giffen, for her continual moral support and encouragement. Judy Jarrow of the Middle East Library and Linda Burns of the interlibrary loans section of the Marriott Library also contributed a great deal to this work through their efficient assistance.

Ragai N. Makar
August, 1988

Chronology

For Ancient Egypt, the table attempts to show some of the commonest terminology used in English at the present, but variations will be found. For some writers, the Old Kingdom begins only with the 4th Dynasty, and for others the Middle Kingdom ends with the 12th. Some include the 25th Dynasty in the Third Intermediate Period: the later term has only recently come into widespread use, and terms such as 'Late Dynastic' are often found applied to the whole period from *c.* 1080-332 BC.

The modern division of pharaonic Egyptian history into numbered 'dynasties' derives from garbled excerpts from the lost history of the Egyptian priest Manetho, who wrote in Greek early in the Ptolemaic period. His primary source was corrupt copies of traditional Egyptian king-lists (fragments of various such compilations survive), which listed families or successions of kings together with the length of each reign. The ancient Egyptians made virtually no use of the idea of a fixed era, and dates in the past could be expressed only by specifying the regnal year of a named king. The many problems posed by this tradition include the fact that contemporary or overlapping royal houses were freely included in the lists, and some subsequent misunderstandings are perpetuated in our apparent sequence of dynasties.

Modern attempts to ascribe absolute dates to earlier pharaonic history depend upon a complex critical re-evaluation of this same tradition, assisted by excavated evidence of all kinds (very uneven in geographical and chronological distribution), and by a few astronomically fixed dates (unfortunately open to a range of interpretations). Debate upon chronological problems continues (the date for the start of the 1st Dynasty listed here is 200 years lower than that which twenty years ago seemed to be becoming established orthodoxy and general opinion may yet come to favour a slightly lower date still). Obviously, therefore, dates before 664 BC are approximate; thereafter, direct links with for example Greek chronology mean that in principle dates may be determined with certainty. Before the Middle Kingdom, it might be prudent to allow a margin of error of up to 100 years. For the Middle Kingdom, present uncertainties suggest a margin of 50 years, and from the New Kingdom onwards few dates are likely to be wrong by more than 20 years. Radio-carbon and other scientifically determined dates are essential for pre-history and useful for predynastic history. Although they are of increasing reliability for the dating of objects from the dynastic period, they are hardly likely to become sufficiently precise to be decisive in work upon dynastic chronology itself.

Muslim historiography of the Islamic period chronicles events according to the Hijri calendar, which takes as the starting-point of the Muslim era the date of Muhammad's migration (Hijrah) from Mecca to Medina on 16 July 622 of the Christian era. As the Muslim year is a lunar one of 354 days, it is steadily advancing on the Christian solar year of 365/6 days, so that Hijri years never coincide exactly with Christian years. In the chronology, Hijri (AH) dates are given in brackets after Christian dates.

PREDYNASTIC PERIOD
The earliest of the various cultures of predynastic Egypt can be traced back to roughly 5000 BC.

EARLY DYNASTIC PERIOD or Protodynastic or Archaic Period

about 2900-2650 AD	1st-2nd Dynasties

OLD KINGDOM

about 2650-2590 BC	3rd Dynasty
about 2590-2475 BC	4th Dynasty
about 2475-2330 BC	5th Dynasty
about 2330-2175 BC	6th Dynasty
about 2175-2150 BC	7th-8th Dynasties

FIRST INTERMEDIATE PERIOD

about 2150-2050 BC	9th and 10th Dynasties (ruling from Herakleopolis) and early 11th Dynasty (Thebes)

MIDDLE KINGDOM

about 2050-1991 BC	later 11th Dynasty

about 1991-1785 BC	12th Dynasty
about 1785-1660 BC	13th-14th Dynasties

SECOND INTERMEDIATE PERIOD

about 1660-1555 BC	15th-16th Dynasties: Hyksos rulers
about 1660-1555 BC	17th Dynasty: Theban kings

NEW KINGDOM

about 1550-1320 BC	18th Dynasty

The 'Amarna Period' flourished about 1377-1361 BC

about 1320-1200 BC	19th Dynasty: earlier Ramesside kings
about 1200-1080 BC	20th Dynasty: later Ramesside kings

THIRD INTERMEDIATE PERIOD

about 1080-945 BC	21st Dynasty: capital at Tanis
about 945-715 BC	22nd Dynasty: Libyan dominion
about 818-715 BC	23rd Dynasty: limited rule from Leontopolis
about 727-715 BC	24th Dynasty: limited rule from Sais and Memphis

LATE PERIOD

about 747-656 BC	25th Dynasty: Kushite, or Ethiopian or Nubian Dynasty

In full control of Egypt about 715-664 BC

664-525 BC	26th Dynasty: Saite kings
525-404 BC	27th Dynasty: First Persian Domination
404-399 BC	28th Dynasty: originating from Sais
399-380 BC	29th Dynasty: originating from Mendes
380-343 BC	30th Dynasty: originating from Sebennytos
343-332 BC	31st Dynasty: Second Persian Domination

GRAECO-ROMAN PERIOD

332-305 BC	Egyptian rule of Alexander the Great and his successors as kings of Macedon
305-30 BC	The Ptolemies
30 BC-AD 395	Roman rule

The Coptic calendar reckons the number of the year from the accession of Diocletian (AD 284: the Era of the Martyrs), in memory of the severe persecutions of his reign.

AD 325	Council of Nicaea: condemnation of Arianism

BYZANTINE PERIOD

AD 395	Division of the Roman Empire: Egypt ruled from Constantinople
AD 431	Council of Ephesus: condemnation of Nestorianism
AD 449	"Robber Council" at Ephesus: unruly behaviour of Egyptian monks – development of split between Alexandria and Constantinople over the nature of Christ
AD 451	Council of Chalcedon: condemnation of the Alexandrian Patriarch Dioscorus – most of Egyptian Christianity henceforward in schism from the Catholic Church of the Eastern Empire: hardening Egyptian adherence to Monophysitism
AD 616	Persian (Sassanian) occupation of Egypt
AD 628	Death of Sassanian king Chosroes: return of Egypt to Byzantine rule
AD 639-642	Arab conquest of Egypt

ISLAMIC CALIPHATE

AD 640-661 (AH 19-40)	"Orthodox" or "rightly-guided" Caliphs: ruling from Medina

AD 661-750 (AH 41-132)	Umayyads: ruling from Damascus
AD 750-1258 (AH 132-656)	Abbasids: ruling from Baghdad

From 868 Egypt was sometimes ruled autonomously or independently

AD 868-905 (AH 254-292)	Tulunids: Turkish dynasty in Cairo
AD 905-909 (AH 292-297)	Abbasid rule restored from Baghdad
AD 909-935 (AH 297-323)	Fatimids: Shi'ite anti-Caliphs ruling from North Africa
AD 935-969 (AH 323-358)	Ikshidids: Turkish dynasty in Cairo
AD 969-1171 (AH 358-567)	Fatimids: from North Africa moved to rule from Cairo
AD 969	Founding of Cairo
AD 1171-1250 (AH 567-648)	Ayyubids: Kurdish dynasty of Salah al-Din (Saladin)
AD 1261-1517 (AH 659-923)	Abbasid Caliphs of Cairo: nominal rulers only
AD 1250-1382 (AH 648-784)	Bahri Mamlukes: Turkish dynasty
AD 1382-1517 (AH 784-922)	Circassian (Burji) Mamlukes

OTTOMAN PERIOD

AD 1517 (AH 922)	Ottoman conquest of Egypt
AD 1517-1879 (AH 922-1297)	Ottoman rule from Constantinople
AD 1798-1801	Napoleon's invasion of Egypt
AD 1805-1953 (AH 1220-1372)	Muhammad Ali's dynasty in Cairo
AD 1869	Suez Canal opened
AD 1879-1936	British control in Egypt
AD 1914-1922	British Protectorate
AD 1952	Free Officers' coup

REPUBLICAN PERIOD

AD 1953	Egypt declared a republic
AD 1954-1970	President Nasser
AD 1959-1961	Union with Syria (United Arab Republic
AD 1970-1981	President Sadat
AD 1979	Treaty with Israel
AD 1981-	President Mubarak

Glossary

Abbasids

The descendants of Abbas Ibn Abdul Mutta-lib, an uncle of the Prophet Muhammad. The great-great-grandson of Abbas overthrew the Umayyad caliphate in 750 AD and founded the Abbasid caliphate. His brother succeeded him and founded Baghdad, which became the caliphal seat of his descendants until it was captured and destroyed by the Mongol Hulagu in 1258. This dynasty saw the highest development of the caliphate, during what is recognized as the Golden Age of Islam.

Akh,
pl. ikhwan

Brother.

'Alim,
pl. 'ulema

An expert, one who knows – used, especially in the plural, to indicate those trained in Islamic Law, and holding a diploma from a teaching institution, such as al-Azhar University in Cairo.

Amir,
pl. umara'

Prince; Mamluke of high rank; distinguished notable.

Ayyubids

The descendants of Saladin (Salah al-Din al-Ayyubi) (d. 1193). The Ayyubids ruled in Egypt, Syria and northern Iraq. They were replaced in Egypt by the Mamlukes in 1250.

Bedouin

Refers generally to Arabic-speaking camel nomads in the Middle East and especially in the Arabian peninsula, but also present in Egypt.

Bey

A Turkish official rank; inferior to pasha (qv). It was given to the Mamluke chiefs who ruled as suzerain princes in Egypt and Syria.

Glossary

Copt	The English words 'Copt(ic)' and 'Egypt(ian)' both derive from the Greek terms for Egypt and its people (Aigyptos, Aigyptios) which in turn come from the Egyptian Hikuptah, an alternative name for the city of Memphis. 'Copt' came into English through Arabic Qibt, which nowadays is used of the Egyptian Christians, members of the Coptic Church.
Deir	Monastery or convent, used for Christian institutions.
Divan (Arabic Diwan)	A word with a long history and various meanings; it was generally used in 19th-century Turkey to signify a secretariat, a department, or a council.
Effendi	Turkish title given to educated persons who were generally government employees.
Eid al-Adha	The Muslim Festival of Sacrifice, which occurs at the time of the Hajj (Pilgrimage to Mecca).
Eid al-Fitr	The festival of the breaking of the fast, at the end of Ramadan, the month of fasting.
Feddan	Measure of land equivalent to 4,201 square metres or just over one acre (1.038 acres).
Fellah, pl. **fellahin**	Peasant.
Firman	A decree of the Turkish Sultan.
Hijrah	The migration of Muhammad and his followers from Mecca to Medina (then called Yathrib) in 622. At Medina the political and social aspects of Muhammad's revelation came to complete fruition. Starting-point of the Islamic calendar.
Imam	A religious teacher. Most often, the term refers to a leader of services in the mosque. In Shi'ism, the term also refers to the leader of the Shi'ite community.
Infitah	The open-door economic policy initiated by President Sadat in 1974.
Jihad	Holy War. This term refers to the obligation of the faithful to extend the *umma* (qv) and protect it from its enemies. *Jihad* has been variously interpreted as actual warfare or spiritual struggle.

Kekhia	An official in both Mamluke and Turkish times whose position was that of a second-in-command, a deputy or a lieutenant, to a more senior official.
Majlis al-shura	An advisory council.
Millets	The religious groups given official status in the Ottoman Empire. In matters of civil conflict among members of the same millet, the conflict would be resolved by the traditional authorities and processes of the respective millet. Thus a Christian man was governed by Christian laws in his dealings with Christians regardless of his physical location in the Ottoman Empire.
Miri	From *amiri*, of the ruler; refers to land over which the government has certain rights. Is also a tax, mainly a land tax.
Mudir	Governor of a province (*mudiriya*).
Muhafaza	Province, under a Governor, formerly called a *mudiriya*.
Nahda	Renaissance.
Omdeh	Village mayor.
Ottomans	Founded by the Turkish leader Osman, the Ottoman state gave rise to the last great Islamic caliphate. Centred in Anatolia, the empire lasted from its founding in the 13th century to the first decade of the 20th century.
Pasha	Title given to certain high civil and military officials in the Ottoman Empire and its provinces. All such titles were cancelled in Egypt in 1952 and were replaced by one title, al-Sayyid (Mister).
Ramadan	The Muslim month of fasting, and one of the lunar months of the Muslim calendar. Fasting during the daylight hours of Ramadan is one of the five 'pillars' of the ritual obligations of Islam.
Ramadan Crescent	New moon that rises on the eve of Ramadan, and signifies the beginning of the month.
Shaikh, pl. mashayikh, shuukh	Elder; bedouin chief; religious dignitary; holy man. *Shaikh al-balad* means a village headman, or native Egyptian.

Glossary

Sham el-Nassim
Arabic for smelling of the breeze. Refers to an Egyptian feast to celebrate the coming of the spring which falls on the Monday after Easter.

Shari'ah
Religious law of Islam.

Shi'ites
The branch of Islam holding the belief that the true successor to the Prophet was the fourth caliph 'Ali and that the imamate (or caliphate) belongs rightly to his successors. Differs on various points of doctrine from the orthodox Sunni majority. Shi'ism, which is concentrated largely in Iraq and Iran, is divided into several different sects.

Sunna, sunnah
Literally a path or way, a manner of life. This term refers to the tradition which records either the sayings or doings of the Prophet Muhammad. The adjectives Sunni and Sunnite are derived from it. All Egyptian Muslims are Sunnis.

Sunnites
The main or orthodox branch of Islam.

Tanzimat
An Arabic and Turkish word meaning reforms, arrangements; commonly used to indicate collectively the 19th-century modernizing and Europeanizing reforms in the administration of the Ottoman Empire. From an Arabic root meaning 'to put in order'.

Umayyads
One of the most powerful and important of the Arab families at the time of Muhammad. The Umayyad caliphate was founded at Damascus by Muawiya, who succeeded to the caliphate in 661 after the death of 'Ali, the last of the four Rightly Guided Caliphs.

Umma
The worldwide community of Islam, which ideally commands a Moslem's loyalty above all considerations of race, kinship, or nationality.

Vali
Turkish word (Arabic: wali) meaning ruler or provincial governor, directly responsible to the sultan.

Vizier
Turkish word (Arabic: wazir) indicating an office of Persian origin whose holder, in Abbasid times, conducted the affairs of state.

	In the Ottoman Empire of the 19th century the grand vizier was roughly equivalent to prime minister, except that, like most Ottoman officials, he was often entrusted with military command. Nowadays wazir means a cabinet minister.
Waqf	Endowed property not subject to normal transactions, its income being assigned by the founder; also covers the act of endowing *waqf*. Refers to religious endowments usually made in perpetuity, which support a specific institution devoted to good works, such as a *madrasah*, a home for orphans, or a religious building.
Zakat	One of the five pillars of the Islamic faith, the obligation on the faithful to support the unfortunate and the needy.

The Country and Its People

1 **Politics and change in the Middle East: sources of conflict and accommodation.**
Ray R. Anderson, Robert F. Seibert, John G. Wagner. Englewood Cliffs, New Jersey: Prentice-Hall, 1982. 307p. 16 maps.

The authors, an economist, a political scientist and a cultural anthropologist, believe that a proper understanding of present events in the Middle East requires a knowledge of the cultural, social and economic as well as the political background of these events. The present work is directed at an audience not specifically acquainted with the Middle East, and Egypt is included as a case study in almost every chapter of the book.

2 **The Middle East remembered.**
John S. Badeau. Washington, DC: Middle East Institute, 1982. 280p.

The author describes in these memoirs half a century of dramatic change and his personal involvement in the events that shaped the modern Middle East. As diplomat, scholar, educator, and missionary, Badeau brings a unique series of different perspectives to bear on the Muslim world, on his role as ambassador to Nasser's Egypt, and in his unvarnished views of Egyptian personalities.

3 **Shahhat: an Egyptian.**
Richard Critchfield, foreword by George M. Foster. Syracuse, New York: Syracuse University Press, 1978. 278p.

This work is the fruit of more than two years spent living as a participant observer in an Upper Egyptian village near Luxor with the family and neighbours of Shahhat, a young *fellah*. It describes in detail, and with an intimacy that is missing from purely academic accounts, the 'fearful and wonderful' life of the Egyptian peasant, a life that is still essentially like that of his ancestors under the pharaohs

1

The Country and Its People

4 **Directory of government and public sector, 1984/86.**
Cairo: Arab Modern House for Foreign Trade, 1986. 477p.

A personnel directory of the government ministries, the public sector companies affiliated to them, of airline companies, foreign banks, tourist companies, and the management of American, British, German, Swedish, Japanese, Italian and other foreign companies in Egypt. Contains addresses of all these organizations.

5 **Egypt.**
Cairo: Lehnert & Landrock; Paris: Editions Marcus, 1976. 408p. maps.

A guide for tourists and students, covering the land and the people, the history of Egypt, Egyptian art and civilization, holidays, Cairo, Alexandria, Luxor, Aswan, the oases and information by region.

6 **The rape of the Nile: tomb robbers, tourists and archaeologists in Egypt.**
Brian M. Fagan. New York: Charles Scribner's Sons, 1975. 399p. map. bibliog.

A vividly written popular account of travellers, collectors, and archaeologists in Egypt from ancient times up to the early 20th century. The substantial second part (p. 95-248) deals with Belzoni and his contemporaries.

7 **Egypt: land of the valley.**
Robin Fedden. London: Michael Haag, 1986. 158p. map. bibliog.

A popular narrative history of Egypt from the earliest times to the Nasser revolution, but chiefly dealing with modern Egypt; first published in 1977 (London: John Murray). Contains illustrations and a brief chronology.

8 **The legacy of Egypt.**
S. R. K. Glanville. Oxford, England: Clarendon Press, 1942. 424p.

Contains fifteen chapters, each written by a specialist, and mostly designed to serve as an introduction for the general reader and student to various aspects of Ancient Egypt, including literature, art, science and technology, law, and the Egyptian contribution to Christianity and Islam. For the completely rewritten second edition, see item no. 145.

9 **The discovery of Egypt.**
Leslie Greener. London: Cassell; New York: Viking Press, 1966. 216p.

This popular but informative book traces the antecedents and early history of Egyptology from the interest taken in monuments of the past by Khaemwese, son of Ramesses II, down to an account of the life of the Egyptologist Mariette (died 1881).

10 **Modern Egypt: studies in politics and society.**
Edited by Elie Kedourie, Sylvia G. Haim. London: Frank Cass,
1980. 136p.

This volume contains eight papers on aspects of modern Egypt, originally
published in a special issue of *Middle Eastern Studies*, vol. 16, no.
2 (May 1980);
the papers are: 'The first Egyptian student mission to France under Muhammad
Ali', by Alain Silvera; 'The Near East in the balance of power: the repercussions
of the Kaulla Incident in 1893', by Gordon Martel; 'The consequences of the
introduction and spread of modern education: education and national integration
in Egypt', by Mahmud A. Faksh; 'Agricultural technology and rural social classes
in Egypt, 1920-1939', by Alan Richards; 'The dilemma of a liberal: some political
implications in the writings of the Egyptian scholar, Ahmad Amin (1886-1954)',
by William Shepard; 'The Iranian settlement in Egypt as seen through the pages
of the community paper *Chihrinima* (1904-1966)', by Mohammad Yadegari; 'Al-
Muwailihi's criticism of Shawqi's introduction', by Mattityahu Peled; and 'Urban
élites and the foundation of municipalities in Alexandria and Istanbul', by Steven
Rosenthal.

11 **Portrait of Egypt.**
Lord Kinross. New York: William Morrow, 1966. 104p.

Consists of four parts which cover respectively Ancient Egypt, Christian Egypt,
Mediaeval Egypt, and Modern Egypt. Interesting and informative reading.

12 **Egypt in transition.**
Jean Lacouture, Simonne Lacouture, translated from the French by
Francis Scarfe. London: Methuen; New York: Criterion Books,
1958. 532p. map. bibliog.

History of modern Egypt from the French campaign of 1798 to the Suez War of
1956. The authors concentrate on the national movement and the 1952 revolution.

13 **Manners and customs of the modern Egyptians.**
Edward William Lane. Cairo: Livres de France; London: East-
West Publications, 1978. Reprint ed. 584p.

First published in 1836, Lane's classic account is still a standard reference work
not merely for the period in which it was written, but for Egyptian, and especially
Cairene, life today, since many beliefs and practices he describes have relevance
for modern times. The 5th edition of 1860 was the last to incorporate corrections
by the author, and therefore is often cited. The 1895 edition, of which this is a
reprint, was particularly well produced and included not only the forty-five
standard illustrations, but also twenty-three full-page engravings omitted from the
cheaper editions.

14 **Egypt.**
Tom Little. London: Ernest Benn, 1958. 334p. map. bibliog.
(Nations of the Modern World).

A readable and sound history of Egypt, principally concerned with rising
nationalism in Egypt under British rule, the background to the coup in 1952, and
Nasser's early years in power.

15 **The land and people of Egypt.**
Zaki Naguib Mahmoud. Philadelphia; New York: Lippincott,
1959. 127p. (Portraits of the Nations Series).

In his first eight chapters the author presents a brief narrative history of Egypt
from the earliest times to the present. The following six chapters discuss Cairo
and Alexandria, agriculture and the countryside, modern industry, the combatting
of illiteracy, women and family life, science, literature and art. Excellent reading
for young people.

16 **The Middle East and North Africa.**
London: Europa Publications, 1948- . annual.

An annual general survey of the region with a section on regional organizations
and a section on each country. A good quick reference source. The section on
each country contains information on the physical and social geography of that
country, its history, economy, statistical survey, directory and bibliography.

17 **The Middle East contemporary survey, 1976/77-**
Tel Aviv, Israel: Tel Aviv University, Dayan Centre for Middle
Eastern and African Studies, Shiloah Institute; Boulder, Colorado:
Westview Press, 1978- . annual.

An annual record and analysis of political, economic, military and international
developments in the Middle East. The series provides scholars, diplomats and
students with a continuing up-to-date record of the rapidly changing events in the
Middle East. Each volume is arranged in two parts; the first includes studies
relating to internal and external issues, both regionally and internationally, and
the subjects explored in detail include Israeli-Arab and inter-Arab relations. The
second part comprises a country-by-country survey which covers the foreign
affairs of each country. Each volume includes several maps.

18 **MERI Report: Egypt.**
Middle East Research Institute, University of Pennsylvania.
London: Croom Helm, 1985. 211p.

An informative report about the country. Chapter one provides background
information, while chapters two to four present respectively political analysis,
economic analysis, and a statistical appendix. The statistics relate to defence,
demography, economy, banking and finance, budget and planning, debt, energy,
industry, agriculture, trade, labour, transport and communications, health,
education and welfare.

19   **Eternal Egypt.**
Pierre Montet, translated from the French by Doreen Weightman.
London: Weidenfeld & Nicolson, 1964. 338p. maps. bibliog.
A general introduction to the civilization and religion of Ancient Egypt.

20   **The land of Egypt.**
Jasper More.   London: Batsford, 1980. 164p. 3 maps.
The first four chapters of this book present an overview of Egyptian history from
Mena to Sadat. The author then provides a description of the Delta and Lower
Egypt, Cairo, Luxor, Karnak, Thebes and Abu Simbel.

21   **The Egypt story: its art, its monuments, its people, its history.**
P. H. Newby, photographs by Fred J. Maroon.   Cairo: American
University in Cairo Press [c.1984]. Reprinted 1985. 259p. (A
Chanticleer Press Edition.)
A beautifully illustrated work which covers the subject in a concise narrative
manner.

22   **Egypt: a country study.**
Edited by Richard F. Nyrop.   Washington, DC: Department of the
Army, 1983. 4th ed. 313p. maps. bibliog. tables.
A well-researched, comprehensive study of the history, geography, politics,
economics and national security of Egypt. Appendices B, C and D give the texts
of the peace agreement with Israel, the Camp David accords, and the peace treaty
itself.

23   **Directory of social scientists in Egypt.**
Aziza Rashad. Cairo: American University in Cairo Press, 1961.
324p.
A who's who of social scientists in Egypt, including all those holding at least a
master of science degree or its equivalent in the following areas: anthropology,
economics, education, geography, history, political science, law, psychology,
public administration, management, social service, sociology, statistics, and
related fields.

24   **Who's who in the Arab world 1986-1987.**
London: Butterworth; Santa Barbara, California: ABC-Clio;
Beirut: Publitec Publications, 1986. 8th ed. 1432p.
The only biographical dictionary for the modern Arab world, in which Egypt is
well represented. Part I contains more than 5,000 biographical sketches of
outstanding personalities and leading national figures; part II presents a country-
by-country survey of the 20 Arab countries; part III gives an outline of the Arab
world.

25 **United Arab Republic of Egypt: its people, its society, its culture.**
    Donald N. Wilber, with the assistance of Fahim Iqubain, Helene L.
    Boatner.   New Haven, Connecticut: Human Relations Area Files,
    1969. 461p. map. bibliog. (Survey of World Cultures, 14).

Covers the culture, history, geography, education, social structure, economics,
agricultural resources and domestic and foreign trade of Egypt, discussing in
detail the changes introduced as a result of the 1952 revolution up to the Arab-
Israeli war of 1967.

Middle East Review.
See item no. 1019.

Geography, Maps and Geology

26 **Environmental profile of Arab Republic of Egypt.**
Arid Lands Information Center. Tucson, Arizona: Office of Arid Lands Studies, University of Arizona, 1980. 108p. maps. bibliog.

A draft environmental report on Egypt prepared for the U.S. Man & the Biosphere Secretariat, Department of State, as part of a series on different countries. The report reviews the information available on the status of Egypt's environment and natural resources, and the major environmental problems it faces, which are: soil damage and loss; water pollution; health hazards (especially water-borne diseases); and pests and weeds (mostly resulting from the introduction of perennial irrigation).

27 **Contributions to the geography of Egypt.**
John Ball. Cairo: Ministry of Finance, Survey and Mines Department, 1939. Reprinted, 1952. 308p. map.

The first chapter of this book presents a brief general view of Egypt. The eight following chapters deal successively with the geographical changes that have taken place in Egypt during past geological ages, the river terraces of the Nile Valley and the evidence they furnish as to past changes in the relative levels of land and sea in the Egyptian region, the high-level (Early Sebilian) silts of the Nile Valley in Upper Egypt and the evidence for the former existence of a great lake in the Sudd region of the Sudan, the solid matter transported by the Nile in solution and suspension respectively, the alluvial land of Egypt, the physical history of the Faiyūm and its lake, and the Birket Qarun fishery. An important contribution to the study of earlier Egypt by the same author was *Egypt in the classical geographers* (Cairo: Government Press, 1942).

Geography, Maps and Geology

28   **The geology of Egypt: an annotated bibliography.**
Farouk el-Baz.   Leiden, The Netherlands: E. J. Brill, 1984. 778p.
This volume provides summaries of published books and papers, in addition to
unpublished theses and reports. The term 'geology' is used in the broadest sense
and the book includes entries of interest not only to geologists, but also to
geophysicists, environmentalists, hydrologists, soil scientists, oceanographers,
marine scientists, biologists and chemists. Each entry comprises a complete
reference citation followed by an abstract.

29   **The High Dam and the transformation of the Nile.**
Richard Elliot Benedick.   *Middle East Journal*, vol. 33, no. 2
(Spring 1979), p. 119-44.
An account of Egyptian attempts to control the waters of the River Nile,
culminating in the construction of the High Dam in the mid-1960s. In spite of the
obvious benefits of the project, it had many ecological drawbacks. It also had
chemical and biological side-effects. The author explains these problems in detail.

30   **The Middle East and North Africa: a political geography.**
Alasdair Drysdale, Gerald H. Blake.   New York; Oxford: Oxford
University Press, 1985. 353p. maps.
This book is intended to serve two objectives simultaneously: to enrich
understanding of political phenomena within the Middle East and North Africa by
offering a spatial perspective, and to help to fill a noticeable gap in the political-
geographic literature of the region. The political geography of Egypt is well
covered throughout the book.

31   **Dams, people and development: the Aswan High Dam case.**
Hussein M. Fahim.   New York; Oxford: Pergamon Press, 1981.
169p. bibliog.
In this book, the author draws together his studies of the Aswan High Dam since
1963. He also examines, at both the conceptual and the policy levels, issues and
problems pertinent to the interrelationships between dams, people, and
development. He views dams as engineering works constructed to serve people,
and although they inevitably have technical specifications and requirements, he
believes their potential humanistic implications should neither be overlooked nor
underestimated: since dams are often associated with development, a task
involving a complex and longitudinal process of concept-making, strategy-building
and implementation, people should form a central theme and a basic element in
this process.

32   **The oases of Egypt.**
Ahmed Fakhry.   Cairo: American University in Cairo Press, 1973-
74. 2 vols.
These volumes by a well-known Egyptian archaeologist provide descriptions of
archaeological discoveries and details of the author's personal experiences as a
traveller and observer, relating them to the accounts of previous travellers in the
area. The result is a survey of the oases' geography and ethnography as well as

their archaeology. Volume one covers Siwa Oasis, volume two covers Bahriya and Farafra Oases. Fakhry never completed a more ambitious project for larger-scale reports on the oases: see *Bahria oasis* (Cairo: Government Press, 1942–52. 2 vols.) and *Denkmäler der Oase Dachla aus dem Nachlass von Ahmed Fakhry* (Mainz am Rhein, FRG: Philipp von Zabern, 1982).

33   The Middle East: a physical, social and regional geography.
William B. Fisher.   London: Methuen, 1978. 7th ed. 596p. maps. bibliog.

A classic study of the geography of the Middle East. The physical, social and regional aspects of the geography of Egypt are discussed in detail along with those of other countries.

34   The Nile: a general account of the river and the utilization of its waters.
H. E. Hurst.   London: Constable, 1952. 326p. map.

A non-technical account of irrigation practice, the different regions of the Nile and the people who depend on it, its hydrology and the various projects that have been proposed to exploit it.

35   Landforms of Egypt.
M. S. Abū al-'Izz, translated by Yūsuf A. Fāyid.   Cairo: American University in Cairo Press, 1971. 282p. 60 maps.

Focusing on the morphology of Egypt's land surface, this book utilizes a regional approach, dividing the country into a number of morphological units each of which is further subdivided. Specific discussions cover the Nile Valley, the Delta, the Fayum, the Western Desert and Sinai, thus providing a reconnaissance study of Egypt's geology and physical geography that points towards a new scheme of geomorphological classification.

36   High Dam at Aswan: the subjugation of the Nile.
Tom Little.   London: Methuen; New York: John Day Company, 1965. 242p. map.

Tells the story of Egypt's struggle to realize its project to build the High Dam – both to secure the financial resources and to construct it. This book also describes the 'doomed land', the Nubians' evacuation and resettlement, and efforts to record and salvage monuments which were to be drowned, of which the most famous is the temple at Abu Simbel.

37   The Nile: the life-story of a river.
Emil Ludwig, translated by Mary H. Lindsay.   London: Allen & Unwin, 1950. 687p. maps.

A detailed description, originally published in 1937, of the River Nile from its Central African sources in Western Ethiopia, Uganda and the Sudan to its mouth at Damietta and Rosetta in Lower Egypt. A 'biography' of the river by a great writer.

38 **Atlas of Christian sites in Egypt.**
Otto Meinardus.   Cairo: Société d'Archéologie Copte, 1962. 7p.
6 maps.

The (rather small-scale) maps in this atlas cover the Nile valley in Egypt and
selected parts of the Eastern Desert and Sinai. The author, drawing upon his own
extensive travels, indicates inhabited, uninhabited, and ruined monasteries,
pilgrim churches, ancient basilica, inhabited and uninhabited hermitages, etc.,
and sites visited by the Holy Family according to Christian or Islamic tradition (cf.
item no. 372). More pretentious series of maps, of varying quality, covering this
period may be found in Wilhelm Berg, *Historische Karte des alten Ägypten* (Sankt
Augustin: Hanz Richarz, 1973); Wolfgang Kosack, *Historisches Kartenwerk
Ägyptens; altägyptische Fundstellen, mittelalterliches arabisches Ägypten,
Koptische Kultur (Delta, Mittelägypten, Oberägypten)* (Bonn: Rudolf Habelt,
1971); and among the publications of the *Tübinger Atlas des Vorderen Orients*
(Wiesbaden, FRG: Reichert, 1977-). See also item no. 127.

39 **The Cairo Nilometer: studies in Ibn Taghri Birdi's chronicles of
Egypt, 1.**
William Popper.   Berkeley, California: University of California
Press, 1951. 269p. bibliog.

A study of the annual rise of the Nile as measured in the well of the Nilometer on
Rauda (Roda), an island in the Nile at Cairo. The author deals in general terms
with the records of the rise during the twelve and a half centuries from 641 to
1890 AD, and in greater detail with those of the first eight centuries of that
period, especially those of the 15th century AD. The author discusses the
information about the Nilometer in the chronicles of the Egyptian historian Abū
al-Maḥāsin Yūsuf Ibn Taghrī Birdī (1411-1470 AD).

40 **The geology of Egypt.**
Rushdi Said.   Amsterdam; New York: Elsevier, 1962. 333p. maps.
bibliog.

A detailed reference work on the geology of Egypt.

41 **South-East Egypt: geographical essays.**
Abdel-Fattah Weheba, Mohamed Riad, M. M. A. Seteha.   Beirut:
Beirut Arab University, 1974. 103p.

Contains three papers: 'Past gold and emerald mining in south-east Egypt', by
Weheba; 'Cultural regions in south-east Egypt', by Riad; and 'Modern mining
industry in south-east Egypt', by Seteha.

42 **Water management models in practice: a case study of the Aswan High Dam.**
Dale Whittington, Giorgio Guariso. Amsterdam; Oxford; New York: Elsevier Scientific Publishing Co., 1983. 223p. bibliog. (Developments in Environmental Modelling, 2).

A study of the development and evaluation of the operating policies for the Aswan High Dam, and their relation to the development of water resources policy in Egypt. This book presents a survey of the hydrology of the Nile, and the history of Nile water management projects, current supply and demand for water in Egypt and Sudan, and an analysis of various management models and their implications for the future.

Tourism and Travel Guides

43 Cairo.

James Aldridge. London: Macmillan; Boston; Toronto: Little, Brown & Company, 1969. 370p. bibliog.

According to the author, a novelist, this book is not an academic study of Cairo nor is it an amateur history; rather it is a biography of the city of Cairo. He treats the subject as a living, breathing entity and tells the full story 'from primitive gestation to modern metropolis'.

44 Guide to Alexandria for newcomers.

American Women of Alexandria. Alexandria, Egypt: American Cultural Center, 1982. 126p.

The target audience for this very useful book is people who are coming to or who have recently arrived in Alexandria for an extended stay. The passing visitor will also find it helpful, especially concerning tourist attractions.

45 Egypt.

Leonard Cottrell. London: Vane; New York: Oxford University Press, 1966. 280p. map.

A well-illustrated travel book. The author includes 'some monuments not normally on the itinerary of conducted tours with advice on how to get to such places and what may be seen there'.

46 Cairo: a practical guide.

Deborah Cowley, Aleya Serour, revised by Arunkumar Pabari. Cairo: American University in Cairo Press, 1984. 4th ed. 248p. maps.

A book designed for the long- or short-term foreign visitor who comes to Cairo either on business or for pleasure. Contains basic information of immediate use to the traveller. This guide is effectively supplemented by *The Fayoum: a practical guide*, by R. Neil Hewison (Cairo: American University in Cairo Press, 1984, reprinted 1985) (cf. item no. 50).

47 The beauty of Cairo: a historical guide to the chief Islamic and Coptic monuments.
G. S. P. Freeman-Greenville.   London: East-West Publications, 1981. 127p. bibliog.

An architectural/archaeological guide to Cairo, organized as a series of walking tours around the city, with historical details, and plans and illustrations of mosques, monuments and churches. A handy up-to-date guide providing both artistic appreciation and practical tourist information. Note also *A guide to the ancient Coptic churches of Cairo* by O. H. E. KHS–Burmester (Giza, Egypt: Société d'Archéologie Copte, 1955) – a short guide with numerous plates, dealing with the history, architecture, and furnishings.

48 Sakkara: a guide to the necropolis of Sakkara and the site of ancient Memphis.
Jill Kamil.   London: Longman, 1978. 172p.

A pocket introduction to the antiquities and excavations of the ancient city of Memphis, of which the step pyramid of Sakkara is the most prominent feature (cf. no. 153).

49 Upper Egypt.
Jill Kamil.   London: Longman, 1983. 224p. maps.

A pocket guidebook to the main archaeological and historic sites of Upper Egypt in the Pharaonic, Graeco-Roman and Early Christian periods, covering the sites of Tel el-Amarna, Abydos, Aswan and Abu Simbel.

50 A guide to the antiquities of the Fayyum.
Mary-Ellen Lane.   Cairo: American University in Cairo Press, 1985. 119p. bibliog.

This guidebook is part of the Fayyum Archaeological Project, an expedition under the direction of Dr. Robert Wenke and the author which is investigating prehistoric sites in the western desert beyond the Fayyum. The book comprises an historical introduction, and descriptions of nineteen sites, with advice on travelling to each. Illahun and sites at the entrance to the Fayyum are included (cf. item no. 46).

51 Frommer's dollarwise guide to Egypt.
Nancy McGrath.   New York: Frommer-Pasmantier, 1982. 246p. maps.

Includes hotels and restaurants that range from the 'super deluxe' to more modest hotels, cafés, coffee shops and special local favourites. Also contains information about culture, shopping and transportation.

52 **The Penguin guide to Ancient Egypt.**
William J. Murnane. London: Allen Lane, Penguin Books, 1983.
367p. maps. bibliog.

A comprehensive and detailed guide which concentrates on the sites tourists are most likely to see. Part one provides an introduction to the land and its antiquities, each chapter covering, in selective fashion, one aspect of Ancient Egypt. Part two gives the site descriptions.

53 **Nagel's encyclopaedia-guide: Egypt.**
English version by James Hogarth. Geneva; Paris; Munich: Nagel
Publishers, 1972. 816p. maps. bibliog.

The most comprehensive travel guide for Egypt, written by an impressive team of distinguished scholars, and covering in great detail Ancient, Christian, and Islamic Egypt. There is a substantial general section, including, inter alia, an historical survey.

54 **Islamic monuments in Cairo: a practical guide.**
Richard Bordeaux Parker, Robin Sabin, revised and enlarged by
Caroline Williams. Cairo: American University in Cairo Press,
1985. 3rd ed. 334p. maps. bibliog.

A comprehensive guide to the Islamic monuments of metropolitan Cairo with an excellent index and glossary of architectural terms.

55 **The Red Sea touristic zones.**
M. E. N. Economic Weekly, vol. 21, no. 4 (22 January 1982), p. 21-4.

Discusses the possible development of tourism on the Egyptian Red Sea coast, with reference both to the advantages of the Red Sea coast as a tourist area and to the obstacles in the way of developing the region for that purpose.

56 **Mediaeval Cairo and the monasteries of Wādi Natrūn: a historical guide.**
Dorothea Russell. London: Weidenfeld & Nicolson, 1962. 368p.
bibliog.

Intended for the visitor to Cairo who is neither scholar nor archaeologist, and for whom this greatest of oriental cities is new ground, this guide is primarily concerned with mediaeval Islamic Cairo; it does not touch on the Ancient Egyptian period, but deals with the city and its story as it grew between the 7th and the 16th centuries AD, and also covers to some extent the Copto-Christian era before this period and the Turkish suzerainty after it.

57 **Fodor's Egypt, 1984**
Day Shawker.   New York: Fodor's Travel Guides, 1984. 259p.
maps.

A concise, up-to-date and practical guide for travellers which provides a brief historical background. A large part of the book is about Cairo. An English-Arabic tourist vocabulary is included.

58 **Egyptian gods: a handbook.**
Alan W. Shorter.   Boston, Massachusetts:Routledge & Kegan
Paul, 1981. 143p.

A brief account of the Ancient Egyptian gods and religion for the traveller in Egypt, or the visitor to Egyptian collections in museums. For a recent handy guide for the general reader, see George Hart, *A dictionary of Egyptian gods and goddesses* (London: Routledge and Kegan Paul, 1986).

59 **Great Cairo: mother of the world.**
Desmond Stewart.   London: Hart-Davis, 1969. 223p. bibliog.

A very readable account of the story of the city, describing the different periods of its long history, starting from ancient times with the old centres of Memphis and Heliopolis, through to the present day. For a more concise account, see by the same author *Cairo* (London: Phoenix House, 1965. Cities of the World, no. 1).

60 **Egypt's untapped tourist potential.**
Susannah Tarbush.   *Middle East* (London), no. 125 (March 1985),
p. 17-20.

An investigative report on the potential for tourism in Egypt.

61 **Travelaid guide to Egypt.**
Michael von Haag.   London: Travelaid Publishing, 1982. 347p.
maps.

A guide to all aspects of Egypt. At the end of each chapter there is a practical information section with details of accommodation, eating places, travel, etc.

62 **Islamic Cairo: endangered legacy.**
Caroline Williams.   *Middle East Journal*, vol. 39, no. 3 (Summer
1985), p. 231-46.

The author explains her concern for the future of the Islamic monuments of Cairo. She makes four proposals: a moratorium on all demolition in the old city should be enforced and sketches, plans, photographs and documentary studies should be undertaken; heavy vehicular traffic and parked cars should be banned from narrow mediaeval streets; revenues from the sales of entry tickets to major monuments should be strictly monitored and returned to the Egyptian Antiquities Organization to be used for restoration programmes; and the Cairo Conservation Agency should be strengthened financially and administratively.

Travellers' Accounts

63   **Voyages en Egypte des années 1597-1601.** (Travels in Egypt in the
      years 1597-1601.)
      Bernardino Amico da Gallipoli, Aquilante Rocchetta, Henry
      Castela, translated from the Italian by Carla Burri, Nadine
      Sauneron, introduction and index by Serge Sauneron. Cairo:
      Institut Français d'Archéologie Orientale du Caire, 1974. 252p.
      map. (Collection of Western Travellers in Egypt, vol. 11).

Gallipoli spent five years in the Holy Land. He gives a short account of a miracle
which took place in Egypt, next to a chapel built by Christians at the Virgin
Fountain in Mataria (near Cairo). Rocchetta's book describes his pilgrimage to
Jerusalem, particularly his travel from Gaza to Egypt. He gives details of the
appearance of villages, customs, the price of food and the population. He
describes the churches of old Cairo, Mataria's holy places, the pyramids, and his
voyage on the Nile back to Alexandria. Castela went on a pilgrimage to
Jerusalem and like Rocchetta he gives a detailed account of his journey between
Gaza and Cairo, mentioning the organization of the caravan, the Arabs of the
desert, the justice of the Turks. He visited Cairo, Mount Sinai, Rosetta and
Alexandria. His book is also useful because he gives details of his expenditure.

64   **Egypt in 1800: scenes from Napoleon's** *Description de l'Égypte.*
      Edited by Robert Anderson, Ibrahim Fawzy.   London: Barrie and
      Jenkins, 1988. 196p. map.

Reproduces 174 selected plates from the *Antiquités* and *État moderne* volumes of
the *Description de l'Égypte*, which began publication in 1809. Each plate is
accompanied by a brief account of its contents and significance.

65   **From Egypt to Palestine through Sinai, the wilderness and the south
      country: observations of a journey made with special reference to the
      history of the Israelites.**
      S. C. Bartlett.   New York: Arno Press, 1977. Reprint ed. 555p.
      maps. (America and the Holy Land Series).

First published in 1879 (New York: Harper and Brothers). Describes a journey
through Sinai, the Negev desert and South Palestine in search of Biblical history
by the author and three Biblical scholars, Jacob Chamberlain, E. M. Williams
and Edwin J. Bartlett. The author's aim was to examine the various routes which
have been ascribed to the Israelites on the basis of the narratives in the Bible.

66   **Voyage en Egypte de Pierre Belon du Mans 1547.** (Travels in Egypt
      by Pierre Belon du Mans, 1547.)
      Pierre Belon du Mans, introduction and notes by Serge Sauneron.
      Cairo: Institut Français d'Archéologie Orientale du Caire, 1970.
      unpaged. (Collection of Western Travellers in Egypt, vol. 1).

After humble beginnings, Belon became a man of the Renaissance, and as a
doctor, he wanted to learn more about plants. This led him to Egypt. In this work
he analyses what he saw, and his descriptions are those of a scholar and a
naturalist. He remarks on animals, fish, plants, even the water of different
regions; he investigates the merchants' quarters of Cairo to research drugs and
plants, and gives significant information about the countryside with emphasis on
nature, boats and navigation; he describes clothes, ways of sitting, talking, and
eating, and religion.

67   **Voyage en Egypte de Gabriel Bremond 1643-1645.** (Travels in Egypt
      by Gabriel Bremond, 1643-1645.)
      Gabriel Bremond, edited and annotated by Georges
      Sanguin.   Cairo: Institut Français d'Archéologie Orientale du
      Caire, 1974. 185p. map. (Collection of Western Travellers in Egypt,
      vol. 12).

We know little about Bremond except that he travelled in the Mediterranean for
14 years. He lived in the Nile valley for 20 months and travelled extensively in the
region. He gives a detailed day-by-day account of walking to St. Catherine's
Monastery and of climbing the Gebel Katarina to Tor. It is believed that
Bremond borrowed many details of his description of Egypt from a book by Jean
Léon, but his remarks about the Sinai and eastern deserts are his own. He
includes amusing anecdotes about the flora and fauna, and gives unusual details
about tombs and mummies; he describes events and people of the period, and the
good relationships he had with Egyptian dignitaries. He shows great tolerance of
Islam and reveals good knowledge of the military and administrative organization
of Egypt.

68 **Voyage en Egypte d'Edward Browne 1673-1674** (Travels in Egypt by Edward Browne, 1673-1674.)
Edward Browne; translated from the English by Marie-Thérèse Bréant, introduction, notes and index by Serge Sauneron. Cairo: Institut Français d'Archéologie Orientale du Caire, 1974. 224p. map. (Collection of Western Travellers in Egypt, vol. 10).

Apart from this book, little is known of the author's life. He was born in England and took an interest in stones, which led him to leave for Egypt. The chronology of his stay of about two years is difficult to unravel. It is believed that the book was completed and edited by a publisher after his death. His account is different from others in that he went to Egypt on business, not as a pilgrim or an ambassador; he mentions the dangers of such an enterprise. The description of Egypt is a word-for-word copy of Prosper Alpin's *Historia Aegypti Naturalis*, which must have been added by the publisher. The rest of the book is authentic: all details of his trip to the Red Sea can be verified. He also gives the first-ever description of the monastery Bir Abou Darag. Brown was in close contact with the population and was able to exchange ideas and hold conversations. He shows respect for foreign customs, and indeed his book is important because it pleads for acceptance by Europeans of the way of life of others.

69 **Up the Nile: a photographic excursion, Egypt 1839-1898**.
Deborah Bull, Donald Lorimer, foreword by Anne Horton. New York: Clarkson N. Potter, 1978. 131p. bibliog.

By the close of the 19th century hundreds of thousands of photographs of Egypt had been taken, but relatively few remain. Those reproduced in this volume are among the best that have survived.

70 **Voyages en Egypte de Jean Coppin 1638-1639, 1643-1646.** (Travels in Egypt by Jean Coppin, 1638-1639, 1643-1646.)
Jean Coppin, introduction and notes by Serge Sauneron. Cairo: Institut Français d'Archéologie Orientale du Caire, 1971. 391p. map. (Collection of Western Travellers in Egypt, vol. 4).

After a journey through the Turkish states and two extensive stays in Egypt, Coppin returned home to become a monk. He emerged from his monastery to call for a crusade, but this never took place. His book is a strategic study for use in case of war, but more interesting is his colourful picture of the Ottoman Empire. He first spent two years in Egypt, then another four years in Damiette as consul of France and England, and this experience lends exceptional quality to his work. He shows little interest in monuments and landscapes but focuses on men (races, military forces, religions) and oriental life; he also gives many details of the life of the European communities in Cairo at the time, which had never been done before. In spite of his hostility to Islam and his desire to fight the Turks, his work indicates some degree of tolerance towards the Arabs.

71 **The man who loved Egypt: Bimbashi McPherson.**
Edited by Barry Carman, John McPherson.   London: British
Broadcasting Corporation, 1985. 313p. bibliog.

This work grew out of a trilogy of radio programmes with the same title, based on
Joseph McPherson's extensive letters. McPherson also wrote *The moulids of
Egypt*, an account of the fairs and fêtes of the Egyptian delta. Originally
published in 1983 under the title *Bimbashi McPherson: a life in Egypt*.

72 **Cairo to Kisumu: Egypt – The Sudan – Kenya Colony.**
Frank G. Carpenter.   Garden City, New York: Doubleday, Page,
1925. 313p. 2 maps. bibliog. (Carpenter's World Travels).

A British traveller's account of his several trips to Egypt, Nubia, the Sudan and
Kenya during the first quarter of the 20th century.

73 **Travels in Upper and Lower Egypt.**
Vivant Denon, translated from the French by Arthur Aikin.   New
York: Arno Press, 1973. Reprint ed. 3 vols. in 1. (The Middle East
Collection).

Originally published under the title *Voyage dans la Basse et la Haute Egypte* and
first published in English in 1803 (London: T. N. Longman & O. Reese), this is
an account of the country and its monuments by an eye-witness of the invasion of
Egypt by Napoléon Bonaparte, 1798-1801. The author was an architect and a
member of the Institute of Cairo who accompanied the French army to Upper
Egypt, compiling a large collection of drawings of monuments throughout Egypt,
many of which were later incorporated into the *Description de l'Égypte*. The work
had a profound impact upon European scholarship, being the first major
publication after the European 'rediscovery' of Ancient Egypt.

74 **Letters from Egypt, 1862-1869.**
Lady Duff Gordon, reedited with additional letters by Gordon
Waterfield.   London: Routledge & Kegan Paul; New York:
Praeger, 1969. 385p. bibliog.

First published in 1865 (London: Macmillan). This new edition includes more
letters and a lengthy introduction about the life and times of the author, who lived
in the Egyptian countryside and vividly recorded the life of the people.

75 **A thousand miles up the Nile.**
Amelia B. Edwards.   London: Century, 1982. Reprint ed. 499p.

First published in 1877 (London: Longmans; New York: Caryell), this is an
extremely detailed account of the great monuments of Ancient Egypt by a British
traveller. Impressed by what she had seen on her visit, Amelia Edwards founded
on her return the Egypt Exploration Fund, later the Egypt Exploration Society,
which still conducts archaeological work in Egypt and publishes the results.

Travellers' Accounts

76 **Le voyage en Egypte de Felix Fabri 1483.** (Travels in Egypt by Felix Fabri, 1483.)
    Felix Fabri, translated from the Latin, introduced and annotated by Jacques Masson, S. J.   Cairo: Institut Français d'Archéologie Orientale du Caire, 1975. 3 vols. (Collection of Western Travellers in Egypt, vol. 14).

Fabri was a Dominican monk who made his first trip to Jerusalem in 1480, and this gave him the desire to return. Hence he made a longer pilgrimage, from April 1483 to January 1484, and his books describe his travels starting at Gaza on his way to Egypt. His narrative is the work of a well-read, knowledgeable humanist who fills out his own memories of events and characters with an encyclopaedic knowledge of the countries he visited. He gives us a good picture of Egypt in the 15th century, although he dramatizes some events, and so what he writes is not always factual. Despite his religious affiliations, he shows sympathy for the Muslims and oriental Christians whom he met during his travels. His work is sometimes weakened by long digressions, but it shows how ignorant Europe was of world geography and stresses the social conditions and customs of Egypt at the time.

77 **Voyage en Egypte du Père Antonius Gonzales, 1665-1666.** (Travels in Egypt by Father Antonius Gonzales, 1665-1666.)
    Father Antonius Gonzales, translated from the Dutch, introduced and annotated by Charles Libois, S. J.   Cairo: Institut Français d'Archéologie Orientale du Caire, 1977. 2 vols. (Collection of Western Travellers in Egypt, vol. 19).

The son of a Spanish family, Gonzales was in 1665-66 the priest to the French consul and merchants in Cairo, although he claimed not to speak French well. He wrote his book immediately after his return. He was interested in the Arab way of life but less so in Islamic culture and monuments. He was also interested in anything related to the Holy Scriptures and nature. He writes as a pilgrim, a visitor not a missionary, although his attitude towards non-Catholic Christians reveals a man of his time, however muted his criticism might be. The work consists of six books. The first, written as a journal, describes the cities and countries he goes through. The second book is the largest and describes the Holy Land, and his wanderings in Jerusalem and the surrounding areas. Each chapter concludes with spiritual considerations. In the third book he describes his walk with a caravan through the desert from Cairo to Jerusalem, while the fourth is particularly interesting as it describes his time as a priest in Cairo with details of the city and the customs of Egypt (populations, illnesses, marriages, etc.). The fifth book relates his journey back to Europe, and the sixth is an account of the biological and mineral curiosities of the Middle East, mainly Egypt.

78 Voyage en Egypte de Christophe Harant de Polžic et Bezdružic,
    1598. (Travels in Egypt of Christophe Harant de Polžic et
    Bezdružic, 1598.)
    Christophe Harant de Polžic et Bezdružic, introduction, translation
    and notes by Claire and Antoine Brejnik. Cairo: Institut Français
    d'Archéologie Orientale du Caire, 1972. 311p. (Collection of
    Western Travellers in Egypt, vol. 5).

The author was a Bohemian nobleman who was finally executed by Ferdinand II
of Habsburg for his rebellion against him. When the Turks invaded Hungary, he
joined the army and became an exceptional soldier. After the war, he left on a
pilgrimage, though it may have been a mission for the king. The book describes
his journey from Venice to Crete and Cyprus, and his arrival in Jaffa. He makes
observations about his trip to Jerusalem, travelling through the lands of the Bible,
describes in detail monuments, churches, chapels and sanctuaries visited by the
pilgrims, and presents a history of Palestine and a general description of the
country. In a second volume, he describes his journey from Jerusalem to Gaza,
Damiette, Cairo, Mount Sinai, St. Catherine's Monastery and Alexandria. He
supplemented his own observations with extensive research – 600 works are
mentioned in his bibliography.

79 **Aspects of Egypt: some travels in the United Arab Republic.**
    Ethel Mannin. London: Hutchinson, 1964. 264p. bibliog.

A journalistic description of Egyptian society of the early 1960s.

80 **Le voyage en Egypte de Balthasar de Monconys, 1646-1647.** (Travels
    in Egypt by Balthasar de Monconys, 1646-1647.)
    Balthasar de Monconys, introduction and notes by d'Henry Amer.
    Cairo: Institut Français d'Archéologie Orientale du Caire, 1973.
    195p. map. (Collection of Western Travellers in Egypt, vol. 8).

Monconys was born to a rich family in Lyons, and his interest in distant countries
was not as a tourist but as a scholar. Because of his scientific mind and passion for
knowledge, he gives a detailed account of oriental flora and fauna, and of his
calculations for establishing the exact dimensions of the great pyramid. As a man
of faith, he was most interested in religious sentiment, and he describes in great
detail the religious services of the Orthodox Greeks and the mystical dances of
the Dervishes. He was also intrigued by the pharaonic civilization. His book
reflects his interest in the foreign customs, ceremonies and parades which he saw
on his tour.

81 **A family in Egypt.**
    Mary Rowlatt. London: Hale, 1956. 226p.

Tells the story of the author's family which has been connected with Egypt for
five generations. A sympathetic account of life in Egypt.

82 **Village life in Egypt, with sketches of the Saïd.**
Bayle St. John. New York: Arno Press, 1973. Reprint ed. 2 vols. in 1.

A detailed account of Egyptian society in the middle of the 19th century, originally published in 1852 (London: Chapman & Hall). Includes descriptions of the Ancient Egyptian monuments, customs, festivals, Cairo by day and by night, women, and relations of the *fellah* to the government, among many other aspects of social life in Egypt.

83 **Voyages en Egypte des années 1611 et 1612.** (Travels in Egypt in the years 1611 and 1612.)
George Sandys, William Lithgow, translated, introduced and annotated by Oleg V. Volkoff. Cairo: Institut Français d'Archéologie Orientale du Caire, 1973. 353p. map. (Collection of Western Travellers in Egypt, vol. 7).

Sandys was born in York, England, was educated at Oxford, and served in the Foreign Office. This journal describes his voyage to the Middle East from Venice via Constantinople to Egypt and back. His account of his stay in Egypt is chronological; his aim is not to give a complete picture of Egypt but to entertain his readers intelligently. He gives a general description of the country and its flora and fauna, and relates his travels to Alexandria, Rosetta, Cairo, Mount Sinai monastery, the pyramids and Memphis. He digresses to write about the Red Sea, the Armenians in Egypt, the Muslim religion and the Nile floods.

84 **Queer things about Egypt.**
Douglas Sladen. Philadelphia, Pennsylvania: Lippincott; London: Hurst & Blackett, 1910. 428p.

A personal view of Egypt in the early 20th century by a British traveller. His account ranges from the life of the varying classes of Egyptian society from Alexandria to Aswan, to descriptions of many of the Ancient Egyptian monuments.

85 **Incidents of travel in Egypt, Arabia Petraea and the Holy Land.**
John Lloyd Stephens, edited and with an introduction by Victor Wolfgang von Hagen. Norman, Oklahoma: University of Oklahoma Press, 1970. 473p.

The author was one of the first Americans to travel to Egypt, and the Egyptian part of his journey covers the first 200 pages of the book. He was in Egypt in 1836, during Muhammad Ali's reign, and the book was first published in 1837 (New York: Harper) and then in Edinburgh in 1839.

86 **Egyptian years.**
L. A. Tregenza. London: Oxford University Press, 1958. 198p.

The memoirs of a British teacher who lived and worked in Egypt from 1927 to 1951.

87 **Voyages en Egypte des années 1589-1590 et 1591.** (Travels in Egypt
    in the years 1589-1590 and 1591.)
    Le Vénitien anonyme, le Seigneur de Villamont, le Hollandais Jan
    Sommer, translated by Carla Burri, Nadine Sauneron, Paul Bleser,
    introduction and notes by Carla Burri, Serge Sauneron.   Cairo:
    Institut Français d'Archéologie Orientale du Caire, 1971. 324p.
    map. (Collection of Western Travellers in Egypt, vol. 3).

Sommer's work focuses on Cairo and the cities of the Delta; he describes the
customs and contemporary civilization of Egypt. The work of the anonymous
Venetian focuses on the Nile valley, Nubia and pharaonic times. It is the earliest
account of a journey made by a European to Upper Egypt and Nubia.

88 **Voyageurs russes en Egypte.** (Russian travellers to Egypt.)
    Oleg V. Volkoff.   Cairo: Institut Français d'Archéologie Orientale
    du Caire, 1972. 344p. (Recherches d'Archéologie, de Philologie et
    d'Histoire, vol. 32).

Gives accounts of nineteen Russian travellers who visited Egypt between 1400
and 1951.

89 **Travels through Syria and Egypt in the years 1783, 1784 and 1785.**
    Constantin François, Comte de Volney.   Farnborough, England:
    Gregg International, 1972. Reprint ed. 2 vols.

First published in English in 1787 (London: G. G. J. and J. Robinson), this is one
of the best-known early travel books. The first nineteen chapters of volume one
give a very detailed account of the physical and political environment in Egypt at
the time, including the economic and social conditions of the people, the state of
government and a description of the ancient monuments.

90 **Desert pilgrimage: journeys to the Egyptian and Sinai deserts.**
    James Wellard.   London: Hutchinson, 1970. 215p. maps. bibliog.

An account of a journey through the deserts of Egypt in the course of which the
author visited many Coptic monasteries. He describes these together with the
beliefs of their inhabitants, the Coptic monks and hermits. Also included is a brief
history of St. Catherine's Monastery in Sinai.

Travellers' Accounts

91 **Voyages en Egypte de Johann Wild, 1606-1610.** (Travels in Egypt by
 Johann Wild, 1606-1610.)
 Johann Wild, translated from the German, introduced and annota-
 ted by Oleg V. Volkoff. Cairo: Institut Français d'Archéologie
 Orientale du Caire, 1973. 259p. map. (Collection of Western
 Travellers in Egypt, vol. 9).

Wild was a German soldier and mercenary who was captured and sold to a Turk.
His book describes his years of adventure as a slave. He mentions his visit to
Mecca, and his participation in some Muslim rituals leads us to believe he may
have converted to Islam. He describes his condition as a slave, and the different
characters he met, and he gives details of cities such as Cairo. The book presents
a detailed account of Egypt in the 17th century, useful to the sociologist and the
historian, with information on such topics as prices, Turkish and Egyptian
customs, ceremonies in Cairo, animals and agriculture.

Flora and Fauna

92   **The weed flora of Egypt.**
Loutfy Boulos, M. Nabil el-Hadidi, illustrated by Magdy el-
Gohary.   Cairo: American University in Cairo Press, 1984. 178p.
bibliog.

Provides the basis for an appreciation of the wide array of species that occur
especially in the gardens, orchards and irrigated areas of the country. The
introductory part of the work summarizes the nature of weeds, their habitats,
distribution, and the means of controlling them.

93   **Handbook of the birds of Europe, the Middle East and North Africa:
the birds of the western palearctic.**
Edited by Stanley Cramp.   Oxford; London; New York: Oxford
University Press, 1977-88. 5 vols.

A comprehensive reference work providing extensive and fully illustrated
accounts of species with sections covering: field characteristics; habitat; distribution; population; movements; food and feeding habits; social patterns and
behaviour; voice; breeding; egg markings; plumage; and flight patterns. The five
volumes so far published deal with: ostriches to ducks; hawks to bustards; waders
to gulls; terns to woodpeckers; tyrant flycatchers to thrushes. The work will
eventually comprise seven volumes.

94   **The birds of Ancient Egypt.**
Patrick F. Houlihan, with the collaboration and a preliminary
checklist to the birds of Egypt by Steven M. Goodman.
Warminster, England: Aris & Phillips, 1986. 191p. bibliog.

Provides a systematic survey of all the bird life depicted by the Ancient Egyptians
in art and hieroglyphic writing, sketches the birds' role in the secular and religious
spheres, and compares their present-day distribution range with that of ancient
times.

95   **The venomous snakes of the Near and Middle East.**
Ulrich Joger.   Wiesbaden, FRG: Ludwig Reichart Verlag, 1984.
115p. 20 maps. bibliog. (Beihefte zum Tübinger Atlas des Vorderen
Orients: Reihe A, Naturwissenschaften, Nr. 12).

A summary description of the taxonomy and distribution of venomous snakes
which occur in the Middle East. There are nine species listed for Egypt, with
another one stated as uncertain (Vipera Palaestinae). The nine are: Naja h. haje,
Naja mossambica pallida, Walterinnesia aegyptia, Atractaspis engaddensis,
Cerastes C. cerastes, Cerastes vipera, Echis coloratus, Echis pyramidum,
Pseudocerastes p. persicum.

96   **Flowers of the Mediterranean.**
Oleg Polunin, Anthony Huxley.   London: Chatto & Windus, 1978.
rev. ed. 257p. map. bibliog.

A revised edition of the work first published in 1965, this is an illustrated guide to
the flora of the Mediterranean basin, including Egypt. Over 700 species are
described, with details on habitat, distribution, time of flowering and uses. The
work is arranged by family, genera, and species. An introductory chapter
discusses the vegetation of the Mediterranean in more general terms. Over 300
plants are illustrated with colour photographs.

97   **Flora of Egypt.**
Vivi Täckholm, Gunnar Täckholm in collaboration with
Mohammed Drar. Cairo: Fuad I University, subsequently Cairo
University, 1941-54. 3 vols.

Volume one (1941) covers Pteridophyta, Gymnospermae and Angiospermae, part
Monocotyledones: Typhaceae-Gramineae.   Volume   two   (1950)   covers
Angiospermae, part Monocotyledones: Cyperaceae-Juncaceae. Volume three
(1954) covers Angiospermae, part Monocotyledones: Liliaceae-Musaceae. Indexes
to Latin and vernacular names are included.

98   **Students' flora of Egypt.**
Vivi Täckholm.   Cairo: Cairo University, 1974. 2nd ed. 790p.

A shorter and more concise flora in one volume for quick identification, including
nearly 600 drawings. Changes in nomenclature have been brought up to date, and
a list of Latin-vernacular names is included. The first edition was published in
1954.

99 **Geobotanical foundations of the Middle East.**
Michael Zohary.   Stuttgart, FRG: Gustav Fischer Verlag;
Amsterdam: Swets & Zeitlinger, 1973. 2 vols. 7 maps. bibliog.

A comprehensive survey of the flora, vegetation and biogeography of the Middle East, including Egypt. The introductory chapters provide an analysis of landforms, climate, soils and plant-geographical regions, including desert vegetation. Detailed chapters outline phytogeographical territories, vegetation units and their ecological interrelations. The role of man as an agent of ecological change is examined.

History

General

100 **Idéologie et renaissance nationale: l'Egypte moderne.** (Ideology
and the national renaissance: modern Egypt.)
Anouar Abdel-Malek.   Paris: Editions Anthropos, 1969. 575p.
bibliog.

Written by a well-known Egyptian socialist scholar, this book studies the
ideological basis of the modernization movement in 19th-century Egypt.

101 **Cairo: 1001 years of the city victorious.**
Janet Abu-Lughod.   Princeton, New Jersey: Princeton University
Press, 1971. 255p. maps. bibliog. (Princeton Studies on the Near
East).

Describes the development, rise and fall of the Islamic city, the foundation of
Fustat, and its evolution into the modern metropolis of Cairo in the 19th century.
Part 3 discusses the growth, structure and problems of the contemporary city. A
fine study of the historical, social and economic development of Cairo.

102 **Urbanization in Egypt, 1820-1907.**
Gabriel Baer. In: *Beginnings of modernization in the Middle East.
The nineteenth century.* Edited by William Polk, Richard L.
Chambers.   Chicago, Illinois: University of Chicago Press, 1968,
p. 155-69.

A well-documented paper about urban development in Egypt in the 19th and
early 20th centuries by a specialist in the social history of Egypt.

103 **Studies in the social history of modern Egypt.**
Gabriel Baer.   Chicago, Illinois: University of Chicago Press,
1969. 246p.

Considers social change, and the evolution of the structure of Egyptian society, in
the years 1800–1914. Various chapters discuss the settlement of the Bedouin, the
changing village structure and the development of the private ownership of land,
and the changes in the political, social and economic life brought about by the
reforms of the Tanzimat period.

104 **Azbakiyya and its environs from Azbak to Ismā'īl 1476-1879.**
Doris Behrens-Abouseif.   Cairo: Institut Français d'Archéologie
Orientale, 1985. 116p. bibliog. (Supplément aux Annales
Islamologiques, cahier no. 6.)

A study of the development of the buildings and growth of the quarter during 400
years, with descriptions of its way of life, the inhabitants' occupations, and the
factors which dictated the area's changing fortunes. There are many drawings and
illustrations.

105 **Egypt and Sinai, eternal battleground.**
Gregory Blaxland.   New York: Funk & Wagnalls, 1966. 327p.
maps. bibliog.

An illustrated history of the Sinai peninsula as the scene of wars for dominion
over Egypt from 535 BC to 1956 AD.

106 **Egypt in Nubia.**
Walter B. Emery.   London: Hutchinson, 1965. 264p. bibliog.

This book is not intended for the specialist, but aims to summarize the history of
archaeological exploration and to present an outline of Nubian history. Special
attention is paid to the author's own excavations (e.g. Ballas and Qustul, and
Buhen), and a number of illustrations are drawn from this work. Emery also
wrote *Archaic Egypt* (Harmondsworth: Penguin Books, 1961 (and reprints)).

107 **Napoleon to Nasser: the story of modern Egypt.**
Raymond Flower.   London: Tom Stacey, 1972. 271p. bibliog.

A succinct history of Egypt from 1798 to 1970, describing how Egypt succumbed
to foreign rule and how Nasser tried to build a new, independent Egypt,
evaluating his initial successes and later defeats.

108 **The Suez Canal: its history and diplomatic importance.**
Charles W. Hallberg.   New York: Octagon Books, 1974. Reprint
ed. 434p.

The purpose of this study, which was first published in 1931 (New York:
Columbia University Press), is not only to present an historical survey of the Suez
route from ancient times to the present but also to show its importance as a factor
in European diplomacy. An attempt is also made to set forth the financial and
commercial development of the canal, its strategic importance and the attempts to
give it a secure juridical status.

109 **Histoire de la nation égyptienne.** (History of the Egyptian nation.)
Gabriel Hanotaux. Paris: Société de l'Histoire Nationale, Librairie
Plon, 1931-1940. 7 vols. maps.

The contents of this work are as follows. Volume one: 'Introduction générale', by
Gabriel Hanotaux; and 'La géographie de l'Egypte à travers les âges', by Charles
de la Roncière. Volume two: 'L'Egypte pharaonique', by Alexandre Moret.
Volume three: 'L'Egypte ptolémaïque', by Pierre Jouquet; 'L'Egypte romaine',
by Victor Chapot; and 'L'Egypte chrétienne et byzantine', by Ch. Diehl. Volume
4: 'L'Egypte arabe de la conquête arabe à la conquête ottomane, 642-1517 A.D.',
by Gaston Wiet. Volume 5: 'L'Egypte turque: pachas et Mameluks du XVI au
XVII siècles'; and 'L'Expédition du Général Bonaparte', by Henri Deherain.
Volume 6: 'L'Egypte de 1801 à 1882', by F. Charles-Roux; and 'Le Saudan
égyptienne de Mohamed Ali à Ismail Pacha', by Henri Deherain. Volume 7: 'Un
mécène royal: S. M. Fouad Iᵉʳ, Roi d'Egypte', by Henri Deherain; 'L'Egypte de
l'occupation anglaise à l'indépendance égyptienne', by F. Charles-Roux; and 'Le
Soudan perdu et reconquis', by Henri Deherain.

110 **Political and social change in modern Egypt: historical studies from
the Ottoman conquest to the United Arab Republic.**
P. M. Holt. London: Oxford University Press, 1968. 400p.

A collection of papers by specialist historians, arranged as follows. Part one
consists of 'Studies in source materials': 'Ottoman Egypt (1517-1798): an account
of Arabic historical sources', by P. M. Holt; 'Alī Mubārak's *Khitat* as a source for
the history of modern Egypt', by Gabriel Baer; 'Turkish source materials for
Egyptian history', by Stanford J. Shaw; 'Ottoman archival materials on nineteenth-
century Egyptian history', by Şinasi Altundağ; 'Documents pertaining to the
Egyptian Question in the Yildiz Collection of the Başbakanlik Arşivi, Istanbul',
by Hasan Adali; 'Some English sources for the study of modern Egyptian history',
by H. S. Deighton; and 'The Hekekyan Papers', by Ahmed Abdel-Rahim
Mustafa. Part two consists of 'Studies in the history of the early modern period
(1517-1798)': 'The pattern of Egyptian political history from 1517 to 1798', by
P. M. Holt; 'Landholding and land-tax revenues in Ottoman Egypt', by Stanford
J. Shaw; 'Quartiers et mouvements populaires au Caire au XVIIIème siècle', by
André Raymond; and 'Some aspects of intellectual and social life in eighteenth-
century Egypt', by Gamal el-Din el-Shayyal. Part three consists of 'Studies in the
history of the nineteenth and twentieth centuries': 'Social change in Egypt: 1800-
1914', by Gabriel Baer; 'The long-term growth of agricultural production in
Egypt: 1821-1962', by Patrick O'Brien; 'The Jews in nineteenth-century
Egypt – some socio-economic aspects', by Jacob M. Landau; 'Law reform in
Egypt: 1850-1950', by J. N. D. Anderson; 'The impact of Egypt on Britain: a
study of public opinion', by H. S. Deighton; 'Notes sur la hiérarchie sociale en
Egypte à l'époque de Muhammad 'Alī', by Nada Tomiche; 'The role of the
ulamā in Egypt during the early nineteenth century', by Afaf Loutfi el-Sayed;
'Egyptian-Yemeni relations (1819-1840) and their implications for British policy in
the Red Sea', by Abdel Hamid el-Batrik; 'The breakdown of the monopoly
system in Egypt after 1840', by Ahmed Abdel-Rahim Mustafa; 'The Egyptian
Nationalist Party: 1892-1919', by Arthur Goldschmidt, Jr.; 'The origins of the
Liberal Constitutionalist Party in Egypt', by Mahmud Zayid; 'The genesis of the
Egyptian constitution of 1923', by Elie Kedourie; and 'Some political conse-
quences of the 1952 revolution in Egypt', by P. J. Vatikiotis.

111 **Pharaoh to Farouk.**
H. Wood Jarvis, with assistance from Walter W. Skeat. London:
John Murray, 1955. 298p.

A history of Egypt, intended for the general reader, from ancient times to 1952.

112 **Historical dictionary of Egypt.**
Joan Wucher King. Metuchen, New Jersey: Scarecrow Press, 1984.
719p. map. bibliog. (African Historical Dictionaries, No. 36).

An historical dictionary which concentrates on Egypt since the Muslim conquest.
The author argues that most readers of the volume will be primarily interested in
the present and the recent past, and thus persons, places, and events are treated
in greater numbers and in greater depth for the more recent periods, with earlier
history covered mainly in terms of important rulers, personalities, and events.
Includes a detailed chronology.

113 **Four aspects of Egypt.**
John Marlowe. London: Allen & Unwin, 1966. 294p.

An account of Egypt written just before the Arab-Israeli war of 1967. The four
aspects of the book's title are the ancient, the mediaeval, modern Egypt and the
Nile.

114 **A short history of modern Egypt.**
Afaf Lutfi al-Sayyid Marsot. Cambridge, England: Cambridge
University Press, 1985. 151p. map. bibliog.

A condensed and well-written history of Egypt, from the Arab conquest in 639
AD to present-day Egypt under President Hosni Mubarak, by a well-known
Egyptian historian.

115 **Dictionary of Egyptian civilization.**
Georges Posener, with the assistance of Serge Sauneron, Jean
Yoyotte, translated from the French by Alex Macfarlane. New
York: Tudor Publishing Company, 1959; London: Methuen, 1962.
324p.

This modest-sized work, first published in French under the title *Dictionnaire de
la civilisation égyptienne*, was compiled by three leading French Egyptologists,
and provides in the form of a dictionary brief accounts of all aspects of Ancient
Egyptian history and culture. A much larger-scale reference work for all
Egyptological topics is *Lexikon der Ägyptologie* founded by Wolfgang Helck and
Eberhard Otto, edited by Wolfgang Helck and Wolfhart Westendorf (Wiesbaden,
FRG: Otto Harrassowitz, 1975-86. 6 vols.). Most entries are in German, but a
proportion are in English.

116 **Themes in the economy of the Bedouin of South Sinai in the nineteenth and twentieth centuries.**
Dan Rabinowitz. *International Journal of Middle East Studies*, vol. 17, no. 2 (May 1985), p. 211–28.
An account of the economy of the Sinai Bedouin in the 19th century, based on historical material, with a description of the main features of that economy, and a comparison with economic trends in the early and later 20th century.

117 **Al-qāmūs al-jughrāfī lil-bilād al-miṣrīyah min 'ahd qudamā' al-miṣrīyīn ilā sanat 1945.** (A geographical dictionary of Egypt from the time of the Ancient Egyptians to 1945.)
Muḥammad Ramzī. Cairo: Maṭbaʿat Dār al-Kutub al-Miṣrīyah, 1953-63. 4 parts in 5 vols. In Arabic.
Volume I of this work covers extinct towns and cities, volumes II-V cover existing towns and cities. Volume II covers the governorates of Qalyubīyah, Sharqīyah and Daqahliyah; volume III the governorates of Gharbīyah, Manufīyah and Buhayrah; volume IV the governorates of Bani Suwayf, Fayyum and Minyā; and volume V the governorates of Assyūt, Jirjā, Qanā, Aswān and the border regions.

118 **Egypt 1798-1952: her advance towards a modern identity.**
J. C. B. Richmond. London: Methuen, 1977. 243p. 7 maps. bibliog.
A political history of Egypt from the French Occupation in 1798 to the Free Officers' revolution in 1952, tracing Egypt's detachment from the Ottoman Empire under Muhammad Ali and takeover by the British. The British attempt to hold on to Egypt eventually failed with the overthrow of the monarchy in 1952.

119 **Conquest and fusion: the social evolution of Cairo, AD 642-1850.**
Susan Jane Staffa. Leiden, The Netherlands: Brill, 1977. 405p. maps. bibliog.
A social history of Cairo from the early foundation of Fustat to the mid-19th century. This book describes the physical development of the city and the economic and social life of the inhabitants, both upper classes and lower orders, including the bureaucracy and the intellectual elite of al-Azhar.

120 **Egypt yesterday and today.**
Georgiana G. Stevens. New York: Holt, Rinehart & Winston, 1963. 234p. bibliog.
A brief sketch of Egypt's earlier history is followed by a detailed description of the revolutionary period (July 1952 to July 1962), which saw the rapid overthrow of both the vestiges of foreign influence and of domestic economic exploitation. This book describes the institutions of the new Egypt and how they are affecting people's lives.

121 **Egypt.**
Gordon Waterfield. London: Thames & Hudson; New York:
Walker & Company, 1967. 230p. maps. bibliog.
A brief general political and social history of Egypt from the Ancient Egyptians to
Nasser which aims to correct some western misconceptions about the country.

Egypt in transition.
See item no. 12.

Manners and customs of the modern Egyptians.
See item no. 13.

Great Cairo: mother of the world.
See item no. 59.

Village life in Egypt, with sketches of the Saïd.
See item no. 82.

The history of Egypt.
See item no. 262.

Cotton and the Egyptian economy, 1820-1914: a study in trade and development.
See item no. 778.

Ancient Egypt to 332 BC

122 **Egypt to the end of the Old Kingdom.**
Cyril Aldred. London: Thames & Hudson; New York: McGraw-
Hill, 1965. 143p. map. bibliog.
Studies the early and later predynastic period in Egypt and how Egyptian
civilization developed up to the dynastic age. The author also examines the
archaic period (Dynasties I and II), and the architecture, sculpture and
civilization of the Old Kingdom. Three other works devoted to the earlier period
are A. J. Arkell *The prehistory of the Nile Valley* (Leiden, The Netherlands;
Cologne, FRG: E. J. Brill, 1975); William C. Hayes *Most ancient Egypt*, edited
by Keith C. Seele (Chicago; London: University of Chicago Press, 1965); and
Michael A. Hoffman *Egypt before the Pharaohs: the prehistoric foundations of
Egyptian civilization* (New York: Knopf, 1979; London; Henley: Routledge &
Kegan Paul, 1980). A recent work for the general reader surveying in

chronological order the pre- and early dynastic period and the Old Kingdom, and freely illustrating the art and monuments, is *In the shadow of the pyramids: Egypt during the Old Kingdom*, text by Jaromir Malek, photographs by Werner Forman (London: Orbis, 1986).

123 **Ancient Egypt in the Metropolitan Museum Journal. Volumes 1-11 (1968-1976).**
Cyril Aldred, Henry G. Fischer, Herman De Meulenaere, Birgit Nolte, Edna R. Russman. New York: Metropolitan Museum of Art, 1977. 201p.

A collection of thirteen reprinted articles aimed at scholars. The articles are as follows: 'Some royal portraits of the Middle Kingdom in Ancient Egypt', by Cyril Aldred; 'An Egyptian glass vessel in the Metropolitan Museum of Art', by Birgit Nolte; 'Some emblematic uses of hieroglyphs with particular reference to an archaic ritual vessel', 'Old Kingdom cylinder seals for the lower classes', 'Sunshades of the marketplace', 'Offering stands from the pyramid of Amenemhet I', and 'Redundant determinatives in the Old Kingdom', all by Henry G. Fischer; 'Le statue d'un chef de chanteurs d'époque saite (The statue of a leading singer from the Saitic period), by Herman de Meulenaere; 'The statue of Amenemope-em-hat', by Edna R. Russmann; and 'The mark of a second hand on Ancient Egyptian antiquities', 'An elusive shape within the fisted hands of Egyptian statues', 'Some early monuments from Busiris, in the Egyptian delta', 'More emblematic uses from Ancient Egypt', and 'Addenda', all by Henry G. Fischer. A *Supplement: volumes 12–13 (1977–1978)*, containing three further articles by Henry G. Fischer, was published in 1980, including Addenda-Corrigenda to the original volume.

124 **The Temple of Dendur.**
Cyril Aldred. New York: Metropolitan Museum of Art, 1978. 80p. map.

An illustrated report about the Temple of Dendur before and after its transference to the Metropolitan Museum of Art in New York in 1968.

125 **The Egyptians.**
Cyril Aldred. London: Thames & Hudson, 1984. rev. & enlarged ed. 216p. bibliog.

Covers the country and the history of its people from the earliest pre-dynastic period to the late period (i.e. from 5000 BC to 525 BC). The author's emphasis is on socio-political developments.

126 **Egyptian mummies.**
Carol Andrews. London: published for the Trustees of the British Museum by British Museum Publications; Cambridge, Massachusetts: Harvard University Press, 1984. 72p. bibliog.

An account of why and how mummies were made by Ancient Egyptians. The book includes descriptions of the coffins and sarcophagi, funerals, tombs and burial equipment, mummies of animals, and particularly famous mummies, all well illustrated, principally by objects in the British Museum. A similar, but longer, book is *Mummies: death and life in ancient Egypt* by James Hamilton-Paterson and Carol Andews (London: Collins, 1978). This also includes sections on funerary equipment and tomb robbery, and a brief history of European attitudes to mummies. A more substantial treatment, still aimed at the general reader, of funerary practice and belief, and of funerary equipment and architecture, is *Death in ancient Egypt* by A. J. Spencer (Harmondsworth, England: Penguin Books, 1982).

127 **Atlas of Ancient Egypt.**
John Baines, Jaromir Malek.   Oxford, England: Phaidon; New York: Facts On File Publications, 1980. 240p. maps. bibliog.
The aim of this atlas is to provide a systematic survey of the most important sites and Ancient Egyptian monuments, to make an assessment of their historical and cultural importance, and briefly to describe their salient features, based on the most up-to-date Egyptological knowledge. Further chapters and special features deal with general aspects of Egyptian civilization. Includes chronological tables, a glossary and a gazetteer, as well as excellent maps and plans.

128 **The tomb-builders of the pharaohs.**
Morris Bierbrier.   London: British Museum Publications, 1982. 160p. bibliog. (A Colonnade Book).
A social study of the life and work of the builders of the New Kingdom royal tombs, who lived in Deir el-Medina on the West Bank at Thebes.

129 **A history of Egyptian archaeology.**
Fred Gladstone Bratton.   London: Robert Hale, 1967; New York: Thomas Y. Crowell, 1968. 312p. map. bibliog.
A description of Egyptian exploration and discovery from Herodotus to the present, a substantial part dealing with monuments and finds.

130 **Armies and enemies of Ancient Egypt and Assyria; 3200 BC to 621 BC.**
Alan Buttery.   Goring by Sea, England: War Games Research Group, 1974. 82p. (War Games Research Group Publication, 4).
The first part of this book (p. 2-35) is devoted to the Egyptians and their enemies. It consists of the following sections: major battles of the period, tactical methods, organization and formations, composition of armies, and dress and arms.

131 **The discovery of the tomb of Tutankhamen.**
Howard Carter, A. C. Mace, with a new introduction by Jon Manchip White.   New York: Dover Publications, 1977. Reprint ed. 231p.
This narrative of the discovery of the tomb of Tutankhamun is a preliminary report by its discoverers in the Valley of the Kings, originally published in 1923. The reprint is of the first of three volumes, designed for the general

reader and not pretending to be a scientific publication of the tomb, together entitled *The tomb of Tut.ankh.Amen* (London: Cassell, 1923, 1927, 1933). The original publication has been reprinted more than once, and translated into several languages. The more interesting portions of the text have also been reprinted more than once. The scholarly publication of Carter's records proceeds slowly in the Tut'ankhamūn's Tomb Series, published by the Griffith Institute at Oxford.

132   **Tutankhamun: the golden monarch.**
       Michael Carter.   New York: David McKay, 1979. 135p.
An account of the discovery of the tomb of Tutankhamun, the man who discovered it, and the disputes and intrigue that surrounded it.

133   **The rediscovery of Ancient Egypt: artists and travellers in the 19th century.**
       Peter A. Clayton.   London: Thames & Hudson, 1982. 192p. map. bibliog.
This well-illustrated book takes the form of a journey up the Nile from Alexandria to Abu Simbel in the company of early travellers. The reader is introduced to the sites and monuments through the eyes of the archaeologists themselves, Napoleon's artists, David Roberts, Edward Lear and others. In all, the work of thirty artists is represented, the most notable of these being Roberts, both for the number of sites and monuments he records and for his method of presentation.

134   **Lady of the two lands: five queens of Ancient Egypt.**
       Leonard Cottrell.   Indianapolis, Indiana: Bobbs-Merrill, 1967. 226p. bibliog.
The queens discussed in this popular work are Hashepsowe (Hatshepsut), who ruled as 'king' in her own right; Tiye, wife of Amenophis III; Nefertiti, wife of Akhenaten; Nefertari, favourite wife of Ramesses II; and Ankhesenamun, wife of Tutankhamun.

135   **The lost pharaohs: the romance of Egyptian archaeology.**
       Leonard Cottrell.   New York: Greenwood Press, 1969. Reprint ed. 256p. bibliog.
A well-written book, first published in 1951 (New York: Philosophical Library), for the non-professional historian or archaeologist. Accurate and interesting.

136   **Egyptian historical records of the later Eighteenth Dynasty.**
       Translated into English by Barbara Cumming.   Warminster, England: Aris & Phillips, 1982-84. 3 vols.
A translation from the original hieroglyphic texts as published in W. Helck, *Urkunden der 18. Dynastie*, Heft 17-19, with reference to Helck's German translation. Published to answer the need of students of both language and history for English translations of basic Egyptian historical texts.

137   **The pyramid builders of Ancient Egypt: a modern investigation of pharaoh's workforce.**
A. R. David.   London: Routledge & Kegan Paul, 1986. 269p. bibliog.

Deals principally with the work of the 'Kahun Project' at the University Museum, Manchester. An account of scientific work carried out on artefacts which were used by the inhabitants of Kahun some 4,000 years ago, which demonstrates how modern research can reveal new details about everyday life in an ancient community.

138   **Who was who in Egyptology.**
Warren R. Dawson, Eric P. Uphill. London: Egypt Exploration Society, 1972. 2nd rev. ed. 315p.

A biographical index of Egyptologists; of travellers, explorers and excavators in Egypt; of collectors of and dealers in Egyptian antiquities; of consuls, officials, authors, benefactors, and others whose names occur in the literature of Egyptology, from the year 1500 AD to the present day, but excluding persons now living.

139   **Life and death of a pharaoh: Tutankhamen.**
Christiane Desroches-Noblecourt, with photographs by
F. L. Kennett, preface by Sarwat Okasha, notes on the colour
plates by Dr. A. Shaukry.   New York: New York Graphic
Society; London: The Connoisseur & Michael Joseph, 1963. 312p.
bibliog.

A well-illustrated biography of King Tutankhamun. An account of the discovery of the tomb, with the historical and religious background to his reign. This book, by a distinguished French Egyptologist, was notable as the first to include a wide range of new and colour photographs of objects from the tomb. Many such fresh sets of illustrations have appeared since in connection with the various Tutankhamun exhibitions; an example with useful photographs and text is *Tutankhamun: his tomb and its treasures* by I. E. S. Edwards (New York: Metropolitan Museum of Art, 1976; London: Victor Gollancz, 1979). A shorter work, dealing with the background to the reign, is *Tutankhamun's Egypt*, by Cyril Aldred (New York: Charles Scribner's Sons, 1972).

140   **The pyramids of Egypt.**
I. E. S. Edwards.   West Drayton (later Harmondsworth),
England: Penguin Books, 1947. 256p.

The most thorough and reliable work devoted to the Egyptian pyramids as a whole. It has been revised several times since 1947, and frequently reprinted, occasionally appearing in a more sumptuous form.

141 **Life in Ancient Egypt.**
Adolf Erman, translated by H. M. Tirard. New York; London:
Benjamin Blom, 1969. Reprint ed. 565p.

An account of the 'manners and customs' of the Ancient Egyptians, first
published in 1894 (London: Macmillan), and amply illustrated, although the range
of material then available to Erman was not great. The revision by Hermann
Ranke of the German edition as *Aegypten und Aegyptisches Leben im Altertum*
(Tübingen, Germany: Mohr, 1923) was a standard work, still not superseded by
any one publication.

142 **The pyramids.**
Ahmed Fahkry. Chicago; London: University of Chicago Press,
1969. 2nd ed. 272p. map.

Describes the impressive development of building techniques that led to the
construction of the pyramids, and the philosophical and religious background to
that development. The author, a prominent Egyptian historian and archaeologist,
provides a new chapter in this second edition describing the use of cosmic ray
muons as X-rays to study the pyramids.

143 **Egypt of the pharaohs: an introduction.**
Sir Alan H. Gardiner. London; New York: Oxford University
Press, 1961. 461p.

In the first part of this book the author, a distinguished Egyptologist principally
noted for his philological works, studies the nature of Egyptian history with
chapters on Egyptology, the Egyptian language and writing, and the natural
resources; in part two he covers the history of the Ancient Egyptian dynasties,
and in part three he considers the prehistory of the country and how Egyptian
civilization developed.

144 **An X-ray atlas of the royal mummies.**
Edited by James E. Harris, Edward F. Wente. Chicago; London:
University of Chicago Press, 1980. 403p.

In 1965, the Michigan-Alexandria expedition went to Egypt to study the ancestral
records of the Nubian people of Gebel Adda, utilizing a cephalometric X-ray
technique. The Egyptian Department of Antiquities invited this team to X-ray the
complete royal collection, and this began in December 1967. Together with the
complete X-ray survey, this volume contains several chapters which suggest the
potential of this method, applied to such a unique collection, for leading to a
better understanding of such subjects as chronology, diseases, physical variation,
mummification and restoration. A useful short work for the general reader on the
scientific study of mummies in general is *The Egyptian mummy: secrets and
science* by Stuart Fleming, Bernard Fishman, David O'Connor, and David
Silverman (Philadelphia, Pennsylvania: The University Museum, University of
Pennsylvania, 1980). This has contributions on the history and religious
background of mummification, but particularly deals with scientific aspects and
the study of health in ancient Egypt. It includes a useful variety of illustrations,
including X-rays, and the objects shown are not confined to the University
Museum.

145 **The legacy of Egypt.**
Edited by J. R. Harris, Oxford: Clarendon Press, 1971. 2nd ed.
510p. bibliog.
This second edition of the work edited by Glanville (see item no. 8) was
completely rewritten, and concentrates to a greater extent than the first edition on
the actual traceable influence of Ancient and Coptic Egypt upon later cultures,
although it remains a useful introduction to many aspects of Egyptology. Each of
the sixteen chapters, written by a wide range of specialists, deals with one topic or
historical period, and, apart from incidental references, nearly every chapter has a
select bibliography.

146 **The scepter of Egypt: a background for the study of the Egyptian
antiquities in the Metropolitan Museum of Art. Part 1: From the
earliest times to the end of the Middle Kingdom. Part 2: The Hyksos
period and the New Kingdom (1675–1080 B.C.).**
William C. Hayes. Cambridge, Massachusetts: Published for the
Metropolitan Museum of Art by Harvard University Press, 1953-
59. 2 vols. maps. bibliog.
Regardless of its subtitle, this substantial work provides an excellent introduction
to the history, culture, religion, and material civilization of Ancient Egypt. The
numerous photographs concentrate upon objects in the Metropolitan Museum of
Art.

147 **Tutankhamun: the untold story.**
Thomas Hoving. New York: Simon & Schuster, 1978. 384p.
bibliog.
A detailed account of the discovery of the tomb of Tutankhamun, also published
in London by Hamish Hamilton in 1979. The book was the first to discuss the
evidence that Carnarvon and his party entered the tomb before its official opening
(except for short articles, one posthumous, by A. Lucas in *Annales du Service des
Antiquités de l'Égypte*, vol. 41 (1942), p. 136-8; vol. 45 (1947), p. 133-4), and that
various objects from the tomb found their way into foreign collections. The role
of the Metropolitan Museum of Art, New York, of which the author was director,
is fully explored.

148 **Imhotep: the vizier and physician of King Zoser, and afterwards the
Egyptian god of medicine.**
Jamieson B. Hurry. New York: AMS Press, 1978. Reprint ed.
211p.
A biography of Imhotep, a distinguished magician-physician and sage who first
appeared on the stage of Egyptian history in the reign of King Zoser of the 3rd
Dynasty, and reemerged at intervals during the next 3,000 years as a demigod and
as one of the full deities of Egypt. Originally published in 1928 (London: Oxford
University Press).

149 **An introduction to Ancient Egypt.**
Edited by T. G. H. James. London: British Museum
Publications; New York: Farrar Straus Giroux, 1979. 286p. bibliog.

The text of this volume is based closely on that of *A general introductory guide to the Egyptian collections in the British Museum* (3rd ed.), first published in 1964. Its aim was to provide an outline of the physical, historical and cultural background of the collection; it was not intended to be a comprehensive catalogue of the 65,000 objects in the Department of Egyptian Antiquities. The title of the present edition emphasizes that the book is essentially an introduction to the culture of Ancient Egypt.

150 **Pharaoh's people: scenes from life in imperial Egypt.**
T. G. H. James. London: Bodley Head, 1984. 282p. bibliog.

A highly readable study of social life in Ancient Egypt, especially during the New Kingdom (1554-1080 BC). The author examines the vizier and his role, the justice system, education and social status, the scribe in action, craftsmen in metal and wood, and domestic economy.

151 **The boat beneath the pyramid: King Cheops' royal ship.**
Nancy Jenkins, special consultant Ahmed Youssef Moustafa, photographs by John Ross. London: Thames & Hudson, 1980. 184p. bibliog.

A detailed popular account of the discovery of the sun-boat in 1954 by Egyptian archaeologist Kamal el-Malakh. The author includes descriptions of the excavations that led to the discovery and reconstruction of the boat. He also includes a chapter on ships and shipbuilding in the Old Kingdom.

152 **The civilization of Ancient Egypt.**
Paul Johnson. London: Weidenfeld & Nicolson, 1978. 240p.

In this popular book, the author argues that the Ancient Egyptians were the first people on earth to create a nation-state; in their world, state, religion and culture formed an indivisible unity. These different elements rose together, fell together, and must be studied together.

153 **Sakkara and Memphis: a guide to the necropolis and the ancient capital.**
Jill Kamil, original photographs by Ann Stuart Anderson.
London; New York: Longman, 1985. 192p. 2nd ed. bibliog.

In this useful guide the monuments of Sakkara are grouped in chronological order. The introduction briefly outlines the history of Memphis, and thus provides a framework for chapter seven, which is specifically about Memphis. In this second edition new material on the recent discovery of New Kingdom tombs has been included and much has been rewritten and updated (cf. no. 48).

154 **Governmental reforms in Old Kingdom Egypt.**
Naguib Kanawati. Warminster, England: Aris & Phillips, 1980.
163p. bibliog.

This study attempts to chart developments in the administration of Old Kingdom Egypt by analysing the loss or gain of administrative or rank titles by the higher officials in the capital and in the provinces of Upper Egypt. The dating of various Old Kingdom tombs is discussed. The same author's *The Egyptian administration in the Old Kingdom: evidence on its economic decline* (Warminster: Aris & Phillips, 1977) attempted to draw some economic conclusions from fluctuations in the size of tombs. An earlier study was that of Klaus Baer, *Rank and title in the Old Kingdom: the structure of the Egyptian administration in the Fifth and Sixth Dynasties* (Chicago, Illinois: University of Chicago Press, 1960). On Ancient Egyptian administration in general, the standard work is Wolfgang Helck *Zur Verwaltung des mittleren und neuen Reichs* (Leiden, The Netherlands; Cologne, FRG: E. J. Brill, 1958). A volume of indexes to Helck's work was published in 1975.

155 **Ancient Egypt: a cultural topography.**
Hermann Kees, edited by T. G. H. James. London: Faber & Faber, 1961. 392p. maps. bibliog.

A historical geography of Ancient Egypt. The book is a translation of *Das alte Ägypten: eine kleine Landeskunde* (Berlin, GDR: Akademie Verlag, 1958. 2nd ed. The text of the '3rd edition' of 1977 appears to be identical – it has merely added a not very substantial index and some trivial corrections). This influential work is an account for a wider audience of how the unique natural characteristics of the Nile Valley formed and affected the nature of Ancient Egyptian civilization. A short general introductory section is followed by a long second part in which an overall picture of Ancient Egyptian life is presented, viewed from a geographical standpoint. The third part contains sketches of a number of major cities and regions.

156 **The third intermediate period in Egypt (1100-650 BC).**
K. A. Kitchen. Warminster, England: Aris & Phillips, 1973.
525p. maps.

A book which aims to reconstruct the basic chronology of the 21st-25th Dynasties, and to present therewith an historical outline incorporating the results gained and serving as a compact, up-to-date survey of the period. A second, revised edition appeared in 1986.

157 **Pharaoh triumphant: the life and times of Ramses II, King of Egypt.**
K. A. Kitchen. Warminster, England: Aris & Phillips, 1982.
272p. map.

This volume by a distinguished historian of the period is 'offered for enjoyment, not study' (p. vii). It describes in narrative style the life of the king and its background. A third, corrected, impression appeared in 1985.

158 **Ships of the pharaohs: 4000 years of Egyptian shipbuilding.**
Björn Landstrom. Garden City, New York: Doubleday, 1970.
159p.

Presents the development of shipbuilding in Ancient Egypt from the predynastic
period to the New Kingdom and the late period. Beautifully illustrated by the
author, who made a long and worldwide study of old ships.

159 **Saqqara, the royal cemetery of Memphis: excavation and
discoveries since 1850.**
Jean-Philippe Lauer. London: Thames & Hudson, 1976. 248p.
bibliog.

An account chiefly of Old Kingdom archaeology. The author reviews the
principal activities of the scholars and archaeologists who either preceded him at
Sakkara or whom he has known there personally, but also presents a well-
illustrated survey of the sites and monuments.

160 **The remarkable women of Ancient Egypt.**
Barbara S. Lesko. Berkeley, California: B.C. Scribe
Publications, 1978. 34p. bibliog.

A brief popular description of the life of Ancient Egyptian women of various
social positions: a member of the royal family, the wife of a pharaoh, a member
of the middle class, a working woman, and a member of the personnel of a
temple. The author stresses the 'equality' of women with men in Ancient Egypt.

161 **Ancient Egyptian materials and industries.**
A. Lucas, J. R. Harris. London: Edward Arnold, 1962. 4th ed.
532p.

The standard work on materials and technology in Ancient Egypt. Topics
included are: adhesives; alcoholic beverages; animal products; beads; building
materials; cosmetics, perfumes, incense; inlaid eyes; fibres; glazed ware; glass;
metals; mummification; oils, fats and waxes; painting materials, writing materials;
pottery; stones, precious and semi-precious; stones other than building stones and
precious stones: stone vessels; and wood. The appendix contains chemical
analyses of many substances. On related topics one might note Somers Clarke and
Reginald Engelbach, *Ancient Egyptian masonry: the building craft* (London:
Oxford University Press, 1930); and a work in English on Ancient Egyptian
medicine: Paul Ghalioungui *The house of life, Per Ankh, magic and medical
science in ancient Egypt* (Amsterdam: B. M. Israël, 1973) – this is effectively the
second edition of the same writer's *Magic and medical science in ancient Egypt*
(London: Hodder and Stoughton, 1963).

162 **Abu Simbel.**
William MacQuitty, foreword by I. E. S. Edwards. New York:
G. P. Putnam's Sons, 1965. 192p.

Describes the saving of the temple at Abu Simbel from the flooding which
resulted from the building of the High Dam at Aswan. Chapter one includes a

history of the temple, which was built by Ramesses II (1292-1225 BC), and various proposed schemes for saving the temple are discussed. Includes photographs by the author, a photographer and film producer.

163 **The gold of Tutankhamen.**
Kamal el-Mallakh, Arnold C. Brackman. New York: Newsweek Books, 1978. 332p.
A book for the general reader about 155 gold and gilt objects found in the tomb of Tutankhamun, now in the Cairo Museum. The first part of the book (p. 1-146) contains the story of the discovery in 1922 by the Earl of Carnarvon and Howard Carter. The second part comprises colour plates showing all these objects with detailed captions describing the function and meaning of each one.

164 **The riddle of the pyramids.**
Kurt Mendelssohn. London: Thames & Hudson, 1974. 224p. bibliog.
In this controversial book, the author, a distinguished physicist, argues that, while it is readily admitted that the pyramids served as royal mausolea, this does not necessarily mean that such usage was the only, or even the principal, purpose of their construction. This book aims to discover what the main purpose was, and the author concludes that it was the activity of building the pyramids which was crucial: the act of construction was the means of achieving a new form of society; the pyramids mark the spot where man invented the state. The author's view that the Medum pyramid collapsed during construction has aroused considerable discussion.

165 **Temples, tombs and hieroglyphics: a popular history of ancient Egypt.**
Barbara Mertz. New York: Dodd, Mead, 1964. rev. ed. 335p.
The author views this work not as a history book, but rather as an informal study of Egyptology, of all things Egyptian.

166 **Red land, black land: the world of the Ancient Egyptians.**
Barbara Mertz. New York: Dell Publishing Co., 1966. 380p. bibliog.
This book might be subtitled 'How to be an Ancient Egyptian', for, if properly studied, it will teach the reader how to make papyrus, how to build a pyramid, how to dress, dine, and furnish a house in the Egyptian manner, and many other skills relating to the culture of the period.

167 **Lives of the pharaohs.**
Pierre Montet. London; New York: World Publishing Company, 1968. 288p. maps.
Presents the history of pharaonic Egypt through the biographies of some of its famous rulers, among them Snorfu, Cheops, Amenemnes I and III, Queen Hatshepsut, Sheshonk I and Amasis.

168 **Everyday life in Egypt in the days of Ramsses the Great.**
Pierre Montet, translated from the French by A. R. Maxwell-Hyslop, Margaret S. Drower. Westport, Connecticut: Greenwood Press, 1974. Reprint ed. 365p. bibliog.

A detailed description of the everyday life of the Ancient Egyptians, first published in 1958 (London: Edward Arnold). The author covers dwelling places, time, the family, life at home, country life, the arts and the professions, travel, the pharaoh, the army and warfare, scribes and judges, the temples and the rites of burial.

169 **Egypt and the Bible.**
Pierre Montet, translated from the French by Leslie R. Keylock.
Philadelphia, Pennsylvania: Fortress Press, 1979. 154p. bibliog.

An account of the Israelites in Egypt. The author includes chapters on first contacts between Israel and Egypt, Moses and the Exodus, Egypt's geography as depicted in the Bible, Egyptian customs in the Bible, magic and superstition, and piety and morality.

170 **Ancient Egypt.**
P. R. S. Moorey. Oxford, England: Ashmolean Museum, 1983. Revised ed. 91p. bibliog.

This book is intended to provide the visitor to the Egyptian Galleries in the Ashmolean Museum with a concise general view of Ancient Egyptian civilization. It is designed not as a comprehensive survey, but as a guide to the wider significance of the objects on display. The bibliography has been brought up to date; otherwise this edition shows only minor changes from the original 1970 publication.

171 **The splendor that was Egypt: a general survey of Egyptian culture and civilization.**
Margaret A. Murray. New York: Philosophical Library, 1949. 354p. map. bibliog.

A wide-ranging book, designed to whet the appetite of the general reader for Egyptology.

172 **Tutankhamun and the Valley of the Kings.**
Otto Neubert. New York: Granada Publishing, 1977. 235p.

A popular book which brings the story of Tutankhamun to life for the modern reader, presenting the whole panorama of Ancient Egypt and its magical cities of Thebes, Luxor and Memphis. First published in German, the book has been translated into sixteen languages.

173 **Warrior pharaohs: the rise and fall of the Egyptian empire.**
P. H. Newby.   London: Faber & Faber, 1980. 212p. bibliog.

A history of the Ancient Egyptian pharaohs' efforts to secure the borders of
Egypt and to extend its frontiers and power. The author discusses among other
historical periods and events the Thutmosids up to the battle of Megiddo, the
Ramesside victories, and the Libyan wars.

174 **Egypt and the Old Testament.**
T. Eric Peet. Liverpool, England: University Press of Liverpool;
London: Hodder and Stoughton, 1922. 236p. bibliog.

A study of the Israelites in Ancient Egypt in the light of Biblical narratives.

175 **A history of Egypt.**
W. M. Flinders Petrie.   London: Methuen; New York: Charles
Scribner's Sons, 1899-1905. 3 vols.

A classic early work on Ancient Egypt. Volume one covers the history of Egypt
from the earliest times to the 15th Dynasty; volume two the history of Egypt
during the 18th and 19th Dynasties; and volume three the history of Egypt from
the 19th to the 30th Dynasties. These volumes were many times revised and
expanded, appearing in their final versions from 1924. They formed a uniform
series with volumes by other authors on the later periods (see item nos. 202, 211,
220).

176 **Egypt and Israel.**
W. M. Flinders Petrie. London: Society for the Promotion of
Christian Knowledge, 1911. 150p. bibliog.

The purpose of this now very dated volume was to illustrate the general historical
setting of the narratives of the Old Testament and Christian times, to see how
they must be understood as part of the history of the period, and to demonstrate
the attitude to these narratives of a general historian.

177 **Social life in Ancient Egypt.**
W. M. Flinders Petrie.   New York: Cooper Square Publishers,
1970. Reprint ed. 210p.

The author describes in this book, first published in 1923, how society was
structured and how it functioned in Ancient Egypt. His chapters study
successively the framework of society, the administrative system, the moral and
ideological system, the private life of the citizens, the economic system, and
construction and defence. This work has been much read, but is both outdated in
approach, and contains many ideas which would now be thought to run counter to
the evidence.

178 **A history of Egyptian mummies and an account of the worship and embalming of the sacred animals by the Egyptians; with remarks on the funeral ceremonies of different nations.**
Thomas Joseph Pettigrew.   Los Angeles: North American Archives, 1983. Reprint ed. 264p.
A classic work, originally published in 1834 (London: Longman, Rees, Orme, Brown and Green) on mummification, its techniques and religious meaning in Ancient Egypt, with observations on the mummies of the Canary Islands, of the Ancient Peruvians, and on other occurrences of this practice.

179 **History and chronology of the Eighteenth Dynasty of Egypt: seven studies**
Donald B. Redford.   Toronto: University of Toronto Press, 1967. 235p.
The author's seven studies cover the following subjects: the accession and coronation of the Ancient Egyptian kings; the family of Ahmose; the coregencies of the early 18th Dynasty; the reign of Hatshepsut; the alleged coregency of Amenhotep III and Akhenaten; the coregency of Akhenaten and Smenkhkare; and the date of the end of the 18th Dynasty.

180 **Romer's Egypt: a new light on the civilization of Ancient Egypt.**
John Romer.   London: Michael Joseph, 1982. 224p. bibliog.
A personal selection of information, opinions and pictures about Ancient Egypt, including the 'hows and whys' of the ancient monuments and the people who made them. Each chapter is intended as an introduction to a different aspect of Ancient Egyptian society.

181 **The sons of Re: cartouches of the kings of Egypt.**
John Rose. Croft, Warrington, England: JR-T, 1985. 175p. maps. bibliog.
Provides a convenient guide to the kings' names found in cartouches in their tombs, on their monuments, and on other Egyptian artifacts, allowing easy identification of the cartouches without any knowledge of the hieroglyphs whatsoever. The author also provides a succinct commentary on the relationship between the kingship and the mythology of Egypt.

182 **The Egyptians: an introduction to Egyptian archaeology.**
John Ruffle.   Ithaca, New York: Cornell University Press; Oxford, England: Phaidon Press, 1977. 224p. bibliog.
An excellent introduction to Egyptian archaeology for non-specialists. Published in Great Britain under the title *Heritage of the pharaohs.*

183 **Daily life in Ancient Egypt.**
Waley-el-dine Sameh, translated from the German by Michael
Bullock. New York; London: McGraw-Hill, 1964. 159p. map.
bibliog.

This book aims to provide a realistic picture of the daily life of Ancient Egypt
based exclusively on contemporary documents and without recourse to any
reconstructions, present-day models or conjecture.

184 **Pharaohs and mortals.**
Torgny Säve-Söderbergh, translated from the Swedish by Richard
E. Oldenburg. New York: Bobbs-Merrill, 1958. 318p.

A series of radio talks and newspaper articles on Ancient Egyptian culture revised
by the author, a distinguished Egyptologist, and published in book form. The
primary goal is not to transmit a mass of facts, but rather to seek out the spirit of
the time and the individual personalities of Ancient Egypt, as reflected in various
situations and milieux.

185 **The Ancient Egyptians and the origin of civilization.**
G. Elliott Smith. London; New York: Harper Brothers, 1923.
rev. ed. 216p.

A classic study based on the 'diffusionist' theory that Egypt was the place from
where human civilization spread.

186 **A visit to Ancient Egypt: life at Memphis and Saqqara (c. 500-30
BC).**
H. S. Smith. Warminster, England: Aris & Phillips, 1974. 92p.

The purpose of this short book is to give to the general reader and to visitors to
Egypt an idea of life at Memphis and Sakkara in the late period. It includes the
texts of two lectures.

187 **Ancient centres of Egyptian civilization.**
Edited by H. S. Smith, Rosalind Hall. London: Egyptian
Education Bureau, 1983. 100p.

A series of essays by several scholars dealing with the great cities of Egypt, and
also with early travellers and with Nubia.

188 **Aspects of the military documents of the Ancient Egyptians.**
Anthony John Spalinger. New Haven, Connecticut: Yale
University Press, 1982. 258p. (Yale Near Eastern Researches, 9).

A comprehensive treatment of the composition and historiographic background of
Ancient Egyptian military inscriptions (ca. 1550 BC to ca. 450 BC), which stresses
analysis of their formal and conventional elements.

189 **When Egypt ruled the East.**
George Steindorff, Keith C. Seele, revised by Keith C. Seele.
Chicago: University of Chicago Press, 1957. 272p.

The emphasis of this work is on the 'Golden Age of Egypt', although the scope
ranges from the earliest times to Alexander the Great. Chapters on art and
religion are included.

190 **The private life of Tutankhamen: love, religion, and politics at the
court of an Egyptian king.**
G. R. Tabouis, with a preface by Theodore Reinach. London:
Routledge, 1929. 322p. bibliog.

An account of the life and times of King Tutankhamun (ca. 1379-1362 BC).

191 **Ancient Egypt: a social history.**
Bruce Trigger, Barry Kemp, David O'Connor, Alan B. Lloyd.
Cambridge, England: Cambridge University Press, 1983. 464p.
bibliog.

This volume provides a fresh perspective on the ancient societies that flourished in
the Nile Valley from the predynastic period to the conquest by Alexander the
Great. From the introduction of a subsistence economy, through the establishment of the first agricultural communities, to the development of urban centres
and the political state, the authors trace the processes of political, social, and
economic change in Egyptian civilization. The first three chapters originally
appeared in Volume I of the Cambridge History of Africa; the fourth was
specially commissioned for this book. The bibliographies are substantial, and the
work has established itself as the first resource for students needing an overall
history of Ancient Egypt in English. Another standard history is provided by the
numerous chapters on Egypt in the Cambridge Ancient History (Cambridge:
Cambridge University Press, second edition still in progress – publication began in
fascicule form in the 1960s). In French, a standard historical survey noted for its
bibliography and exposition of the major problems is *L'Égypte* by Étienne
Drioton and Jacques Vandier (Paris: Presses Universitaires de France, 1962, 4th
enlarged edition, also reprinted with a supplement). One of the most respected
straightforward histories is in German: W. Helck, *Geschichte des alten Ägypten*
(Leiden, The Netherlands; Cologne, FRG: E. J. Brill, 1968, reprinted with
corrections and additions 1981). A convenient brief history in English forms part
of *The ancient Near East: a history* by William W. Hallo and William Kelly
Simpson (New York: Harcourt Brace Jovanovich, 1971).

192 **Nefertiti: an archaeological biography.**
Philip Vandenberg, translated from the German by Ruth Hein.
New York: Lippincott, 1978. 161p. map. bibliog.

A biography of the great Ancient Egyptian queen Nefertiti, wife of Akhenaten
(Amenhatep IV). She was given eighteen epithets by her people, clearly
indicating a queen both extremely beautiful and popular.

193 **The Hyksos: a new investigation.**
John van Selers.   New Haven, Connecticut; London: Yale
University Press, 1966. 220p. bibliog.

This book originated in a doctoral dissertation for Yale University. In it, the author sets out to review all the well-known problems of the Hyksos period. He places the study of the Hyksos in the general context of Bronze Age archaeology, and considers all aspects of our evidence. Recent Austrian excavations directed by Manfred Bietak at Tell el-Dab'a have now opened a new chapter in our understanding of the Hyksos.

194 **Index of Egyptian administrative and religious titles of the Middle Kingdom with a glossary of words and phrases used.**
William A. Ward.   Beirut: American University of Beirut, 1982.
221p.

This work grew out of the author's awareness of the need of researchers in Egyptology for a guide to individual administrative titles.

195 **The life and times of Akhnaton pharaoh of Egypt.**
Arthur Weigall.   London: Thornton Butterworth, 1922. new rev.
ed. 255p.

An account of the rise and fall of Akhenaten and his religion of the Aton.

196 **Serpent in the sky: the high wisdom of Ancient Egypt.**
John Anthony West.   New York; London: Harper & Row, 1979.
253p. bibliog.

This book presents a revolutionary, exhaustively documented reinterpretation of the civilization of Ancient Egypt; it is a study of the life work of the philosopher, orientalist and mathematician, the late R. A. Schwaller de Lubicz.

197 **The burden of Egypt: an interpretation of Ancient Egyptian culture.**
John A. Wilson.   Chicago, Illinois: University of Chicago Press,
1951. 332p.

A standard survey of Ancient Egyptian civilization. Although it deals with each chronological period in order, it does not claim to be a history. It traces developments in Egyptian culture, discussing the nature of our evidence and our approaches to it.

198 **Signs and wonders upon pharaoh: a history of American Egyptology.**
John A. Wilson.   Chicago; London: University of Chicago Press,
1964. 243p. bibliog.

The first part of this book covers the general history of Egyptology; the second part covers the rôle of the American Egyptologists Breasted, Reisner, Winlock and others in promoting the study of Egyptology.

199 **Thousands of years: an archaeologist's search for Ancient Egypt.**
John A. Wilson. New York: Charles Scribner's Sons, 1972. 218p.

An account, in the form of memoirs, of Professor Wilson's experiences in the field of Egyptology.

Dictionary of Egyptian civilization.
See item no. 115.

From the Greeks to the Arab Conquest, 332 BC-640 AD

200 **Egyptian antiquities in the Nile Valley: a descriptive handbook.**
James Baikie. New York: Macmillan, 1932. 874p.

A thorough survey of the remains of Egyptian architecture and large-scale art still to be found *in situ* in Egypt and Nubia. The illustrations are valuable although rather small-scale by modern standards.

201 **Egypt from Alexander the Great to the Arab conquest.**
H. Idris Bell. Oxford, England: Clarendon Press, 1948. 168p. bibliog.

The text of four lectures delivered at the University College of Wales, Aberystwyth, November 1946. The lectures are about papyri and the science of papyrology; the Ptolemaic period; the Roman period; and the Byzantine period. The work still forms the handiest introduction for students to the history of the period. Note also by the same author *Cults and creeds in Graeco-Roman Egypt* (Liverpool, England: University Press, 1953, also reprinted Chicago, Illinois: Ares Press, 1975).

202 **A history of Egypt under the Ptolemaic dynasty.**
Edwyn Bevan. London: Methuen, 1927. 409p. map.

Still the standard history of the period in English. This was a complete rewriting of a work of the same title by J. P. Mahaffy (London: Methuen, 1899), which appeared in a uniform series with Petrie's *History of Egypt* (item no. 175) and Milne's volume on Roman Egypt (item no. 211). Egypt during this period is set in a wider context in F. W. Walbank, *The Hellenistic world* (London: Fontana Paperback, 1981, also published by Harvester Press).

203 **Egypt after the pharaohs, 332BC-AD642: from Alexander to the Arab conquest.**
Alan K. Bowman. London: British Museum Publications; Berkeley, California: University of California Press, 1986. 264p. bibliog.

Viewed from the standpoint of the Egyptologist, the Graeco-Roman period may seem to lack the grandeur and romance which relics of the pharaohs possess, but it was during the millennium between the conquest by Alexander and the Arab invasion that Egypt made its most significant contribution to the classical world and itself absorbed that world's crucial influences. It is a period which is, by the standards of the ancient world, exceptionally well documented, and the author explains the impact of the presence of the Greeks and the Romans in Egypt on its people and culture in a narrative which avoids the 'proliferation of footnotes replete with documentation, bibliography and argument'.

204 **Cleopatra.**
Ernie Bradford. New York: Harcourt Brace Jovanovich, 1972. 279p. bibliog.

A biography of Cleopatra, Queen of Egypt and the last of the Ptolemies.

205 **The large estates of Byzantine Egypt.**
Eduard Rochie Hardy. New York: Columbia University Press, 1931. 162p. bibliog.

After an introductory chapter on Byzantine Egypt, its political organization, tax system, local government and the Egyptian nation, the author studies the history of the Apion Family, other proprietors of the period, feudalism and serfdom, estate management and the estates in the social and economic life of Egypt.

206 **Byzantine Egypt: economic studies.**
Allan Chester Johnson, Louis C. West. Amsterdam: Adolf M. Hakkert, 1967. Reprint ed. 344p. bibliog.

Originally published in 1949 (Princeton, New Jersey: Princeton University Press), this remains one of the few general studies of economic conditions in Egypt under Byzantine rule. Based on material from literature, papyri, and excavations relating to Egypt from the age of Diocletian to the Arab conquest, the book consists of four parts dealing in turn with the land, the people, defence and taxation.

207 **Life in Egypt under Roman rule.**
Naphtali Lewis. Oxford, England: Clarendon Press, 1983. 240p. map.

A study which concentrates on the people who wrote and figure in thousands of the private and official papyri and ostraca of Roman date found in the ruins of ancient towns and villages. The author presents a picture of what life was like for the inhabitants of Egypt when it was a Roman province. The same writer has also published *Greeks in ptolemaic Egypt: case studies in the social history of the Hellenistic world* (Oxford, England: Clarendon Press, 1986).

208 **Daily life in Roman Egypt.**
Jack Lindsay. London: Frederick Muller, 1963. 392p. bibliog.

In this work, of value to the student as well as the general reader, the author
concentrates on the main issues of daily life in the cities and villages of Egypt,
largely ignoring Alexandria, which was a world of its own. The period covered is
essentially the first three centuries AD.

209 **Cleopatra.**
Jack Lindsay. New York: Coward McCann & Geoghegan, 1970.
560p. bibliog.

Cleopatra was the most famous Egyptian queen, and the author believes that
Cleopatra deserves her pre-eminent position; the activities of none of the other
queens were of comparable importance. An interesting account of her life.

210 **L'Organisation militaire de l'Egypte byzantine.** (Military
organization in Byzantine Egypt.)
Jean Maspero. New York; Hildesheim, GFR: Georg Olms
Verlag, 1974. 157p. bibliog. (Bibliothèque de l'Ecole des Hautes
Etudes, Sciences Historiques et Philosophiques, fasc. 201.)

A description of the structure and functions of the Byzantine army in Egypt,
originally published in 1912 (Paris: Librairie Honoré Champion). The book
covers: the situation of Egypt in the Byzantine Empire; the defence system of the
province; the different elements of the army of Egypt; the organization of the
forces; the interior organization of the ethnic quota; and the practical value of the
Byzantine defence system.

211 **A history of Egypt under Roman rule.**
J. Grafton Milne. London: Methuen, 1924. 3rd ed., revised and
enlarged. 331p.

This work has not been superseded as a straightforward history of the period. It
formed part of a uniform series with Bevan's volume on Ptolemaic Egypt (item
no. 202) and Petrie's *History of Egypt* (item no. 175).

212 **Sunrise of power: Ancient Egypt, Alexander and the world of
Hellenism.**
Joyce Milton, preface by William Kelly Simpson. New York:
HBJ Press, 1980. 167p.

Ancient Egyptian history (p. 9-88) is followed by a history of Alexander and the
dynasties that succeeded him in the Middle East and Egypt; the book is
beautifully illustrated.

213 **Women in Hellenistic Egypt: from Alexander to Cleopatra.**
Sarah B. Pomeroy. New York: Schocken Books, 1984. 241p.
map. bibliog.

A social and political history of women and their roles in Hellenistic Egypt (322
BC-30 BC).

The Islamic Dynasties, 640-1250

214 **The reign of al-Hakim bi Amr Allah (386/996-411/1021): a political study.**
Sadik A. Assaad. Beirut: Arab Institute for Research and Publication, 1974. 192p. bibliog.
A political biography of the Fatimid caliph who ruled Egypt for twenty-five years which were enormously difficult for the country.

215 **The Arab conquest of Egypt and the last thirty years of the Roman dominion.**
Alfred J. Butler, edited by P. M. Fraser. Oxford, England: Clarendon Press, 1978. 2nd ed. 563p. 2 maps. bibliog.
An important classic work on the Arab invasion of Egypt in 639 AD and the immediate political context in which it occurred. This edition includes forty additional pages of critical bibliography, and studies by the author entitled 'The treaty of Miṣr in Ṭabarī: an essay in historical criticism', and 'Babylon of Egypt: a study in the history of old Cairo'.

216 **Saladin**
Andrew S. Ehrenkreutz. Albany, New York: State University of New York Press, 1972. 238p. bibliog.
A biography of Saladin (Salah al-Din al-Ayyubi), who was ruler of Egypt 564-89 AH (1169-93 AD), divided into the following chapters: Egypt before Saladin; Saladin before the Egyptian expedition; Saladin and the campaigns of Shirkuh in Egypt; Saladin's accession to the Fatimid vizirate; Saladin as Fatimid vizir; The new master of Egypt and Nur al-Din; Saladin's first campaign in Syria; Consolidation of power in Egypt and Syria; Saladin's war against Mosul; The showdown with the Crusaders; The final six months; and Saladin in historical perspective: a dissenting view.

217 **The agrarian administration of Egypt from the Arabs to the Ottomans.**
Gladys Frantz–Murphy. Cairo: Institut Français d'Archéologie Orientale, 1986. 118p. (Supplément aux Annales Islamologiques, cahier no. 9).
A study of the agrarian administrative system of Egypt based on a chapter in the treatise on taxation written in the 12th century by al-Makhzūmī. Tracing the origins and evolution of the system which he describes establishes the history of agrarian administration from approximately the Arab conquest to the Ottoman conquest of Egypt. An edited text and translation of the relevant part of al-Makhzūmī's treatise is included.

218 **The Fatimids.**
Abbas Hamdani. Karachi: Pakistan Publishing House, 1962. 82p.
A brief history of the Fatimid caliphs, 297-567 AH (909-1171 AD). Of the sixteen
caliphs, twelve ruled in Egypt, from 969-1171 AD. These were al-Muizz, al-Aziz,
al-Hakim, al-Zahir, al-Mustansir, al-Mustaali, al-Amir, the Tayyibi Baawa, al-
Hafiz, al Zafir, al-Faiz and al-Adid.

219 **The governors and judges of Egypt.**
Muhammad Ibn Yusuf El Kindî, translated from the Arabic by
Rhuvon Guest. London: Luzac; Leiden, The Netherlands: Brill,
1912. 72 + 686p. (E. J. W. Gibb Memorial Series, Vol. 19).
Biographies of the governors and judges of Egypt from the Muslim conquest in
640 AD to 860 AD. The author lived in the 10th century AD and the book's
original title was *Kitāb al-umarā' (al-wulah) wa-kitāb al-qudāh* (The book of
governors and the book of judges).

220 **A history of Egypt in the Middle Ages.**
Stanley Lane-Poole. New York: Haskell House, 1969. Reprint
ed. 382p. map.
A classic study by a British historian, first published in 1901 (London: Methuen).
It covers the history of Egypt from the Arab conquest in 640 AD to its annexation
by the Ottoman Turks in 1517. Sources, mainly Arabic, are listed at the beginning
of each chapter. The London editions of this work formed part of a uniform series
with Petrie's *History of Egypt* (item no. 175).

221 **The origins of Ismā'īlism: a study of the historical background of
the Fatimid caliphate.**
Bernard Lewis. Cambridge, England: W. Heffer, 1940. 100p.
bibliog.
The importance of the Ismā'īlī sect was enhanced by its connection with the rise
of the Fatimid dynasty, the most powerful in mediaeval Egypt. The book's four
chapters cover respectively Ismā'īlī origins; the hidden *imāms* and their helpers;
the Carmathians of Bahrain; and the social significance of Ismā'īlism.

222 **Saladin: the politics of the Holy War.**
Malcolm Campbell Lyons, D. E. P. Jackson. Cambridge,
England: Cambridge University Press, 1982. 434p. maps. bibliog.
A detailed history of Saladin's political dealings and military campaigns. The early
part of the book deals with his conquest and rule of Egypt, and the situation there
always remained a factor in his prosecution of the war against the crusaders in
Palestine and Syria.

223 **A history of the Ayyubid sultans of Egypt.**
al-Maqrizi, translated from the Arabic, with introduction and
notes, by R. J. C. Broadhurst. Boston, Massachusetts: Twayne
Publishers, 1980. 376p. bibliog. (Library of Classical Arabic
Literature, vol. V).
An account of the history of the Ayyubid dynasty, which ruled from 1169 to
1242 AD in Egypt, written by the most famous of the Mamluke historians.

224 **A short history of the Fatimid khalifate.**
DeLacy O'Leary. London: Kegan Paul, Trench & Trubner; New
York: E. P. Dutton, 1923. 267p. bibliog.
A history of the Shi'ite dynasty of the Fatimids, who ruled Egypt and North
Africa from 297 to 567 AH (909-1171 AD). Includes a list of original sources,
primarily Arabic and Persian historians; the author depended on these 'so as to
present a picture which, though inaccurate in some points, nevertheless shows the
other side not perceived by the historians who wrote the narrative of the Crusades
from a western standpoint'.

225 **The financial system of Egypt AH 564-741/AD 1169-1341.**
Hassanein Rabie. London: Oxford University Press, 1972. 197p.
bibliog. (London Oriental Series, vol. 25).
A detailed study of the *iqṭā'* system, by which land revenues were awarded by the
state to officials in lieu of salaries, taxation, other sources of revenue, and the
financial administration and monetary system of mediaeval Egypt.

226 **The Fatimid theory of state.**
Panayiotis J. Vatikiotis, foreword by Majīd Khaddūri. Lahore,
Pakistan: Orientalia Publishers, 1957. 223p.
Discusses the Fatimid political ideology and the Fatimid theory of state, which
were based on the Ismā'īlī doctrinal teachings. The author divides his analysis as
follows: firstly, the Fatimid propaganda (*da'wa*): syncretic origins and early
history; secondly, the Fatimid propaganda (*da'wa*): basic doctrine (A) – concept
of the *imama*; (B) – the concept of law; (C) – executive authority in the Fatimid
state; (D) – the concept of the *jihad*; thirdly, the apocalyptic nature of the
Fatimid state: introductory (A) – the *mahdi* idea: gnostic trends and universalist
tendencies; (B) – the theocratic principle; fourthly, the form of the Fatimid state:
(A) – period of *satr*, i.e. concealment; (B) – period of *kashf*, i.e. apocalypse;
(C) – period of chiliastic frustrations and the rise of dissident Puritans.

**Recueil de firmans impériaux Ottomans adressés aux valis et aux Kedives
d'Egypte, 1006-1322 H (1597 J.-C.-1904 J.-C.). Réunis sur l'ordre de Sa
Majesté Fouad Ier, Roi d'Egypte.** (Catalogue of Imperial Ottoman edicts
addressed to the valis and khedives of Egypt. Compiled at the order of
His Majesty King Fuad I of Egypt.)
See item no. 989.

Mamluke and Turkish Rule, 1250-1798

227 The crusade in the later Middle Ages.
Aziz S. Atiya. New York: Kraus Reprint Corporation, 1965.
Reprint ed. 604p. bibliog.

A classic study, first published in 1938, of the crusades by an internationally known historian of the period. Egypt played an important part in this eventful period in the Middle East, and the author covers among other topics the Egyptian conquest of Cyprus, the Egyptian conquest of Armenia, the Mamluke army, the Mongols and Egypt, and the Turkish conquest of Egypt.

228 Gunpowder and firearms in the Mamluk kingdom: a challenge to a mediaeval society.
David Ayalon. London: Vallentine, Mitchell, 1956. 111p.

The main subject of this study is not the technical side of firearms but the historical and social aspects of these weapons, and, above all, a description and analysis of the clash between the deeply-rooted antagonism of a military ruling class of horsemen to firearms, on the one hand, and the steadily growing and inescapable necessity of employing them, on the other. The author's ultimate aim is to prove that superiority in firearms was the main factor which enabled the Ottomans to incorporate Western Asia and Egypt in their dominions.

229 Studies on the Mamlūks of Egypt (1250-1517).
David Ayalon. London: Variorum Reprints, 1977. 360p. bibliog.

This volume contains ten studies in English or French on topics related to Mamluke Egypt, entitled as follows: 'Studies on the structure of the Mamlūk army'; 'The Wafidiya in the Mamlūk kingdom'; 'Le régiment Bahriya dans l'armée mamelouke' (The Bahriya regiment in the Mamlūk army); 'The Circassians in the Mamlūk kingdom'; 'The plague and its effects upon the Mamlūk army'; 'The Mamlūks and naval power – a phase of the struggle between Islam and Christian Europe'; 'The Muslim city and the Mamlūk military aristocracy', 'The system of payment in Mamlūk military society'; 'Studies on the transfer of the Abbasid caliphate from Baghdad to Cairo'; and 'Studies in al-Jabartī: I. Notes on the transformation of Mamlūk society in Egypt under the Ottomans'.

230 The Mamlūk military society: collected studies.
David Ayalon. London: Variorum Reprints, 1979. 364p.

Eleven studies by the author in English or French with the following titles: 'L'esclavage du Mamelouk' (Mamluke slavery); 'Notes on the Furūsiyya exercises and games in the Mamlūk sultanate'; 'The eunuchs in the Mamlūk sultanate'; 'Names, titles and *nisbas* of the Mamlūks'; 'Discharges from service, banishments and imprisonments in Mamlūk society'; 'A reply to Professor J. R. Partington'; 'One of the works of Jean Sauvaget'; 'The European-Asiatic steppe: a major reservoir of power for the Islamic world'; 'Preliminary remarks on the Mamlūk military institution in Islam'; 'Aspects of the Mamlūk phenomenon: the importance of the Mamlūk institution'; 'Aspects of the Mamlūk phenomenon: Ayyūbids, Kurds and Turks'; and 'The historian al-Jabartī and his background'.

231 **Syria and Egypt under the last five Sultans of Turkey: being experiences, during fifty years, of Mr. Consul-General Barker, chiefly from his letters and journals edited by his son Edward B. B. Barker, Her Majesty's Consul.**
Edited by Edward B. B. Barker. New York: Arno Press, 1973.
Reprint ed. 2 vols. in 1.
This work was first published in 1876 (London: Samuel Tinsley). The editor argues that the materials he collected throw light on the history and character of the countries and times his father lived in as an efficient, patriotic and zealous public servant.

232 **History of Egypt 1382-1469**
Ibn Taghrī Birdī, translated from the Arabic by William Popper.
Berkeley, California: University of California Press, 1954-60.
7 vols. (University of California Publications in Semitic Studies, vols. 13, 14, 17-19, 22, 23).
This history was written by Ibn Taghrī Birdī, an Egyptian historian who lived from 1411 to 1470 AD, and in it he gives an account of part of the rule of the Circassian (Burji) Mamlukes who reigned over Egypt from 1382 to 1517. He is regarded as one of the most reliable historians of the period.

233 **The roots of modern Egypt: a study of the regimes of 'Ali Bey al-Kabir and Muhammad Bey Abu al-Dhahab, 1760-1775.**
Daniel Crecelius. Minneapolis; Chicago: Bibliotheca Islamica, 1981. 182p. maps. bibliog.
A study of Ottoman Egypt which covers the military and administrative organization of Ottoman Egypt, the consolidation of Qazdughli power by 'Ali Bey al-Kabir and his elaboration of a new foreign policy for Egypt, the transformation of the Qazdughli Bait into an autonomous regime, and the foreign relations of Muhammad Bey.

234 **Ottoman Egypt in the age of the French Revolution.**
Huseyn Efendî, translated from the Arabic, with introduction and notes, by Stanford J. Shaw. Cambridge, Massachusetts: Harvard University Press, 1964. 197p. (Harvard Middle Eastern Monographs, XI).
A simple bureaucrat describing the forms of administration as they existed at the end of the 18th century, the author provides a unique and valuable glimpse into the Ottoman hierarchy of his day.

235 **The office of qâḍî al-quḍât in Cairo under the Bahri Mamlūks.**
Joseph H. Escovitz. Berlin, FRG: Klaus Schwarz Verlag, 1984.
279p. bibliog. (Islamkundliche Untersuchungen, vol. 100).
Examines the important position held by the chief justice during the rule of the
Bahri Mamlukes, who reigned in Egypt from 648 to 792 AH (1250-1390 AD).

236 **The internal affairs in Egypt during the third reign of Sultan
al-Nasir Muhammad B. Qalawūn 709-741 AH (1309-1341 AD).**
Hayat Nasser al-Hajji. Kuwait: Kuwait University, 1978. 235p.
bibliog.
This work, originally written as a doctoral thesis, consists of an introduction and
seven chapters, which cover in turn the Abbasid caliphate; the administrative
divisions; the political plots; the non-Muslim subjects; Bedouin revolts; the
taxation system; and famines and epidemics.

237 **An urban history of Būlāq in the Mamluk and Ottoman periods.**
Nelly Hanna. Cairo: Institut Français d'Archéologie Orientale,
1983. 112p. bibliog. (Supplément aux Annales Islamologiques,
no. 3).
In this extensively researched history of the Egyptian town of Bulaq, the author
has in succinct fashion reconstructed the story of Bulaq's emergence, urban life,
spatial development and architecture. Wholesale trade in particular brought about
the apogee of Bulaq's importance in Ottoman times, but the area declined quickly
during the 19th century to become a neighbourhood of the greatly expanded
metropolis of Cairo. The economic factors and architectural aspects of change are
important contributions of this research which is based on *awqaf* deeds and
contemporary histories in manuscript.

238 **Egypt and the Fertile Crescent, 1516-1922: a political history.**
P. M. Holt. Ithaca, New York: Cornell University Press, 1966.
337p. bibliog.
Describes the internal developments of the various constituent parts of the
Ottoman Empire in the Arab East and the relationship between Egypt and the
Syrians, Lebanese and Iraqis from Muhammad Ali to the First World War.

239 **Studies in the history of the Near East.**
P. M. Holt. London: Cass, 1973. 261p.
The third part of this book contains the following studies in Egyptian
history: 'Ottoman Egypt (1517-1798): an account of Arabic historical sources';
'al-Jabartī's introduction to the history of Ottoman Egypt'; 'The Beylicate in
Ottoman Egypt during the seventeenth century'; 'The exalted lineage of Ridwān
Bey: some observations on a seventeenth-century Mamlūk genealogy'; and 'The
career of Küçük Muḥammad (1676-94)'.

240 **'Ajā'ib al-āthār fī al-tarājim wa-al-akhbār.** (Wonderful traces in biographies and events.)
'Abd al-Raḥmān ibn Ḥasan al-Jabartī.   Cairo: Lajnat al-Bayān al-'Arabī, 1959-67. 7 vols.
An important historical source for Egypt in the 18th century.

241 **Baibars the first: his endeavours and achievements.**
Abdul-Aziz Khowaiter.   London: Green Mountain Press, 1978. 210p. maps. bibliog.
An account of the life of the Mamluke sultan Baibars I (1260-77), his endeavours, and his political, military and social achievements as the founder of the Bahri Mamluke dynasty.

242 **Saracenic heraldry: a survey.**
Louis A. Mayer.   Oxford, England: Clarendon Press, 1933. 302p.
An illustrated examination of the heraldry of the Mamlukes of Egypt and Syria.

243 **The Mameluke or slave dynasty of Egypt: 1260-1517 A.D.**
Sir William Muir.   London: Smith, Elder & Company, 1896. 245p. map.
A classic work which surveys the Mamluke dynasty from its start under Baibars in 1260 to 1517 when it was brought to a close by the Ottoman sultan Selim.

244 **The judicial administration of Ottoman Egypt in the seventeenth century.**
Galal H. el-Nahal.   Minneapolis; Chicago: Bibliotheca Islamica, 1979. 99p. bibliog.
Discusses the composition of the judiciary, aspects of court administration, criminal justice, civil cases, family law, the role of the court in urban administration, rural administration and the administration of *awqaf*.

245 **Ottoman Egypt in the eighteenth century: the Nizâmnâme-i Miṣir of Cezzâr Aḥmed Pasha.**
Cezzar Ahmed Pasha, edited and translated from the Turkish by Stanford J. Shaw.   Cambridge, Massachusetts: Harvard University Press, 1962. 61p. bibliog. (Harvard Middle East Monographs, no. 7).
A unique and invaluable document for understanding conditions in Egypt during the time of Ottoman rule.

246 **The civilian élite of Cairo in the later Middle Ages.**
Carl F. Petry. Princeton, New Jersey: Princeton University Press, 1981. 435p. maps. bibliog.

A study of the civilian élite of Cairo based on the contents of two biographical dictionaries compiled during the 15th century under the rule of the Mamlukes. The élite staffed the bureaucratic, legal, educational and religious offices of the state and determined the course of intellectual inquiry. This book examines their geographical origins and patterns of residence in Cairo, and their occupations there.

247 **Egypt and Syria under the Circassian sultans, 1382-1468 AD: systematic notes to Ibn Taghri Birdi's chronicles of Egypt. Part I.**
William Popper. Los Angeles; Berkeley, California: University of California Press, 1955. 22 maps. 54 & 123p. (University of California Publications in Semitic Philology, vol. 15).

Section one of this book covers the geography of the Mamluke Empire, with reference to boundaries, provinces, districts, capital cities, routes and post stations. Section two describes the government of the Circassian sultans; it includes an outline of the system of government, the officials and their functions, the *emirs*, and office holders in the Egyptian and Syrian provinces.

248 **Egypt and Syria under the Circassian sultans, 1382-1468 AD: systematic notes to Ibn Taghri Birdi's chronicles of Egypt. Part II.**
William Popper. Los Angeles; Berkeley, California: University of California Press, 1957. 123p. (University of California Publications in Semitic Philology, vol. 16).

A description of Egyptian and Syrian society under the Circassian sultans. The author includes details of the different ethnic communities, names and titles in use, the calendar, weights and measures, currency, food, income and salaries.

249 **The financial and administrative organisation and development of Ottoman Egypt, 1517-1798.**
Stanford J. Shaw. Princeton, New Jersey: Princeton University Press, 1962. 403p. map. bibliog.

A detailed study of the system of administration maintained by the Ottoman rulers of Egypt from the time of their conquest in 1517 until the French occupation in 1798. It attempts to indicate the basic objectives of Ottoman rule in Egypt, and the extent to which they were fulfilled in practice. In terms of revenue, both the landed wealth and the urban wealth of Egypt are discussed, and Ottoman expenditures in administration and on the pilgrimage are examined.

250 **The budget of Ottoman Egypt 1005-1006/1596-1597.**
Stanford J. Shaw. The Hague; Paris: Mouton, 1968. 208p.

The most important concrete expression of the Ottoman administrative-financial system was the annual budget, which was a year-end summary of the revenues and expenditures of the Treasury of Istanbul, as well as of the various provincial treasuries under its jurisdiction. The Ottoman budget in Egypt was divided into three main sections: revenues, expenditure, and balance. This study gives a summary, transcription and translation of the Ottoman budget for Egypt for 1596-97 together with an explanatory introduction. Photographs of the document are appended.

251 **Money, prices and population in Mamluk Egypt, 1382-1517.**
Boaz Shoshan. PhD thesis, Princeton University, 1978. 281ff.
(Available from University Microfilms International, Ann Arbor, Michigan. Order No. 78-18396.)

In this doctoral thesis the author stresses the importance of several changes in the monetary system of 15th-century Egypt. He also notes an inflationary trend in food prices during the last decades of Circassian rule and suggests that this trend coincided with an increasing influx of copper to Egypt from the West. He argues that the shift from silver to copper currency had important consequences and brought on a deterioration in the economic conditions of large segments of Egyptian society. He also stresses the relationship in Mamluke Egypt between certain economic factors and social and political changes.

The agrarian administration of Egypt from the Arabs to the Ottomans.
See item no. 217.

The financial system of Egypt AH564-741/AD1169-1341.
See item no. 225.

Society and religion in early Ottoman Egypt.
See item no. 405.

Fihrist wathā'iq al-Qāhirah ḥattā nihāyat 'asr salātīn al-mamālik 239-922 AH (853-1516 AD) ma'a nashr wa-taḥqīq tis'ah namādhij. (Index of the documents in Cairo archives until the end of the Mamluke sultanate, 239-922 AH (853-1516 AD), with detailed study of nine documents.)
See item no. 956.

Recueil de firmans impériaux Ottomans adressés aux valis et aux Kedives d'Egypte, 1006-1322 H (1597 J.-C.-1904 J.-C.). Réunis sur l'ordre de Sa Majesté Fouad Ier, Roi d'Egypte. (Catalogue of Imperial Ottoman edicts addressed to the valis and khedives of Egypt. Compiled at the order of His Majesty King Fuad I of Egypt.)
See item no. 989.

French Occupation and Muhammad Ali, 1798-1848

252 **Egypt: imperialism and revolution.**
Jacques Berque, translated from the French by Jean Stewart.
London: Faber & Faber, 1972. 674p. bibliog.

Originally published in 1967 (Paris: Editions Gallimard) under the title *L'Egypte: impérialisme et révolution*, this is an important work, tracing the modern social, economic and political history of Egypt by describing the realities of the countryside, the capital, the social structure and political heritage of the people. Part 1 introduces the people and institutions, Part 2 the 18th century colonial period, Part 3 the nationalist wave of 1919, Part 4 the inter-war period and Part 5 the Second World War and the period up to the coup in 1952.

253 **Bonaparte: Governor of Egypt.**
F. Charles-Roux, translated from the French by E. W.
Dickes. London: Methuen, 1937. 359p. maps. bibliog.

Describes the aims and course of Napoleon's Egyptian expedition, his policy towards the Egyptians and Islam, the activities of the French academics and artists, the insurrection at Cairo, and the French administration until Napoleon's abrupt departure.

254 **The writing of history in nineteenth-century Egypt: a study in national transformation.**
Jack A. Crabbs. Cairo: American University in Cairo Press;
Detroit, Michigan: Wayne State University Press, 1984. 227p.
bibliog.

The author aims in this book to present a clearer understanding of the process of national transformation, using historiography as the primary, but not exclusive, tool of analysis.

255 **The founder of modern Egypt: a study of Muhammad 'Ali.**
Henry Dodwell. Cambridge, England: Cambridge University
Press, 1967. Reprint ed. 276p.

A detailed political history of the life of Muhammad Ali (1805-46), originally published in 1931.

256 **The beginnings of the Egyptian question and the rise of Mehemet Ali: a study in the diplomacy of the Napoleonic era based on researches in the British and French archives.**
Shafik Ghorbal, with a preface by Arnold J. Toynbee. New York; London: AMS Press, 1977. 318p. bibliog.
An account of the diplomatic history of 1798-1812 and the events which led to the rise of Muhammad Ali, the founder of modern Egypt. First published in 1928 (London: Routledge).

257 **The predominance of the Islamic tradition of leadership in Egypt during Bonaparte's expedition.**
Samir Girgis. Bern: Herbert Lang; Frankfurt am Main: Peter Lang, 1975. 124p. bibliog. (European University Papers, Series 3; History, Paleography & Numismatics, vol. 47).
Argues that, contrary to the ideas of many historians, it was the profound influence of the Islamic tradition of leadership and the idea of the caliphate and the one-ness of authority which undermined the authority of the French in Egypt, and stunted the self-governing institutions which were transplanted there.

258 **Islamic roots of capitalism, Egypt, 1760-1840.**
Peter Gran. Austin, Texas; London: University of Texas Press, 1979. 278p. bibliog.
This study seeks to redefine the relationship between the West and the Middle East in both cultural and material terms, with principal reference to the Industrial Revolution. The author considers the role of the *ulama* (religious scholars) in developing capitalism and supporting its ideology during that period.

259 **Bonaparte in Egypt.**
J. Christopher Herold. New York: Harper & Row, 1962; London: Hamish Hamilton, 1963. 424p. maps. bibliog.
Describes the French expedition under Napoléon Bonaparte. The author discusses the military and political aims of the expedition, and how it was carried out, in detail.

260 **Spoiling the Egytians.**
John Marlowe. London: André Deutsch, 1974. 277p. bibliog.
Describes the technical, financial and economic colonization of Egypt by Western Europe, beginning with Bonaparte's invasion in 1798 and ending with the British invasion in 1882. The author argues that the strategic interest in Egypt was almost exclusively British, while the economic and financial interests were international.

261 **Egypt in the reign of Muhammad Ali.**
Afaf Lutfi al-Sayyid Marsot. Cambridge, England: Cambridge University Press, 1984. 300p. bibliog.
A well-documented history of Egypt from 1805 to 1848, based on archival research in Egypt, England and France.

262 **The history of Egypt.**
P. J. Vatikiotis. London: Weidenfeld & Nicolson; Baltimore, Maryland: Johns Hopkins University Press, 1986. 3rd ed. 560p. maps. bibliog.

Three major themes dominate this work: the elements of continuity in Egyptian society from ancient times to the present day; the effect of the Islamic religion in shaping the collective and individual beliefs of the Egyptian people and their view of the world; and the encounter, in the 19th and 20th centuries, between the Egyptian and European civilizations. The book concentrates on the internal political and social development of Egypt since 1805 and the development of the new social order created by the revolution. The first edition was published under the title *The modern history of Egypt: the history of Egypt from Muhammad Ali to Sadat.*

The agricultural policy of Muḥammad 'Alī in Egypt.
See item no. 840.

British Occupation and the Successors of Muhammad Ali, 1848-1952

263 **The truth about Egypt.**
J. Alexander. London: Cassell and Company, 1911. 384p.

Describes year by year the political events that took place in Egypt between 1906 and 1910; the author was a British eye-witness.

264 **Ismailia: a narrative of the expedition to Central Africa for the suppression of the slave trade organized by Ismail Khedive of Egypt.**
Sir Samuel W. Baker. London: Macmillan, 1874. maps. 2 vols.

Account of a military campaign in Central Africa inaugurated by Khedive Ismail of Egypt to put an end to the slave trade. The author was a major-general and governor-general of the Equatorial Nile Basin who worked for some time for the Egyptian government.

265 **Secret history of the English occupation of Egypt; being a personal narrative of events.**
Wilfred Scawen Blunt. Cairo: Arab Center for Research and Publishing, 1980. Reprint ed. 606p.

The memoirs of one of the lawyers who defended Urabi, first published in 1907 (London: T. Fisher Unwin). An important work for students of the Urabi revolution of 1881-82.

266   **How we defended Arabi and his friends: a story of Egypt and the**
       Egyptians.
       A. M. Broadley, illustrated by Frederick Villiers.   Cairo: Arab
       Center for Research and Publishing, 1980. Reprint ed. 507p.
This book, first published in 1884 (London: Chapman and Hall), was written by
one of Urabi's lawyers; it gives a detailed account of his defence and a partial
outline of his cause. Based on documents submitted by Urabi himself to the
author.

267   **Ibrahim of Egypt.**
       Pierre Crabites.   London: George Routledge, 1935. 254p.
The biography of Ibrahim Pasha, the eldest son of Muhammad Ali, highlighting
the important role the son played during the life of his father, and tracing his
military career.

268   **Modern Egypt.**
       The Earl of Cromer.   London: Macmillan, 1908. 2 vols.
In this book the author aimed firstly to place on record an accurate narrative of
some of the principal events which occurred in Egypt and the Sudan after 1876,
and secondly to explain the results for Egypt of the British occupation of the
country in 1882. The book reflects the official British view of the period on these
subjects.

269   **Abbas II.**
       The Earl of Cromer.   London: Macmillan, 1915. 84p.
An account of political events in Egypt from January 1892 to 1907, when the Earl
of Cromer left Egypt. The topics covered include the accession of Abbas II,
the Mustafa Fahmi crisis, the Riaz and Nubar ministries, and the methods of
Abbas II.

270   **The practical visions of Ya'qub Sanu'.**
       Irene L. Gendzier.   Cambridge, Massachusetts: Harvard
       University Press, 1966. 175p. (Harvard Middle Eastern
       Monographs, 15).
A study of the thought of Ya'qub Sanu', an Egyptian active in the proto-
nationalist movement of the 1870s. He lived in France from 1878 until 1912 as a
political exile, and there he took the opportunity to act as unofficial
representative of the Egyptian nationalists; this book is concerned with his period
in exile.

271 **Egypt, Islam and the Arabs: the search for Egyptian nationhood, 1900-1930.**
Israel Gershoni, James P. Jankowski. New York; Oxford, England: Oxford University Press, in cooperation with the Dayan Centre and the Shiloah Institute for Middle Eastern and African Studies, Tel Aviv University, 1986. 346p. bibliog.
A study of nationalism in modern Egypt which aims to present firstly, an understanding of the perceptions that constituted that nationalism, secondly, an account of the interplay of nationalist ideas and actions, and thirdly, an explanation of how historical circumstances influenced nationalist doctrines and behaviour.

272 **Egypt under the Khedives (1805–1879): from household government to modern bureaucracy.**
F. Robert Hunter. Pittsburgh, Pennsylvania: University of Pittsburgh Press, 1984. 283p. bibliog.
This study examines the evolution of the new state system after the death of Muhammad Ali in 1849, the development of a bureaucratic elite, and the efforts made by Egypt's viceroys to maintain themselves in the face of financial crises and humiliations by Europe, until the rapid collapse of viceregal bureaucracy between 1875 and 1879.

273 **Al-Jabarti's chronicle of the first seven months of the French occupation of Egypt, Muharram-Rajab 1213 AH (15 June-Dec. 1798).**
Abdul Rahman al-Jabarti, edited and translated by S. Moreh.
Leiden, The Netherlands: E. J. Brill, 1975. 116 & 131p. In English and Arabic. bibliog.
A translation of al-Jabarti's *Tārīkh muddat al-Faransīs bi-Miṣr* (History of the stay of the French in Egypt), an important text for anyone studying the modern history of Egypt.

274 **Nationalism in twentieth-century Egypt.**
James P. Jankowski. In: *The Middle East Reader*, edited by Michael Curtis. New Brunswick, New Jersey; Oxford, England: Transaction Books, 1986, p. 193-204.
A condensed review of the development of nationalism in Egypt from the middle of the 19th century to the mid-20th century. Discusses the different nationalistic trends, which have ranged between Pharaonicism, Egyptianism, Arabism and Islamism.

275 **Between two seas: the creation of the Suez Canal.**
Lord Kinross. London: John Murray, 1968. 283p. maps. bibliog.
Tells the story of the creation of the Suez Canal, and of the political and personal forces involved in it. De Lesseps was a Frenchman and the British steadfastly

opposed its creation for fear of French predominance in Egypt. In the midst of all the diplomatic intrigue was the Egyptian government, trying to defend its own perceived interests.

276 **The Killearn diaries, 1934-1946.**
     Sir Miles Lampson, edited and introduced by Trefor E.
     Evans.   London: Sidgwick & Jackson, 1972. 400p. map.

These diaries present the personal and diplomatic memoirs of Sir Miles Lampson, later Lord Killearn, who was successively Great Britain's High Commissioner and Ambassador to Egypt; they provide an authoritative account of the Egyptian and Middle Eastern political situation as viewed against world events during a critical period.

277 **Bankers and pashas: international finance and economic**
     imperialism in Egypt.
     David S. Landes.   Cambridge, Massachusetts: Harvard
     University Press, 1979. 354p. 2nd ed. bibliog. (Studies in
     Entrepreneurial History, published in cooperation with the
     Research Center in Entrepreneurial History, Harvard University.)

Tells the intricate story of European international business activities in Egypt in the second half of the 19th century. The book is based on the unusually large and intimate correspondence between two businessmen of the period: Alfred Andé, a leading international financier, and Edouard Dervieu, private banker to the Viceroy of Egypt. Originally published in 1958 (London: Heinemann).

278 **The Suez Canal: letters and documents descriptive of its rise and**
     progress in 1854-1856.
     Ferdinand De Lesseps, translated from the French by N.
     D'Anvers.   Wilmington, Delaware: Scholarly Resources Inc.,
     1976. Reprint ed. 311p.

A facsimile reprint of the 1876 edition (London: Henry S. King) of De Lesseps' letters and memoranda about the building of the canal. For an account of the building of the canal, see John Pudney's *Suez: De Lesseps' canal*, published in 1969 (London: Readers Union, J. M. Dent & Sons), with one map and 39 contemporary engravings of the construction of the canal.

279 **Farouk of Egypt: a biography.**
     Barrie St. Clair McBride.   South Brunswick, New York: A. S.
     Barnes, 1968. 238p. bibliog.

An account of the life of King Farouk, who reigned from 1936 to 1952, which makes reference to his struggle against overwhelming odds including a sycophantic court, two unsuccessful marriages and numerous affairs, his humiliation at the hands of a domineering British ambassador, and his conflict with an ageing prime minister. Also discussed are political problems such as the rising nationalism of the clandestine Free Officers' movement led by Nasser, and the sinister Moslem Brotherhood; the Egyptian army's abortive campaign against the Jews in Palestine; guerilla warfare against the British garrisons; the Black Saturday burning of Cairo in 1952; and, finally, the coup d'état and Farouk's life in exile.

280   **The boycott of the Milner mission: a study in Egyptian nationalism.**
      John McIntyre, Jr.   New York: Peter Lang, 1985. 214p. bibliog.
      (American University Studies, Series 9: Vol. 10).

The first two chapters of this account are introductory in nature, and cover the period between 1882 and the active revolt of March 1919 which led to the British Government decision to send the Milner mission. Chapters 3 to 6 examine the respective roles in the boycott movement of the Central Committee of the Wafd, Muslim and Coptic religious leaders and institutions, Egyptian women, and students. Contains a good bibliography.

281   **The last pharaoh: the ten faces of Farouk.**
      Hugh McLeave.   London: Michael Joseph, 1969. 319p. bibliog.

A very readable account of the life of King Farouk, the last king of Egypt, who was caught between the British and the nationalists and was eventually deposed by the Free Officers' coup in 1952 and sent into exile.

282   **Cromer in Egypt.**
      John Marlowe.   London: Elek Books, 1970. 332p. maps. bibliog.

A well-documented history of the British occupation of Egypt. Chapter 9 covers the reconquest of the Sudan.

283   **Egypt and Cromer: a study in Anglo-Egyptian relations.**
      Afaf Lutfi al-Sayyid (Marsot).   London: John Murray; New York: Praeger, 1968. 236p. bibliog.

This book represents an attempt to show to what extent the strength and weakness of men's characters dominated the course of Anglo-Egyptian relations in the late 19th and early 20th centuries. The intrigues, power struggles, aspirations, and especially the conflicting ambitions of the Egyptians and the British Consul-General are described in detail and set in their context.

284   **Egypt's liberal experiment: 1922-1936.**
      Afaf Lutfi al-Sayyid (Marsot).   Berkeley, California; London: University of California Press, 1977. 276p. bibliog.

A detailed study of the period which saw a struggle between the king and the nationalist leaders of the Wafd Party with the British still trying to control the scene. The socio-economic background is well explained.

285 **The military clauses of the Anglo-Egyptian treaty of friendship and alliance, 1936.**
Laila Marsy. *International Journal of Middle East Studies*, vol. 16, no. 1 (March 1984), p. 67–97.
The Anglo-Egyptian treaty of 1936 liquidated a military occupation in principle while allowing it to continue in fact. The treaty recognized Britain's special interest in the security of the Canal, accepted the legitimacy of British forces stationed on Egyptian soil, and provided for a permanent military alliance with the added security afforded by a friendly Egypt. The military were profoundly thankful to have achieved a treaty which provided the basis on which the entire British position in the Middle East in World War II was to depend.

286 **Sir Eldon Gorst: the overshadowed proconsul.**
Peter Mellini. Stanford, California: Hoover Institution Press, 1977. 315p. bibliog. (Hoover Colonial Studies.)
Gorst was His Majesty's Agent and Consul-General in Egypt from 1907 to 1911. This book is a study of the failure of British imperial vision, and also a study of a man who was too clever for his own good, who did not share the confusion of many of his contemporaries about the realities of imperial power, and who was congenitally unable to mask his talents in an age when success in higher office depended to a great extent on both self-deception and hypocrisy.

287 **In the land of the pharaohs: a short history of Egypt from the fall of Ismail to the assassination of Boutros Pasha.**
Duse Mohamed, with a new introduction about the author by Khalil Mahmud. London: Frank Cass, 1968. Reprint ed. 380p. (Africana Modern History, no. 4).
A history of Egypt between 1879 and 1910, first published in 1911, by an Egyptian nationalist who was educated in England, describing the social background as well as the political and international intrigues of the period.

288 **With Kitchener in Cairo.**
Sydney A. Moseley. London: Cassell, 1917. 252p.
A critical view of Lord Kitchener's actions in Egypt by a Briton who worked with him there.

289 **Great Britain in Egypt.**
Major E. W. Polson Newman, foreword by General the Rt. Hon. Sir J. G. Maxwell. London: Cassell, 1928. 303p. 2 maps.
Describes Anglo-Egyptian relations from the days of Ismail Pasha to 1928. The author was able to draw upon certain official unpublished documents, as well as valuable private diaries, and the letters and notes of reputable eye-witnesses, both British and Egyptian.

290 **Egypt for the Egyptians: the socio-political crisis in Egypt 1878-1882.**
Alexander Schölch, with a foreword by Albert Hourani. London: Ithaca Press, 1981. 386p. 2 maps. bibliog. (St. Antony's Middle East Monographs, No. 14.)

This study of the British occupation of Egypt, first published in German (Atlantis Verlag, 1972) is based on the Egyptian archives, French, German and British consular reports and a large number of contemporary memoirs and histories. It is a major work on the period, describing the destruction of the old socio-political order, the short-lived establishment of a new Egyptian order – Urabi and his associates – and the expansion of British economic and political power. The English translation includes additional bibliography, but fewer explanatory and documentary notes.

291 **Fuad, King of Egypt.**
Sirdar Ikbal Ali Shah. London: Herbert Jenkins, 1936. 317p.

A readable, if somewhat fulsome, biography of King Fuad, who reigned from 1917 to 1936. He had to steer a precarious course between the British, who wished to dictate policy to him, and rising Egyptian nationalism principally led by the Wafd Party.

292 **Modernization and British colonial rule in Egypt, 1882-1914.**
Robert L. Tignor. Princeton, New Jersey: Princeton University Press, 1966. 417p. bibliog.

This study assumes that in general the British administration had a modernizing impact on Egypt. It does not argue, however, that the British administrators were bent upon the complete modernization of Egyptian society. Indeed, the reverse was the case in many crucial areas of Egyptian development. The author tries to show in what areas the British administrators did serve as modernizers, in what areas they had little or no effect, and in what areas they even impeded the pressures for change.

293 **The defense statement of Ahmad 'Urabi.**
Ahmad 'Urabi, translated from the Arabic and edited by Trevor Le Gassick. Cairo: American University in Cairo Press, 1982. 110p.

An edition of the Arabic text, together with a translation and explanatory introduction of Urabi's apologia of his political activities. He wrote this while he was imprisoned awaiting trial and revised it later in exile. He was a leading nationalist of the 1870s.

294 **Egypt and the Egyptian question.**
D. Mackenzie Wallace. New York: Russell & Russell, 1967. Reprint ed. 521p.

Originally published in 1883, one year after the British occupation of Egypt, this book discusses conditions in Egypt on the eve of the British intervention. It describes the Egyptian administration and its shortcomings and the social conditions of the Egyptian population, the majority of whom were peasants (*fellaheen*). The author also discusses the occupation and the nature of British interests, and summarizes the various opinions on these matters expressed in Great Britain at the time.

295 **Imperialism and nationalism in the Middle East: the Anglo-Egyptian experience 1882-1982.**
       Edited by Keith M. Wilson. London: Mansell Publishing, 1983.
       172p.
Consists of eight papers by British historians relating to the British occupation of Egypt and Anglo-Egyptian relations between 1882 and the Suez War of 1956. The titles of the papers are as follows: 'Britain and Egypt 1882-1914; the containment of Islamic nationalism', by David Steele; 'Constantinople or Cairo: Lord Salisbury and the partition of the Ottoman Empire 1886-1897', by Keith M. Wilson; 'Negotiating the Anglo-Egyptian relationship between the World Wars', by Oded Eran; 'The Suez Canal and the British economy, 1918-1960', by Richard C. Whiting; 'British diplomacy and the crisis of power in Egypt: the antecedents of the British offer to evacuate, 7 May 1946', by Eran Lerman; 'Egypt, the Arab states and the Suez expedition, 1956', by Elie Kedourie; 'Collusion and the Suez crisis of 1956', by Geoffrey Warner; and 'The significance of the Suez Canal for Western strategy since 1956', by Edward M. Spiers.

296 **Egypt.**
       George Young. London: Ernest Benn, 1927. 352p.
Describes the development of Egyptian nationalism during the 19th century and relations between Britain and Egypt.

297 **Egypt's struggle for independence.**
       Mahmud Y. Zayid. Beirut: Khayats, 1965. 258p. map. bibliog.
An historical study, based on Arabic and English sources, of the negotiations which finally led to the Anglo-Egyptian Treaty of 1936.

Portrait of Egypt.
See item no. 11.

Egypt: imperialism and revolution.
See item no. 252.

The Egyptian élite under Cromer, 1882-1907.
See item no. 558.

Americans in the Egyptian army.
See item no. 734.

Nasser and His Successors, 1952-

298 **Nasser of the Arabs: an Arab assessment.**
Nejla M. Abu Izzeddin. London: Third World Centre for Research & Publishing, 1981. 444p. bibliog.

A critical study of Nasser's achievements in three principal areas: internal development; domestic and foreign relations – especially Suez and non-alignment; and inter-Arab relations. A thorough assessment of the Nasser era.

299 **The October War: documents, personalities, analyses and maps.**
Compiled by An-Nahar Arab Report Research Staff, edited by Riad N. el-Rayyes, Dunia Nahas. Beirut: An-Nahar Press Service, 1973. 295p. maps.

This book includes a day-by-day account and analysis of the fighting on the Egyptian and Syrian fronts with Israel in October 1973, explains how oil emerged as a political weapon, and describes superpower contacts concerning the conflict, and Arab solidarity during the war. It also includes profiles of the senior military hierarchy in Egypt, Syria and Israel.

300 **Mubarak's Egypt.**
Hamied Ansari. *Current History*, vol. 84, no. 498 (Feb. 1985), p. 21–4, 39–40.

Argues that the Mubarak regime seems stable, but that continuity has been secured by sacrificing reform.

301 **Egypt, the stalled society.**
Hamied Ansari. Albany, New York: State University of New York Press, 1986. 308p. bibliog.

An in-depth examination of the effects of ideological and policy changes on individuals and classes in Egyptian society during the last fifteen years. The author explains in political, social, and economic terms the effects of shifting from the secular ideas of Nasser, which underpinned Pan-Arabism and socialism, to the approach of Sadat with his open-door policy, religious beliefs and sectarian attitudes.

302 **Egypt's uncertain revolution under Nasser and Sadat.**
R. W. Baker. Cambridge, Massachusetts: Harvard University Press, 1978. 290p.

An historical survey and analysis of the development policies pursued by Nasser and Sadat.

303   **The Israeli-Egyptian war of attrition 1969-1970: a case study of limited local war.**
Yaacov Bar-Siman-Tov. New York: Columbia University Press, 1980. 428p.

The author considers the Israeli-Egyptian war of attrition to have been a major confrontation, and that therefore it deserves more study than it has previously received. He views it as a special case of limited local war and studies it as such.

304   **The making of a war: the Middle East from 1967 to 1973.**
John Bulloch. London: Longman, 1974. 220p. 2 maps.

A description of events in the Arab world between the wars of June 1967 and October 1973, giving a detailed account of the political struggles and alliances which were brought into play, and contributed to the growing impetus towards war. This is a very useful study of the complex politics of inter-Arab relations.

305   **The transformation of Egypt.**
Mark N. Cooper. London; Canberra: Croom Helm; Baltimore, Maryland: Johns Hopkins University Press, 1982. 278p.

An in-depth analysis of the political economy of Egypt between 1967 and 1977. Utilizing the concepts and categories of political sociology, the author conducts an empirical analysis of the period from the June War of 1967 to Sadat's 'mission of peace' to Jerusalem in November 1977, during which time the country lived through the death of Nasser and the dramatic liberalization of the country's economic structures.

306   **Egypt under Nasir: a study in political dynamics.**
R. Hrair Dekmejian. London: University of London Press; Albany, New York: State University of New York Press, 1971. 310p. bibliog.

This study traces the evolution of the Egyptian political system from the 1952 revolution, through the June 1967 war, to Nasser's death and its aftermath. The primary focus of the inquiry is on the leader himself as he interacted with the political environment of the 1950s and 1960s. An excellent piece of political analysis.

307   **Sadat and his statecraft.**
Felipe Fernandez-Armesto. Windsor Forest, England: Kensal Press, 1983. 2nd ed. 179p. bibliog.

A study of Sadat's policy and achievements as a statesman, both at home and abroad, within the constraints of Egypt's domestic pressures and international position.

308 **Sadat and Begin: the domestic politics of peacemaking.**
Melvin A. Friedlander. Boulder, Colorado: Westview Press, 1983. 338p. bibliog.

This book demonstrates how domestic factors affecting policy decisions made in both Cairo and Jerusalem prevented Sadat and Begin from embracing a structure that would yield a more comprehensive arrangement. Sadat, for example, confronted an anti-peace movement in Egypt, while Begin was opposed by Israeli conservatives who saw the Camp David formulas as leading to a peace that would jeopardize Israel's security. Both leaders, the author concludes, were able ultimately to guide their nations toward approval of the peace initiative primarily because of their mastery of the techniques of domestic intra-élite bargaining.

309 **Suez: the double war.**
Roy Fullick, Geoffrey Powell. London: Hamish Hamilton, 1979. 227p. maps. bibliog.

Based on the memoirs of the participants, both published and as recounted to the authors in letters and interviews, and on their own personal knowledge of the events of the summer of 1956. This book details the political and diplomatic intrigues and the carrying out of the operation.

310 **The real Suez crisis: the end of a great nineteenth century work.**
Jacques Georges-Picot, translated from the French by W. G. Rogers. New York; London: Harcourt Brace Jovanovich, 1978. 200p.

First published in French in 1975 (Paris: Editions de la R.P.P.). The early chapters of this book cover Egypt's political evolution and its consequences for the Suez Canal Company in the ten years preceding the crisis, and this is followed by a summary of the Company's attitudes to the West and its own reputation on the eve of the crisis. The crisis itself is described essentially from the point of view of the Company, although the attitudes of Egypt, Great Britain, France, the United States and other countries are not ignored.

311 **Revolutions and military rule in the Middle East: Egypt, the Sudan, Yemen, and Libya. Vol. 3.**
George M. Haddad. New York: Robert Speller, 1973. 444p. bibliog.

Egypt is covered in the first 173 pages of this volume; chapter one deals with the conditions in Egypt that led to the 1952 revolution and the early years of conflict thereafter; chapter two considers the methods and results of Nasser and Nasserism.

312 **Nasser: the Cairo documents.**
Mohamed Heikal. London: New English Library; Garden City,
New York: Doubleday, 1972. 328p. Reprinted with an introduction
by Edward R. F. Sheehan. Garden City, New York: Doubleday,
1973. 357p.

This book 'is largely the story of Nasser's personal relations with twelve men,
giants of the international scene, rebels and statesmen, whom he met in conflict or
friendship – and occasionally both', written by Nasser's confidant and close
adviser. The later edition's introduction is about the author himself.

313 **The road to Ramadan.**
Mohamed Heikal. London: Collins, 1975. 285p.

Traces the inevitable descent into war in 1973 after the defeat of 1967, and the
failure to achieve any diplomatic progress towards the recovery of Egypt's
conquered territories.

314 **Autumn of fury: the assassination of Sadat.**
Mohamed Heikal. London: André Deutsch; New York: Random
House, 1983. 290p.

A controversial interpretation of Sadat's reign and the factors leading to his
assassination, explaining why a man so admired in the West was so isolated in his
own world, and why a man mourned as a hero in the West found hardly any
mourners in his own country. Mohamed Heikal was a close associate of Nasser
and later of Sadat until the October war of 1973. He was imprisoned during
Sadat's mass arrests in September 1981.

315 **The war of atonement.**
Chaim Herzog. London: Weidenfeld & Nicolson; Boston: Little,
Brown, 1975. 300p. 9 maps.

A full account of the war from an Israeli viewpoint. For another account from the
Israeli side, see Zeev Schiff *October earthquake: Yom Kippur 1973*, published in
1974 (Tel Aviv: University Publishing Projects).

316 **Sadat.**
David Hirst, Irene Beeson. London: Faber & Faber, 1982. 384p.
maps. bibliog.

A political biography which concentrates on Sadat's decade as Egyptian head of
state, and on his foreign and domestic policies. A critical and provocative
judgement of the former president.

317 **Egypt and Nasser.**
Edited by Dan Hofstadter. New York: Facts on File, 1973.
3 vols.

The first of these three volumes describes Nasser's overthrow of King Farouk, his
elimination of his major domestic enemies, his negotiation of the withdrawal of
British troops from Egyptian soil, his unsuccessful bid for American credits to

finance a new Nile dam at Aswan and his subsequent break with the USA, his nationalization of the Suez Canal, which led to the Suez Canal crisis of 1956, and the aftermath of this crisis. Volume 2 takes the story from January 1957 to December 1966. This period was one of unprecedented domestic peace, economic development and expanded foreign prestige for Egypt. It was also, however, the era of two major Egyptian fiascos in the Arab world – the ill-fated union with Syria (1958-1961) and the disastrous military involvement in the Yemeni Civil War (1961-1967). Volume 3 deals with the period from January 1967 to August 1972, covering the rapid deterioration of the Middle Eastern political scene preceding the June war of 1967, the death of Nasser in September 1970, and President Sadat's expulsion of most Soviet military advisors in July and August 1972.

318 **Egypt – the crucible: the unfinished revolution of the Arab world.**
Harry Hopkins.   London: Secker & Warburg, 1969. 513p. map.
bibliog.

Describes the events leading up to the revolution of 1952, and the pressures within Egypt for change during Nasser's time. This book provides a picture of the aspirations of ordinary Egyptians and what they thought and wanted.

319 **The Yom Kippur War.**
Insight Team of the London *Sunday Times*.   Garden City, New York: Doubleday, 1974. 514p.

An in-depth journalistic report derived from the extensive coverage of the Arab-Israeli war in the London *Sunday Times* during October 1973. Research into the causes and conduct of the war continued, however, for some time after the cease-fire. In this American edition the authors incorporated considerable material not previously available and corrected errors of fact and interpretation which appeared in the original version.

320 **The public diary of President Sadat.**
Edited by R. Israeli.   London: E. J. Brill, 1979. 3 vols.

The three volumes of this diary are entitled respectively 'The road to war' (Oct. 1970-Oct. 1973); 'The road of diplomacy' (Nov. 1973-May 1975); and 'The road of pragmatism' (June 1975-Oct. 1976). The text consists of passages from transcripts of original addresses, some of which were given in English; these are placed in their proper historical context to underline their significance, and to outline the development of the president's thinking.

321 **Man of defiance: a political biography of Anwar Sadat.**
Raphael Israeli, Carol Bardenstein.   London: Weidenfeld & Nicolson; Totowa, New Jersey: Barnes & Noble, 1985. 314p.
bibliog.

Following Sadat's assassination a number of biographies were published, some of them rather hurriedly; the authors of this book disagree with many of them about both 'facts' and judgements, and believe that in some cases injustice was done to the late president out of political or personal bias. They present in this book an 'inner' and 'subjective' rather than an 'outer' and 'judgemental' biography of

Sadat, on the basis that it is no less important to comprehend why he acted as he acted than to pronounce a sometimes unwarranted verdict on the quality of his reasoning or the results thereof.

322   Nasser: the rise to power.
Joachim Joesten.   London: Odhams Press, 1960. 224p.
A biography of Nasser which is critical of his policies.

323   Frogs and scorpions, Egypt, Sadat and the media.
Doreen Kays.   London: Frederick Muller, 1984. 277p.
The author of this book argues that both the American and the Middle Eastern views of Sadat are accurate. Anwar Sadat was both hero and villain, a man of two worlds, 'frog and scorpion'. The book deals with Sadat's career as a media superstar from the time of his trip to Jerusalem until his death.

324   The Sadat assassination: background and implications.
Jihad B. Khazen.   Washington, DC: Georgetown University, Center for Contemporary Arab Studies, 1981. 10p.
An interesting analysis of the assassination by an Arab journalist and political scientist.

325   The demigods: charismatic leadership in the Third World.
Jean Lacouture, translated from the French by Patricia Wolf.   New York: Knopf; London: Secker and Warburg, 1970. 300p.
Nasser is one of the Third World leaders the author studies in this book.

326   Nasser: a biography.
Jean Lacouture.   London: Secker & Warburg, 1973. 394p.
bibliog.
First published in French in 1971, this is a detailed biography of Nasser, his rise to power, and his troubled domestic revolution. His attempts to promote Egypt's development and his foreign policy successes and disasters are discussed.

327   Egypt and the West: salient facts behind the Suez crisis.
E. V. Lawrence.   New York: American Institute of International Information, 1956. 85p.
The author adopts the view that the principal factor in the Suez crisis resulting from Nasser's nationalization of the Suez Canal is Soviet penetration of the Middle East on a scale threatening the displacement of the West. He stresses the uncompromising policies of Nasser and the new Russian influence in the Middle East, both of which were threats to the interests of the West and Israel. The book represents a veiled invitation to the West to interfere in the Suez Canal, and such interference indeed occurred just one month after the book was published.

History. Nasser and His Successors, 1952-

328 Suez: the twice-fought war.
Kennett Love.   New York; Toronto: McGraw-Hill, 1969. 767p.
maps. bibliog.

The most comprehensive account of the Suez war, written by a *New York Times* correspondent who was working in the Middle East during the crucial years. Includes detailed maps and a chronology from 1798 to 1968.

329 Nasser's Egypt.
Peter Mansfield.   Harmondsworth, England; Baltimore,
Maryland: Penguin Books, 1965. 222p. map. (Penguin African
Library, AP 16).

A very good, short history of the first decade of Nasser's revolution of 1952, and the historical, social and political background to it. See also by the same author *Nasser* (London: Methuen, 1969. Makers of the Modern World, no. 1).

330 Middle East in crisis: a historical and documentary review.
Syracuse, New York: Syracuse University Press, 1959. 213p.

A review of the events of the time, with particular reference to the Israeli invasion of Sinai on 29 October 1956 and world reaction to it. The description of events is supported by 48 documents and speeches.

331 Suez: ten years after – broadcasts from the BBC Third Programme.
Edited by Peter Calvocoressi and others, introduced by Anthony
Moncrieff.   New York: Pantheon Books, 1967. 160p.

Contains the texts of eight programmes about the Suez war of 1956 which Peter Calvocoressi prepared for the BBC Third Programme in 1966.

332 Egypt's liberation: the philosophy of the revolution.
Gamal Abdel Nasser, introduction by Dorothy
Thompson.   Washington, DC: Public Affairs Press, 1955. 119p.

Nasser sets out in this book the goals of the 1952 revolution under his leadership.

333 The philosophy of the revolution.
Gamal Abdel Nasser, introduction by John S. Badeau,
biographical sketch by John Gunther.   Buffalo, New York:
Economica Books, 1959. 102p.

This volume is the result of a careful study by Economica Books of several versions of Nasser's text. The translation used is one published by Dar Al-Maaref in Egypt, and given by President Nasser in Cairo to the editor.

334 **Nasser speaks: basic documents.**
Gamal Abdel Nasser, rendered into English by E. S.
Farag. London: Marssett Press, 1972. 176p.

A direct insight into events between 1952 and 1970 cannot be better gained than
from the writings of the man who was so largely instrumental in their making.
This book consists of two main parts: The Philosophy of the Revolution, p. 11-58;
and The Charter, p. 59-167.

335 **Egypt's destiny.**
Mohammed Neguib. London: Victor Gollancz, 1955. 273p.

An account of the 1952 revolution in Egypt, written by the first prime minister of
that revolution, who was in power between July 1952 and March 1954.

336 **Egypt under Sadat: the contours of asymmetrical interdependence.**
Salua Nour, Carl F. Pinkele. In: *The contemporary Mediterranean
world*. Edited by Carl F. Pinkele and Adamantia Pollis. New
York: Praeger, 1983, p. 276-96.

A discussion of Sadat's internal and external policies. The authors try to explain
the reasons behind Sadat's shifts of policy and the way in which he tried to 'de-
Nasserize' Egypt.

337 **The electronic war in the Middle East 1968-70.**
Edgar O'Ballance. London: Faber & Faber; Hamden,
Connecticut: Archon Books, 1974. 148p. 4 maps.

Describes the war of attrition between Egypt and Israel and how the two sides
waged it during the period after the 1967 war. Also contains references to the role
of the superpowers in that period.

338 **Return to Sinai: the Arab–Israeli war, 1973.**
Major-General D. K. Palit. Salisbury, England: Compton
Russell, 1974. 142p.

A description of the 1973 war from an Indian viewpoint. Although details of
operations were obtained from Arab sources, the overall framework is based on
the generally anti-Arab world press. The book is limited to a study of the military
campaign; although the political and strategic reasons that led to President Sadat's
decision to go to war are discussed, the details of political developments such as
superpower involvement and the oil strategy of the Arabs are dealt with only in
so far as they pertain to the course of the war. For another straightforward
military account, see Edgar O'Ballance, *No victor, no vanquished; the Yom
Kippur war*, published in 1979 (London: Barrie & Jenkins).

339 **Nasserite ideology: its exponents and critics.**
Nissim Rejwan. New York: John Wiley; Jerusalem: Israel
Universities Press, 1974. 271p.

An analysis of the ideology of Nasser's regime. Contains a translation of the
important document 'The Charter of National Action' (*Al-Mithaq*), p. 192-265.

79

340 **International crises and the role of law: Suez 1956.**
Robert R. Rowie.   New York; London: Oxford University Press,
1974. 148p.

This study of the Suez crisis of 1956 seeks to explore what part international law,
norms, or agencies played in the decisions and actions of the major protagonists.
How did such rules, norms or agencies influence what was done or how it was
done? How were they used for legitimizing political actions, for rallying support,
or for imposing restraints? What role did they play in resolving the crisis? The
author's aim is to answer these questions rather than to recount the history of the
crisis in detail.

341 **Memoirs from the women's prison.**
Nawal el Sa'adawi, translated from the Arabic by Marilyn
Booth.   London: Women's Press, 1986. 197p.

Nawal el Sa'adawi was arrested along with many others by President Sadat a
month before he was assassinated. She was eventually released about three
months later. This is a powerful account of her time in prison, the conditions
there, and the other women imprisoned with her, including political radicals and
veiled Islamic conservatives.

342 **Revolt on the Nile.**
Anwar El Sadat, with a foreword by President Nasser.   London:
Allan Wingate; New York: John Day Company, 1957. 159p.

The role of Anwar el-Sadat in the 1952 Egyptian revolution, as described by
himself.

343 **In search of identity.**
Anwar el-Sadat.   London: Collins, 1978. 343p.

An autobiography of his life up to the time of his trip to Jerusalem and the
negotiations with Israel, giving Sadat's version of the role he played in the Nasser
years and as President. Five appendices give the texts of important documents
and speeches, including his letter to Brezhnev of 30 August 1972 at the time of
the expulsion of the Russians from Egypt, and his speech to the Israeli Knesset on
20 November 1977.

344 **My father and I.**
Camelia Sadat.   New York: Macmillan, 1985. 203p.

The personal memoirs of Sadat's daughter by his first wife, portraying from the
inside the problems and complexities of family politics.

345 **The boss.**
Robert St. John.   London: Arthur Barker; New York: McGraw-
Hill, 1960. 325p.

A readable and informal biography of Nasser.

346   **The Suez Canal in peace and war, 1869-1969.**
Hugh J. Schonfield.   London: Vallentine Mitchell; Coral Gables,
Florida: University of Miami Press, 1969. Revised ed. 214p.
The author aims in this book to answer the question of how, if the Canal belongs
to Egypt, but also belongs to mankind, it can effectively serve these two masters.
The appendices contain the texts of the international agreements relating to the
Suez Canal of 1854, 1856, 1888, 1936, 1949, and 1954, and the Suez Canal
Company Nationalization Law of 1956.

347   **The crossing of the Suez.**
Lt.-General Saad el-Shazly.   London: Third World Centre for
Research and Publishing; San Francisco, California: American
Mideast Research, 1980. 333p. maps.
A military memoir by the chief of staff of the Egyptian armed forces during the
Arab-Israeli war of October 1973. The author is very critical of Sadat's conduct of
the war. For another account from the Egyptian side, see Hassan El Badri, Taha
El Magdoub, Mohammed Dia El Din Zohdy, *The Ramadan war, 1973*, published
in 1979 (Dunn Loring, Virginia: T. N. Dupuy Associates).

348   **Egypt: portrait of a president, 1971-1981. The counter revolution in
Egypt. Sadat's road to Jerusalem.**
Ghali Shoukri.   London: Zed Press, 1981. 465p.
An important historical account which focuses solely upon political life within
Egypt during the period and is well documented. The author analyses the
development of a growing opposition to President Sadat within Egypt in terms of
events, ideology and actions.

349   **Nasser: a political biography**
Robert Stephens.   London: Allen Lane, The Penguin Press; New
York: Simon & Schuster, 1971. 631p. 4 maps. bibliog.
The aim of this book is to give a coherent account of Nasser's life and career for
the general reader and to describe the historical circumstances which helped to
form his political character and ideas. The author also aims to distinguish what, if
anything, were Nasser's own distinctive contributions to political thought and
practice. A very good, sympathetic account.

350   **Down into Egypt: a revolution observed.**
John Sykes.   London: Hutchinson, 1969. 190p.
An account of Egypt by an English writer who visited it after the 1967 defeat. A
portrait of a society facing crisis.

351 **The multinational force and observers in the Sinai: organization, structure and function.**
Mala Tabory, foreword by Dr. Ruth Lapidoth. Boulder, Colorado; London: Westview Press, 1986. 179p. maps.

This book describes the MFO with reference to its conception, creation, structure and organization, functions, duties and rights, in order to test its suitability for its assigned tasks and evaluate its chances of success. The appendices contain the text of the peace treaty and attached documents.

352 **Egypt since the revolution.**
Edited by P. J. Vatikiotis. New York: Praeger; London: Allen & Unwin, 1968. 195p.

Includes most of the papers delivered at the September 1966 conference held by the Centre of Middle Eastern Studies, School of Oriental and African Studies, University of London, and also subsequent contributions by scholars who had attended. The purpose of the conference was to discuss the economic, political and cultural problems of Egypt since 1952. The papers included are as follows: 'Planning and economic growth in the UAR, 1960-5', by Bent Hansen; 'The Egyptian economy and the revolution', by Galal Amin; 'Agricultural production in historical perspective: a case study of the period 1890-1939', by Roger Owen; 'Economic and institutional organization of Egyptian agriculture since 1952', by M. Riad El-Ghonemy; 'The political system', by Maxime Rodinson; 'Egyptian foreign policy and the revolution', by Malcolm H. Kerr; 'Foreign policy since 1952: an Egyptian view', by Khaled Mohieddin; 'Cultural and intellectual developments in Egypt since 1952', by Louis Awad; 'Literary trends in Egypt since 1952', by David Cowan; and 'Some Western views of the Egyptian revolution', by Derek Hopwood.

353 **Nasser and his generation.**
P. J. Vatikiotis. London: Croom Helm, 1978. 369p.

A political study of Nasser, seen as a representative of a whole generation of Egyptians. Part 1 discusses the political forces in Egypt which arose in the 1930s, which influenced most of Nasser's generation. Part 2 considers the Free Officers' road to power, the eventual emergence of Nasser as sole ruler, and the disintegration of the old political order. Later parts deal with Nasser's relations with the Arabs, Israel and the rest of the world, and his style at home as absolute ruler of Egypt.

354 **The Egypt of Nasser and Sadat: the political economy of two regimes.**
John Waterbury. Princeton, New Jersey: Princeton University Press, 1983. 475p. bibliog.

Presenting a balance sheet of thirty years of revolutionary experiment, this book undertakes a comprehensive analysis of the failure of the socialist transformation of Egypt during the regimes of Nasser and Sadat. Testing recent theories of the nature of the developing states and their relation both to indigenous class forces and to external pressures from advanced industrial societies, the author describes the limited but complex choices available to Egyptian policy-makers in their attempts to reconcile the goals of reform and capital accumulation.

355 **Nasser's new Egypt: a critical analysis.**
Keith Wheelock. London: Stevens & Sons; New York: Praeger, 1960. 326p.
A critical review of Nasser's military regime, which discusses developments in Egyptian society between 1952 and 1959. Agriculture, education and social development, economics and industrialization, the High Dam project, and the political policies adopted by the regime are reviewed in turn.

The *Jihad*: an 'Islamic alternative' in Egypt.
See item no. 393.

The Arabs and the world: Nasser's Arab nationalist policy.
See item no. 678.

The Arab cold war: Gamal 'Abd al-Nasir and his rivals, 1958-1970.
See item no. 684.

The road to war 1967: the origins of the Arab–Israeli conflict.
See item no. 704.

The third Arab–Israeli war.
See item no. 708.

The Suez War.
See item no. 722.

The Suez Canal settlement.
See item no. 724.

Warriors at Suez.
See item no. 727.

No end of a lesson: the story of Suez.
See item no. 728.

Crisis: the inside story of the Suez conspiracy.
See item no. 729.

Suezkanal-bibliographie: eine Auswahl des europäisch-sprachigen Schrifttums seit 1945. Bibliography on the Suez Canal: a selection of literature in European languages since 1945.
See item no. 955.

Religion

Ancient Egyptian

356 **Akhenaten, pharaoh of Egypt – a new study.**
Cyril Aldred.   London: Thames & Hudson, 1968. 272p. bibliog.
An account of Akhenaten (1378-1362 BC) and his cult, based on seventeen years' study of the pharaoh and the Amarna period. Includes numerous illustrations and a chronology.

357 **Gods and myths of ancient Egypt.**
Robert A. Armour, with the research assistance of Alison Baker.   Cairo: American University in Cairo Press, 1986. 207p. bibliog.
The author aims in this book to present the most interesting tales, based on the most reliable sources. As he points out in his preface, many of the earlier scholars, such as E. A. Wallis Budge, Flinders Petrie, and James Frazer, collected material that remains valuable for anyone compiling an anthology of Egyptian mythology, although their interpretations have often been modified by more recent scholarship.

358 **Ancient Egyptian religion.**
Jaroslav Černý.   London: Hutchinson's University Library, 1952. 159p.
The most useful straightforward account of the subject in English.

359   **Ancient Egyptians: religious beliefs and practices.**
      A. Rosalie David.   Boston, Massachusetts: Routledge & Kegan
      Paul, 1982. 260p.

This introduction to the religion of Egypt places beliefs and practices in their
social and historical settings. The author includes extensive bibliographies as well
as a table of Egyptian history and a list of major archaeological sites.

360   **Ancient Egyptian religion: an interpretation.**
      H. Frankfort.   New York: Columbia University Press; London:
      Oxford University Press, 1948. 172p.

The author presents a new interpretation of Ancient Egyptian religion based on a
rigorous new analysis of the religious texts of the period. Chapters cover in turn
the Egyptian gods, the Egyptian state, the Egyptian way of life, the Egyptian
hope as regards death, and change and permanence in literature and art. Two
wider-ranging books by the same author contain much on Egyptian religion: *The
intellectual adventure of ancient man* (Chicago, Illinois: Chicago University Press,
1946) and *Kingship and the gods* (Chicago, Illinois: Chicago University Press,
1958).

361   **Conceptions of god in Ancient Egypt: the one and the many.**
      Erik Hornung, translated from the German by John
      Baines.   Ithaca, New York: Cornell University Press, 1982. 296p.

The author studies the Ancient Egyptians' conceptions of god, basing his account
on a thorough reappraisal of the primary sources. He seeks to answer two basic
questions: How did the Egyptians themselves see their gods? Did they believe
there was an impersonal, anonymous force behind the multiplicity of their deities?

362   **Egyptian mythology.**
      Veronica Ions.   New York: Peter Bedrick Books, 1983. Revised
      ed. 144p.

After an introductory chapter on cults and divinities in Ancient Egypt, the author
studies the creation of the world in the mythology of the different periods of
Ancient Egyptian history. She also studies pharaonic divinities and divinities of
creation, fertility and birth. In the final section she considers life after death and
the spread of the Osiris cult.

363   **Akhenaten: the heretic king.**
      Donald B. Redford.   Princeton, New Jersey: Princeton University
      Press, 1984. 255p. bibliog.

This work examines afresh the history of King Akhenaten and the twilight of the
Thutmosid house, using the results of recent research at Karnak, Amarna and
elsewhere in the Middle East. Much of the material is based on the work of the
Akhenaten Temple Project which has, since 1966, concerned itself with the
remains of the period at Karnak and Luxor.

364 **Myth and symbol in Ancient Egypt.**
R. T. Rundle Clark. London: Thames & Hudson, 1959. 292p.
map.

An account of the spiritual life of the Ancient Egyptians. The author covers the
history of the various gods and deities who were worshipped by the Ancient
Egyptians, especially Osiris, and he also includes chapters on myths about the
great gods, and on mythological symbols.

365 **Isis and Osiris: the myth and the stage.**
Aziz al-Shawan. *Prism: Quarterly of Egyptian Culture*, vol. 10
(October-December 1984), p. 9-11. illus.

Describes how the author, an Egyptian musician, tried to present this legend on
stage in the form of a ballet.

366 **Myths and legends: ancient Egypt.**
Lewis Spence. Boston, Massachusetts: David D. Nickerson
[n.d.]. 326p.

In this volume the religious history of Ancient Egypt is reviewed in the light of
the findings of modern mythology.

367 **Egyptian saints: deification in pharaonic Egypt.**
Dietrich Wildung. New York: New York University Press, 1977.
110p.

The author carefully traces Imhotep's gradual acceptance into the Egyptian array
of deities over a period of a millennium. He shows how the great creative abilities
of Imhotep as an architect and builder were mainly responsible for his ultimate
deification.

Christianity

368 **A history of Eastern Christianity.**
Aziz S. Atiya. Millwood, New York: Kraus Reprint, 1980.
Reprint ed. 492p. 7 maps. bibliog.

This book, first published in 1968 (London: Methuen; Notre Dame, Indiana:
University of Notre Dame Press), was enlarged and updated by the author for this
edition. It is a very authoritative history of which the first 167 pages cover the
Copts and their Church: the origins of Coptic Christianity, the Copts and the
world, the Copts under Arab rule, the Copts in modern times, Coptic faith and
culture, and the Copts abroad.

369 **The flight into Egypt.**
William Farid Bassili. Cairo: El-Mahaba Bookstore, 1968. 2nd ed. 121p.

A brief history of the flight of the Holy Family into Egypt. The author describes the journey, the traditional sites visited by the Holy Family, and the miracles which are said to have happened throughout the journey.

370 **Nubian antiquities in the Coptic Museum.**
Mounir Basta. *Prism: Quarterly of Egyptian Culture*, vol. 11 (1985), p. 6-7.

A brief report on the discovery by a Dutch mission in 1963-64 of a church which was built in Nubia in the middle of the 8th century AD.

371 **Coptic Egypt.**
New York: Brooklyn Institute of Arts and Sciences, The Brooklyn Museum, 1955. 58p.

This volume contains six papers originally read at a symposium held under the joint auspices of New York University and the Brooklyn Museum, 15 February 1941, in connection with the exhibition 'Paganism and Christianity in Egypt'. The papers are: 'On the background of Coptism', by William Linn Westermann; 'Later Egyptian piety', by Arthur Darby Nock; 'Romano-Coptic Egypt and the culture of Meroë', by Dows Dunham; 'Problems of Coptic art', by John Ducey Cooney; 'Some aspects of Coptic painting', by Sirarpie Der Nersessian; and 'Classification of Coptic textiles', by Maurice Sven Dimand.

372 **In the steps of the Holy Family from Bethlehem to Upper Egypt.**
Otto F. A. Meinardus. Cairo: Dar Al-Maaref, 1963. 66p. maps.

The author traces in this book the birth of Christ, the flight of the Holy Family to Egypt and their eventual return to Palestine. He relates the sites of churches and monuments existing today to the original legend (cf. item no. 38).

373 **Christian Egypt: ancient and modern.**
Otto F. A. Meinardus. Cairo: Cahiers d'Histoire Egyptienne, 1965. 518p. bibliog.

An authoritative survey of the history of the major Christian sects that covers the whole of Egypt from Alexandria to Sohag. Included are detailed studies of the Orthodox Churches (Coptic, Greek, and Armenian), the Catholic Churches (Armenian, Greek, Latin, Maronite and Syrian rites) and the Coptic Evangelical Church. Special sections cover the monastic movement and the legend of the Holy Family in Egypt. All major monuments and feasts are described.

374 **Christian Egypt: faith and life.**
Otto F. A. Meinardus. Cairo: American University in Cairo Press, 1970. 514p. bibliog.

A companion volume to the author's *Christian Egypt: ancient and modern*, this book is intended to serve as an introduction to selected issues in Coptic theology and ethics. The approach is multidisciplinary, employing the methods of history, theology, sociology, psychology and anthropology to distinguish between the 'official' and the 'folk' religions of the Copts and to discuss such questions as the relationship of the Coptic Church to the family, to the state, and to its own historic mission.

375 **New discoveries in Nubia: proceedings of the colloquium on Nubian studies, The Hague, 1979.**
Edited by Paul von Moorsel. Leiden, The Netherlands: Nederlands Instituut voor het Nabije Oosten, 1982. 129p.

This book consists of twelve complete papers, résumés of four others, and three lectures on Christian Nubia, including the following: 'Late hunter-gatherers of Central Sudan: the site of Saggai', by Isabella Caneve, Annalisa Zarattini; 'The mosque building in Old Dongola', by Wlodzimierz Godlewski; 'Loopholes in theory: feudal Nubian architecture', by Thomas E. Higel; 'An ancient scheme to build a pyramid at Meroë', by Friedrich W. Hinkel; 'A brief account of the churches of old Dongola', by Stefan Jakobielski; 'Habitation mounds in Shilluk Land', by Else Johansen Kleppe; 'Salih, medieval Nubia: retrospects and introspects', by Ali Osman Mohed; 'Nubian Christian numerical cryptograms: some elucidations', by J. Martin Plumley; 'The Christian period in Nubia as represented in the site of Qasr Ibrim', by J. Martin Plumley; 'The visit of a Nubian king to Constantinople in A.D. 1203', by Bozena Rostkowska; 'Linguistic aspects of Greater Nubian history', by Robin Thelwall; and 'The interpretation of the earliest evidence of lungfish *Protopterus sp.* in the Nile Valley, El-Zakyab Site, Central Sudan', by A. Tigani el-Mahi.

376 **The roots of Egyptian Christianity.**
Edited by Birger A. Pearson, James E. Goehring. Philadelphia, Pennsylvania: Fortress Press, 1986. 319p.

The first part of this book deals with sources preserved in Greek, Coptic and Arabic; part 2 deals with the environment of early Christianity in Egypt; part 3 deals with the emergence of Christianity in Egypt; part 4 is devoted to studies in theology; and part 5 deals with various aspects of Egyptian monasticism.

377 **Manuscript, society and belief in early Christian Egypt.**
Colin H. Roberts. London: Oxford University Press for the British Academy, 1979. 88p. (Schweich Lectures of the British Academy, 1977).

Considers the first century and a half of Christianity in Egypt, with reference to why so little is heard and known about the Church in Egypt during that period, and whether there was Jewish influence on the Church in Egypt at that time. The author is a distinguished Greek papyrologist, and much of the book is concerned with the 'manuscript' part of its title.

Atlas of Christian sites in Egypt.
See item no. 38.

Islam

378 **Islam and modernism in Egypt: a study of the modern reform movement inaugurated by Muḥammad 'Abduh.**
Charles Clarence Adams. New York: Russell & Russell, 1968. Reprint ed. 283p. bibliog.
Describes the modernizing efforts of the religious leader Muhammad Abduh, and contains a chapter on Jamal al-Din al-Afghani, the predecessor of Abduh, and on Rashid Rida, his successor. Originally published in London in 1933.

379 **In the pharaoh's shadow: religion and authority in Egypt.**
Fouad Ajami. In: *Islam in the political process.* Edited by James P. Piscatori. Cambridge, England: Cambridge University Press, 1983, p. 12-35.
A study of the relationship between religion and political authority as expressed by three modern Egyptian Muslim writers (Shaykh 'Abd al-Halim Mahmud, Shaykh al-Azhar, and Khalid Muhyi al-Din), a leftist party leader, and Sayyid Qutb, a Muslim Brother ideologist.

380 **The reformers of Egypt: a critique of al-Afghani, 'Abduh and Ridha.**
Zaki Badawi. Slough, England: Open Press, 1976. 95p. (Muslim Institute Papers, no. 2).
Discusses in turn the views of three major leaders of the Reform School in Egypt: Jamal al-Din al-Afghani, Muhammad Abduh, and Rashid Rida. The reformists, as opposed to the Westernizers and the revivalists, represent a form of synthesis of various trends within the Muslim political community and their influence was much greater than their numbers warranted.

381 **Five tracts of Hasan al-Banna: a selection from *Majmu'at Rasa'il Hasan al-Banna*.**
Hasan al-Banna, translated from the Arabic and annotated by Charles Wendell. Berkeley, California: University of California Press, 1978. 180p. bibliog. (University of California Publications on Near Eastern Studies, vol. 20).
In these five well-known essays Hasan al-Banna (1906-1949), the founder of the Moslem Brothers of Egypt, explains the Brotherhood's moral position, social purpose and goals, and role vis-à-vis the West.

382 **Memoirs of Hasan al-Banna Shaheed (1906-1949)**
Hasan al-Banna, translated from the Arabic by M. N. Shaikh. Karachi: International Islamic Publishers, 1981. 224p.
The memoirs of the founder of the Muslim Brothers of Egypt.

383   **Islamic political activity in modern Egyptian history: a comparative analysis.**
Gabriel Baer. In: *Islam, nationalism and radicalism in Egypt and the Sudan*. Edited by Gabriel R. Warburg and Uri M. Kupferschmidt.   New York: Praeger, 1983, p. 33-54.
A study of the role played by Islam in Egyptian politics in the first half of the 20th century.

384   **Islam in Egypt today: social and political aspects of popular religion.**
Morroe Berger.   New York: Cambridge University Press, 1970. 131p. bibliog.
Discusses religious behaviour and the organization of religious life in Egypt today, the mosque and its relations with government, Sufi brotherhoods and activities, and the various voluntary benevolent societies.

385   **Aspects of the political involvement of *Sufi* orders in twentieth-century Egypt (1907-1970): an exploratory stock-taking.**
Fred de Jong. In: *Islam, nationalism and radicalism in Egypt and the Sudan*. Edited by Gabriel R. Warburg and Uri M. Kupferschmidt.   New York: Praeger, 1983, p. 183-212.
This paper presents a number of cases illustrating the forms of involvement of the Sufi orders in Egyptian politics in the era before and after the 1952 revolution and up to 1970.

386   **Islam in revolution: fundamentalism in the Arab world.**
R. Hrair Dekmejian.   Syracuse, New York: Syracuse University Press, 1985. 249p. bibliog.
The primary concern of this book is to examine the historical roots and patterns of Islamic resurgence and the forms of its manifestation in the crisis milieu of present-day Muslim society. The case of Egypt is thoroughly discussed in chapter 6. A well-documented study.

387   **The resurgence of Islamic organizations in Egypt: an interpretation.**
Ali E. Hillal Dessouki. In: *Islam and power*. Edited by Alexander S. Cudsi and Ali E. Hillal Dessouki.   London: Croom Helm, 1981, p. 107-19.
Written by an Egyptian professor of political science, this chapter analyses the reasons behind the revival of Islamic organizations in Egypt since 1967.

388 Egypt, Islam and social change: al-Azhar in conflict and
     accommodation.
     A. Chris Eccel.   Berlin: Klaus Schwarz Verlag, 1984. 611p.
     bibliog. (Islamkundliche Untersuchungen, vol. 81).
An academic study of Muslim religious institutions in Egypt, especially al-Azhar,
the principal centre of Muslim learning not only for Egypt, but, even today, for
the entire Sunni Muslim world. The book examines al-Azhar's functioning during
the Ottoman period, its changing relationship with the ruling authority, the
challenges posed by the Islamic reformers and, later, the secularists and discusses
how the institution has responded to these challenges and adapted itself to
changes in the state and society.

389 Islam and politics.
     John L. Esposito.   Syracuse, New York: Syracuse University
     Press, 1984. 273p. bibliog.
This volume provides the historical background to and the context in which to
understand Islamic politics today, describes the role of Islam in modern Muslim
politics, and analyses the major obstacles and issues which attend the
establishment of Islamically-oriented states and societies. The case of Egypt is
discussed in every chapter.

390 Saint and Sufi in modern Egypt: an essay in the sociology of
     religion.
     Michael Gilsenan.   Oxford, England: Clarendon Press, 1973.
     241p. bibliog.
Describes religious practice among Egyptians belonging to the Sufi brotherhoods
and discusses the transformation of the position of the Sufi orders in Egypt since
the turn of the century and the decline of their activities and importance in the
wider society.

391 The world turned inside out: forms of Islam in Egypt.
     Michael Gilsenan. In: *Recognizing Islam: an anthropologist's
     introduction.*   London: Croom Helm, 1982, p. 215-50.
An account of religious movements in Cairo, with particular reference to the
Muslim Brothers and Sufi Tariqa.

392 Islamic fundamentalism in Egypt during the 1930s and 1970s:
     comparative notes.
     Ahmed M. Gomaa. In: *Islam, nationalism and radicalism in Egypt
     and the Sudan.* Edited by Gabriel R. Warburg and Uri M.
     Kupferschmidt.   New York: Praeger, 1983, p. 143-58.
The author believes in the continuity of Islamic fundamentalism in 20th century
Egypt, and argues that, although it has emerged the loser in all its confrontations
with the authorities (1948, 1954, 1965, 1981), this does not detract from its actual
or potential importance as an ongoing phenomenon in Egyptian society and
politics.

393   **The Jihad: an 'Islamic alternative' in Egypt.**
Nemat Guenena.   Cairo: American University in Cairo Press,
1986. 103p. (Cairo Papers in Social Science, vol. 9, monograph 2).
This is an analysis, based on court records, of the ideology, leadership, organization and social profile of the members of the Jihad group which was responsible for killing Sadat.

394   **Nationalism and revolution in Egypt: the role of Muslim Brothers.**
Christina Phelps Harris.   The Hague: Mouton for the Hoover
Institution on War, Revolution and Peace, 1964. 276p. bibliog.
This study is primarily concerned with the Muslim Brotherhood founded by Hasan al-Banna in 1928 and the development of its role in Egyptian politics. The かかかかか かかか かかかかか かかか かかかかかか かかかかかか かかか かかかかかか かかかかかかかかかか かかかかかかかかか and Nasser's regime.

395   **Religious and political trends in modern Egypt.**
J. Heyworth-Dunne.   Washington, D.C.: J. Heyworth-Dunne,
1950. 111p.
A useful description of the background and rise of the Muslim Brotherhood, and its relations with the political authorities, and with other political groups both inside and outside Egypt, together with a summary of Hasan al-Banna's political doctrines.

396   **Islam in Egypt under Nasir and Sadat: some comparative notes.**
Raphael Israeli.   In: *Islam and politics in the modern Middle East.*
Edited by Metin Heper and Raphael Israeli.   London: Croom
Helm, 1984, p. 64-78.
A comparison between Nasser's secularism and Sadat's opportunism as exemplified by their treatment of the Muslim Brothers of Egypt.

397   **The neglected duty: the creed of Sadat's assassins and Islamic
resurgence in the Middle Ages.**
Johannes J. G. Jansen.   New York: Macmillan; London: Collier
Macmillan, 1986. 245p.
A book which is required reading for anyone interested in the Islamic militant movement in Egypt today. It contains a translation of the document entitled 'The Neglected Duty' which is 'a call for Muslims to take up arms in fulfillment of their religious duty to submit to the will of God and to bring the world into subjection to him'.

398 **Nubian ceremonial life: studies in Islamic syncretism and cultural change.**
Edited by John G. Kennedy. Berkeley, California: University of California Press; Cairo: American University in Cairo Press, 1978. 249p.

A full-scale study of Nubian religious beliefs and practices, based on salvage ethnography of Old Nubia and field study in New Nubia by a team of American and Egyptian anthropologists.

399 **The Prophet and pharaoh: Muslim extremism in Egypt.**
Gilles Kepel. London: Al Saqi, 1985. 251p.

First published in French in 1984, this is a study of the historical background of Muslim radicalism in the years 1954-1966, the works and life of Sayyid Qutb, and the development in the 1970s of new groups which spread into the universities and fomented trouble with the Coptic community in Egypt, and finally were responsible for the assassination of Sadat.

400 **The beginnings of modernization among the rectors of al-Azhar, 1798-1879.**
Afaf Lutfi al-Sayyid Marsot. In: *Beginnings of modernization in the Middle East: the nineteenth century.* Edited by William R. Polk, Richard L. Chambers. Chicago; London: University of Chicago Press, 1968, p. 267-80.

The author argues in this paper that whereas in past centuries al-Azhar had been capable of adapting itself to doctrinal changes while remaining at the forefront of the intellectual life of Islam, the 19th century, bringing Westernization in its wake, caused al-Azhar to fear modernization of any kind. The period of Muhammad Ali proved to be such a traumatic experience that it took al-Azhar a whole century to overcome its distrust of the government's motives in attempting to modernize it, and to realize that modernization did not imply extinction but that, on the contrary, extinction was the threat that lurked behind entrenchment in the citadel of tradition.

401 **Milestones.**
Sayyid Qutb. Cedar Rapids, Iowa: Unity Publishing, 1980. 160p.

A translation of *'Alamat 'Ala al-Tariq*, the most important book by Sayyid Qutb, the ideologist of the Muslim Brothers.

402 **The concept of *jihad* in Egypt: a study of *Majallat al-Azhar* (1936-1982).**
Hannah R. Rahman. In: *Islam, nationalism and radicalism in Egypt and the Sudan.* Edited by Gabriel R. Warburg and Uri M. Kupferschmidt. New York: Praeger, 1983, p. 249-61.

An attempt to explain the concept of *jihad* in Islam in theory and practice as it was presented in the periodical *al-Azhar* published by al-Azhar University in Cairo.

403 **Islam and the search for social order in modern Egypt: a biography of Muhammad Husayn Haykal.**
Charles D. Smith. Albany, New York: State University of New York Press, 1983. 249p. bibliog.
Haykal saw popular opinion and political participation as threats to the landowning class to which he belonged. He envisaged Islam as an individualistic faith for intellectuals – a faith which imposed on the masses the acceptance of the socioeconomic status into which they had been born. His opinions brought him into conflict with official and popular Muslim organizations which sought to preserve Islam's traditional role and to improve social conditions. In this book the author revises previous accounts of Egyptian intellectual history in the inter-war period, and argues that the conflicts experienced by Muhammad Husayn Haykal still exist in today's Egypt.

404 **Islam, nationalism and radicalism in Egypt and the Sudan.**
Edited by Gabriel R. Warburg, Uri M. Kupferschmidt. New York: Praeger, 1983. 383p.
A group of studies of political trends and ideologies in Egypt and the Sudan during the twentieth century. Thirteen of the papers deal specifically with Egypt, and individual entries for some of these are given in this bibliography.

405 **Society and religion in early Ottoman Egypt: studies in the writings of 'Abd al-Wahhāb al-Sha'rānī.**
Michael Winter. New Brunswick, New Jersey: Transaction Books, 1982. 345p. bibliog.
The author uses the works of 'Abd al-Wahhab al-Sha'rani, one of the important and fruitful Sufi writers in Egypt in the 16th century, to examine the religious and social order in Egypt at the beginning of the Ottoman period. He reviews topics such as: orthodox Islam compared to Sufism; relations between the Sufis and the Ottoman rulers; the status of women; and the attitude of Muslim society towards Jews and Christians – topics which are still relevant to Egypt today.

406 **Militant Islam in Egypt: some socio-cultural aspects.**
Rivka Yadlin. In: *Islam, nationalism and radicalism in Egypt and the Sudan*. Edited by Gabriel R. Warburg and Uri M. Kupferschmidt. New York: Praeger, 1983, p. 159–82.
A detailed analysis of the dilemma that has long faced the Egyptians: *asala* versus *mu'asara* (traditionalism versus modernity). Traditionalism has been revived by the débâcle of 1967 and the decline of Nasserism. The author studies the socio-cultural background of the revival of religiosity as expressed by militant Muslims, and the contradictions that prevailed on the Egyptian scene during that process.

The Islamic militants in Egyptian politics.
See item no. 613.

Sectarian conflict in Egypt and the political expediency of religion.
See item no. 614.

The impact of the Egyptian Muslim Brotherhood's political Islam since the 1950s.
See item no. 622.

Islamic movements in Egypt, Pakistan and Iran: an annotated bibliography.
See item no. 973.

Population

407 **Review and evaluation of studies on the determinants of fertility in Egypt.**
Hamed Abou-Gamrah.   Cairo: Population and Family Planning
Board, Research Office, 1981. 74p. bibliog.

The author, an Egyptian population specialist, presents a critical review and an
evaluation of studies on the determinants of fertility in Egypt.

408 **Urban in-migration and out-migration in Egypt: an analytical study
of birthplace data in 1976 cenus.**
Ahmad Seif al-Nasr, Muhammad Attiya. *Population Bulletin of
ECWA*, no. 26 (June 1985), p. 9-37.

A detailed case study was carried out by the authors to examine the role of urban
areas as both receivers and senders of migrants in Egypt. The analysis shows that
almost all such areas in Egypt are sources of out-migration, and that the
variations between them are far less in this respect than as centres of in-migration,
in which capacity they vary greatly. In addition, the analysis shows that the three
largest cities, Cairo, Alexandria and Giza City, draw the majority (over 70 per
cent) of their immigrants from other cities and not from rural areas.

409 **The estimation of recent trends in fertility and mortality in Egypt.**
Committee on Population and Demography, National Research
Council.   Washington, DC: National Academy Press, 1982. 144p.
bibliog. (Committee on Population and Demography, Report
no. 9).

The panel on Egypt which produced this report included eight population
specialists from Egypt and the United States.

410 **Is there hope? Fertility and family planning in a rural Egyptian community.**
Saad M. Gadalla. Chapel Hill, North Carolina: University of North Carolina; Cairo: American University in Cairo, 1978. 262p. bibliog.
Based upon a long-term in-depth study of a typical three-village rural Egyptian community, this book relates local circumstances, attitudes and knowledge to the general problem of fertility control, and recommends a programme of positive action.

411 **Population and development in Egypt: new hopes for old problems.**
Charles F. Gallagher. *American Universities Field Staff Reports*, no. 31 (1981), p. 1-14; no. 32 (1981), p. 1-21.
A quantitative analysis in two parts of population trends in Egypt from the late 1960s to the year 2000. An important article which provides an understanding of the increasing imbalance between population and economic resources.

412 **Old ills and new remedies in Egypt: a comprehensive review of the different measures adopted in recent years to deal with the problems resulting from overpopulation.**
Eva Garzouzi. Cairo: Dar Al-Maaref, 1958. 157p. maps. bibliog.
Poverty, ignorance and disease are the natural results of overpopulation unless there are matching increases in economic resources. This book explains the scope of the overpopulation problems, how much has been done to solve them, and how much still remains to be done.

413 **An action research on the promotion of conventional methods of contraceptives among Egyptian married couples.**
Mary Taylor Hassouna. Cairo: Population and Family Planning Board, 1981. 134p. (Final Report of Barrier Method Study, no. 2; Research Monograph Series, no. 3).
This project, known as the Barrier Method Study, sought to identify factors affecting the acceptability of barrier methods. Acceptability of a method is a function of the attitudes, beliefs and perceptions of potential and actual clients and of delivery system factors affecting acceptability. The project also sought to remove factors which have inhibited family planning service delivery in the country and have thus affected the level of programme participation.

414 **Internal migration in Egypt: a critical review.**
Saad Eldin Ibrahim. Cairo: Population and Family Planning Board, Research Office, 1982. 86p. bibliog. (Research Monograph Series, no. 5).
Reviews what is known about internal migration in Egypt: its volume, trends and directions, factors leading to it and consequences of it.

415 **Family planning in rural Egypt: a report on the results of the Egypt Contraceptive Prevalence Survey.**
Atef M. Khalifa, Hussein Sayed, M. Nabil el-Khorazaty, Ann A. Way. Cairo: Population and Family Planning Board, Westinghouse Health Systems, 1982. 221p. bibliog.

This report presents the findings of the Egypt Contraceptive Prevalence Survey conducted by the Population and Family Planning Board in November and December 1980. The survey was part of an ongoing worldwide Contraceptive Prevalence Survey (CPS) designed to institutionalize the monitoring of levels of contraceptive awareness, availability and use in order to provide an improved data base for evaluating family planning programmes. Additional information on this survey and on family planning activities in Egypt can be obtained from the Population and Family Planning Board, P.O. Box 1036, Cairo, Egypt.

416 **Population and development in rural Egypt.**
Allen C. Kelley, Atef M. Khalifa, M. Nabil el-Khorazaty. Durham, North Carolina: Duke University Press, 1982. 252p. bibliog. (Studies in Social & Economic Demography).

Analyses the pattern of population growth in Egypt, and the factors influencing family size and fertility. The relative success and failure of attempts to control population growth are evaluated.

417 **Egyptian population studies: annotated bibliography until 1979.**
Edited by Sarah F. Loza. Cairo: Population and Family Planning Board, Research Department, 1979-83. 3 vols.

The third volume of this annotated bibliography supplements and updates volumes 1 and 2 which surveyed Arabic and English literature up to 1976. Volume 3 comprises references published during the period 1977-79 and material missing from volumes 1 and 2. The entries are serially numbered throughout the three volumes, which all follow the same pattern of organization. The volumes include 1,438 entries in English and 2,993 entries in Arabic, covering all aspects of population studies in Egypt. The author, title and subject indexes are in English and Arabic.

418 **Industrialization and population dynamics and characteristics.**
Sarah F. Loza. Cairo: Population and Family Planning Board [n.d.]. 232p. bibliog. (Research Monograph Series, no. 9).

An investigation of the relationship between industrialization and fertility, which started work in January 1977 and is largely based on fieldwork. The findings discuss the reproductive behaviour of groups experiencing industrialization, with reference to such factors as age at marriage, and also the relationship between socio-economic variables and fertility differentials.

419 **Internal migration and structural changes in Egypt.**
Mostafa H. Nagi. *Middle East Journal*, vol. 28, no. 3 (Summer
1974), p. 261-82.

The author identifies a number of streams of migration which include: rural-
metropolitan centres; rural-urban (movement of large numbers of students and
workers); rural-industrial (movement from villages to major industrial centres in
Aswan, Giza, etc.); and a traditional movement from Upper to Lower Egypt.
After studying these streams based on the 1966 census, he concludes that
population explosion is a major factor in rural-urban migration; rural-urban
migration has contributed greatly to urbanization; that Egypt is an over-urbanized
country; and that in Egypt urbanization as a form of structural change is at a stage
well advanced from urbanism as a way of life.

420 **Egypt: population problems and prospects.**
Edited by Abdel R. Omran. Chapel Hill, North Carolina:
University of North Carolina, Carolina Population Center, 1973.
434p. bibliog.

A collection of 22 papers, divided into 7 parts, written by specialists on the
population problems of Egypt. Part I, Demographic Profiles of a Changing
Society, contains 'The population of Egypt, past and present', 'The mortality
profile', and 'The fertility profile', all by Abdel R. Omran; 'Population
movements and distribution over time and space', by Sandra K. Burden; and 'An
annex to the demographic profiles: population projections', by Abdel R. Omran,
with Nader Fergany. Part II, Economic and Sociocultural Profiles of a Changing
Society, comprises 'Economic development', by Haifaa Shanawany; 'Islam and
fertility control', by Abdel R. Omran; and 'Status of women and family planning
in a developing country – Egypt', by Aziza Hussein. Part III, Development of a
Population Policy and Program Implementation, includes 'Stages in the
development of a population control policy', by Haifaa Shanawany; 'The family
planning effort in Egypt: a descriptive sketch', by Abdel R. Omran, Malek el-
Monrossey; 'A note on the assets and difficulties of Egypt's family planning
program', by Khalil Mazhar; 'Some research needs of the national family planning
program', by Aziz Bindary; 'Estimates of the family planning program's effects on
fertility in the 1970's', by Nader Fergany; and 'Benefits and costs of a prevented
birth: conceptual problems and application to Egypt', by George C. Zaidan. Part
IV, Medical Research on Population Control in Egypt, includes 'Research in
family planning in Alexandria', by H. K. Toppozada; 'Clinical studies of
contraception at Ain Shams University', by Aly M. Makhlouf, Shawky Z.
Badawy; and 'Clinical studies of lactation and contraception', by Ibrahim Kamal.
Part V, Selected Studies in Population Dynamics and Family Planning, contains
'Childhood mortality experience and fertility performance', by Shafick S. Hassan;
'Social studies on fertility and contraception in Alexandria', by Zahia Marzouk;
'A study on abortion in Cairo University Hospital', by I. Kamal, M. A. Ghoneim,
M. Talaat, M. Abdallah, M. Eid, Laila Shukry el-Hamamsy; and 'Experience
with abortion in a private practice', by H. K. Toppozada, M. K. Toppozada. Part
VI, Prospects for Accelerating the Transition in Egypt, consists solely of
'Prospects for accelerating the transition in Egypt', by Abdel R. Omran; and
finally part VII is 'Egypt: a selected bibliography'.

Population

421 Report on the Egyptian state information service's mass media campaign to support population and family planning.
Marshal D. Rothe, Douglas Larson. Washington, DC: American Public Health Association, 1981. 55p. (U.S. AID Doc. No. PN-AAJ-483).

Explains the need for and the methods of utilizing the mass media to educate the Egyptian people in the importance and goals of family and population planning.

422 The population and development program in Egypt: a problem in program impact measurement.
H. Abdel-Aziz Sayed, J. Mayone Stycos, Roger Avery. Cairo: Cairo Demographic Centre, 1984. 26p. (Working Paper, no. 8).

In addition to promoting family planning services, this programme mobilizes local resources and upgrades management capabilities at the village level in order to stimulate economic development, slow down population growth and improve the health and welfare of the community. Initiated on an experimental basis in 1977, by 1978 the project was operating in over 800 villages, by 1979 in about 1,500, and by the end of 1980 in nearly 3,000 of Egypt's roughly 4,000 villages.

423 Rural resettlement in Egypt's reclaimed lands: an evaluation of a case study in the northwestern Nile delta.
Helmi R. Tadros. Cairo: American University in Cairo, 1978. 66p. bibliog. (Cairo Papers in Social Science, Monograph 4).

This evaluative study had three major objectives: to describe the land reclamation and resettlement area; to consider the demographic aspects of the populations in the resettlement areas that were the subject of the research, with reference to family size, fertility levels and knowledge, attitudes and practices related to family planning; and to evaluate the rehabilitation process in relation to changes in economic conditions, social development of the transferred families, community services and community development.

424 Urbanization and migration in some Arab and African countries.
Cairo: Cairo Demographic Centre, 1973. 528p. (Research Monograph Series, no. 4).

The following papers in this volume relate to Egypt: 'Internal migration and urbanization in Egypt', by Abdel Fattah Nassef; 'Characteristics of recent migrants and non-migrants in Cairo', by Shafick S. Hassan, Mohammed A. el-Dayem; 'Characteristics of migrant families in Cairo', by Shafick S. Hassan; and 'Some demographic, social and economic aspects of settlers in Tahrir Province, Egypt', by S. Zaghloul, A. Sallam, Adel Bayyoumi.

425 **Population analysis of Egypt (1935-70) with special reference to mortality.**
V. G. Valaoras, with the assistance of N. Mahgoub, M. Farag. Cairo: Cairo Demographic Centre, 1972. 63p. (Occasional Paper, no. 1).

The author aims in this study to reconstruct the sex/age structure of the population and of those dying, in five-year periods from 1935, on the basis firstly of material published in the last three official censuses (1937, 1947 and 1960) and secondly, of the number of deaths registered by age and sex for the years from 1936 to 1968.

426 **Egypt: burdens of the past, options for the future.**
John Waterbury. Bloomington, Indiana; London: Indiana University Press, in association with the American Universities Field Staff, 1976. 318p. bibliog.

An economic and political portrait of Egyptian society in the 1970s by a specialist in Egyptian affairs. Part 1 deals with population and resources, part 2 with strategies and solutions.

Population Studies.
See item no. 1020.

Minorities

427 **Jews and Christians in Egypt: the Jewish troubles in Alexandria and the Athanasian controversy.**
Edited by H. Idris Bell, W. E. Crum. London: British Museum, 1924. 104p.

This book is of interest to students of Roman administration, Jewish antiquities, the ecclesiastical history of the 4th century and the origins of the Coptic Orthodox Church of Egypt; the subject is presented through texts from Greek papyri in the British Museum, and three Coptic texts. Note also E. R. Hardy *Christian Egypt: Church and people, Christianity and nationalism in the patriarchate of Alexandria* (New York: Oxford University Press, 1952) and William H. Worrell *A short account of the Copts* (Ann Arbor, Michigan: University of Michigan Press, 1945).

428 **The Copts in Egyptian politics.**
B. L. Carter. London: Croom Helm, 1986. 328p. bibliog.

The most important study in English of the role in Egyptian politics of the largest Christian minority in the Middle East. The author provides a scholarly and well-documented study of how the Egyptians restructured the system of governmental relationships between the majority and the minority in a changing system and what factors influenced that restructuring.

429 **The Coptic community in Egypt: spatial and social change.**
E. J. Chitham. Durham, England: Centre for Middle Eastern and Islamic Studies, 1986. 121p. bibliog. (Occasional Papers Series, no. 32).

In chapter one the author presents a general discussion of Copts as a minority group. Using standard statistical methods, he then studies in chapters 2-5 the numerical strength of the Copts, their spatial distribution, their urbanism and the Coptic population of Cairo. In chapter 6 he considers the sectarian conflict under Sadat (1972-81) and its implications for the future.

430   **The institutionalization of Palestinian identity in Egypt.**
Maha Ahmed Dajani.   Cairo: American University in Cairo Press, 1986. 133p. (Cairo Papers in Social Science, vol. 9, monograph 3).

The first two chapters of this book deal with the theoretical definition of Palestinian-ness and its evolution in the Egyptian context. The next two chapters examine the formal Palestinian institutions within the PLO apparatus in Egypt, while the fifth chapter reviews Palestinian economic enterprises. In the final chapter, the effectiveness of this Palestinian institutional presence in Egypt is assessed according to four variables: adaptability, complexity, coherence, and autonomy.

431   **The socioeconomic role of the local foreign minorities in modern Egypt, 1805-1961.**
Marius Deeb.   *International Journal of Middle East Studies*, vol. 9, no. 1 (February 1978), p. 11-22.

The local foreign minorities of this paper's title are the Greeks, the Armenians, the Italians and other Europeans who emigrated to Egypt during the 19th and early 20th centuries, kept their language and culture, and did not become assimilated into Egyptian society. This paper examines only their socio-economic role, which was essentially their *raison d'être* in Egypt. The author discusses firstly their economic activities and the social classes and groups to which they belonged and secondly, the repercussions their activities had for the rise and development of indigenous social classes and groups in Egypt.

432   **Egyptian Nubians: resettlement and years of coping.**
Hussein M. Fahim.   Salt Lake City, Utah: University of Utah Press, 1983. 183p. bibliog.

A follow-up study of the resettlement of the Nubians which was undertaken because of the building of the Aswan High Dam in 1963. The author has been associated with the relocation of the Nubians from the beginning, which is why he succeeded in documenting Nubian activities long after the transitional period.

433   **Religious strife in Egypt: crisis and ideological conflict in the seventies.**
Nadia Ramsis Farah.   New York; London: Gordon & Breach, 1986. 135p. bibliog.

A description of religious tension between Muslims and Christians in Egypt under Sadat. Facing mounting opposition from all political groups, the government used religious strife as an excuse to justify wide arrests in September 1981.

434   **The Egyptian Nubian: a study in social symbiosis.**
Peter Geiser.   Cairo: American University in Cairo Press, 1986.
254p. map. bibliog.

This book documents one of the major undertakings in the history of modern
Egypt: the resettlement that followed the flooding of Nubia. The author provides
a scholarly study of the displacement of an ancient people and the effects of this
displacement on tradition, identity, and family-community relationships.

435   **Ghagar of Sett Guiranha: a study of a gypsy community in Egypt.**
Nabil Sobhi Hanna.   Cairo: American University in Cairo Press,
1982. 113p. (Cairo Papers in Social Sciences, Vol. 5,
Monograph 1).

Apart from giving a detailed description of the Ghagar of Sett Guiranha, the
study attempts to reveal the dynamics of integration of this gypsy group with the
society around it through examination of forms of social contact and avoidance;
similarities and contrasts between the gypsy group and the local community; and
some aspects of the social structure and prevailing culture of both the Ghagar and
their host community.

436   **The Copts in Egyptian society and politics, 1882-1919.**
Subhi Labib. In: *Islam, nationalism and radicalism in Egypt and the
Sudan*. Edited by Gabriel R. Warburg, Uri M.
Kupferschmidt.   New York: Praeger, 1983, p. 301-20.

A review of the role of the Copts in Egyptian politics in the 19th and 20th
centuries. The author is a Coptic historian teaching in West German universities.

437   **The Egyptian nationalist movement and the Syrians in Egypt.**
Zachary Lackman.   *Immigrants and Minorities* (London), vol. 3,
no. 3 (November 1984), p. 233-51.

A study of the relationship between the emerging nationalist movement and the
Christian Syrian community in Egypt from the late 19th century to the First
World War. The major role of the Syrians in government, press, and business
caused resentment among educated young nationalists, and the support of the
Syrian press for the British occupation resulted in accusations that the Syrians
were agents of imperialism. After the 1919 revolution assimilation into Egyptian
society became easier for the Syrians.

438   **Jews in nineteenth-century Egypt.**
Jacob M. Landau.   London: University of London Press; New
York: New York University Press, 1969. 334p. bibliog.

A study of the period from the fall of the Mamluke regime to the end of the First
World War, when the rise of extreme nationalism led to the undermining of the
Jewish community and altered its circumstances. The author discusses in turn the
Jewish population and its institutions, its relations with the non-Jews, its
intellectual and religious life, education in Egypt and early Zionism there. A
number of documents are reproduced in an appendix.

439   **Modern sons of the pharaohs: a study of the manners and customs of the Copts of Egypt.**
      S. H. Leeder.   New York: Arno Press, 1973. Reprint ed. 355p. bibliog.

The first part of this volume covers the people and their customs (p. 3-168), while the second discusses their oriental Orthodox Church, their great dignitaries and their social and political position (p. 169-344). Now somewhat out of date, but of historical interest. Originally published in 1918 (London: Hodder & Stoughton).

440   **Monks and monasteries of the Egyptian deserts.**
      Otto F. A. Meinardus.   Cairo: American University in Cairo Press, 1961. 436p. map. bibliog.

A detailed description of the still-inhabited Coptic monasteries of Egypt. Every monastery in the book is dealt with separately so that the history of each can be traced through the centuries. A study of the Cult of St. Antony is included in order to convey the international and ecumenical impact of that Egyptian hermit.

441   **Copts and Moslems under British control: a collection of facts and a resumé of authoritative opinions on the Coptic question.**
      Kyriakos Mikhail.   Port Washington, New York; London: Kennikat Press, 1971. Reprint ed. 146p.

Written by a representative of the Coptic press in London and first published in 1911 (London: Smith, Elder & Co), this book presents a record of facts and opinions on the Coptic question and the grievances of the Copts.

442   **L'Egypte et ses juifs: le temps révolu (XIXe et XXe siècle).** (Egypt and its Jews in the 19th and 20th centuries.)
      Maurice Mizrahi.   Geneva, Switzerland: L'Imprimerie Avenir, 1977. 267p.

The memoirs of a man who was born in Syria of a Jewish family and later moved to Egypt, where he lived for fifty-five years until 1960. This book describes the life of the Jewish community in Egypt, and its contribution to Egyptian culture and development, which the author did not wish to be forgotten now that most of that community had left the country.

443   **The Copts in modern Egypt.**
      J. D. Pennington.   *Middle Eastern Studies*, vol. 18, no. 2 (April 1982), p. 158-79.

An analytical study of the position of the Christians of Egypt in modern times in the light of the rise of Islamic fundamentalism. The paper includes an introduction, studies of the Copts in pre-revolutionary Egypt, under Nasser, and under Sadat, and a conclusion.

444 **The Syrians in Egypt 1725-1975.**
Thomas Philipp.   Stuttgart, FRG: Franz Steiner-Verlag, 1985.
176p. bibliog. (Berliner Islamstudien, vol. 3).

There were two major waves of Syrian immigration to Egypt, the first around
1730-1780, and the second from the mid-19th century to the outbreak of the First
World War, at which time the Syrian population numbered about 35,000 persons.
They were predominantly Greek Catholics, with large numbers also of Maronites
and Greek Orthodox, while the remainder were Muslims and members of other
Christian communities. This book examines the reasons for their immigration,
their relations with the Egyptians, and their economic, cultural and political
activities and impact.

445 **The Copts and Muslims of Egypt.**
Makram Samaan, Soheir Sukkary. In: *Muslim-Christian conflicts:
economic, political and social origins.* Edited by Suad Joseph,
Barbara L. K. Pillsbury.   Boulder, Colorado: Westview Press;
Folkestone, England: Dawson, 1978, p. 129-55.

A brief and objective review of the relations between Muslims and Copts in
Egypt. Includes a good bibliography.

446 **La communauté juive en Egypte.** (The Jewish community in
Egypt.)
Marlène Shamay.   *Peuples Méditerranéens*, no. 16 (July 1981),
p. 93-100.

A study of the Jewish community in Egypt up to 1949. The author views this
community as an example of a minority group faced with a society undergoing
change. Although the Jews in Egypt were relatively well adapted, the pan-Arabist
political trends in Egypt were not conducive to their social integration. The
community itself was divided by class, and the poorer groups emigrated to Israel
while the richer ones emigrated to Europe and the United States.

447 **Cairo memories.**
Magdi Wahba.   *Encounter*, vol. 62, no. 5 (May 1984), p. 74-9.

An Egyptian writer reminisces about the foreign communities and élites in Egypt
during the period from 1919 to 1956. The Greek and British communities were
self-contained, while the Italians supported fascism; Jews, who spoke French,
were active in trade, banking and the arts, and were also the first proponents of
Egyptian Marxism; Syrian Christians were active in journalism but stayed outside
the mainstream, while Syrian Muslims became integrated into Egyptian society.
Membership of the élite class was based on political stature rather than family
affiliation.

448 **A lonely minority: the modern story of Egypt's Copts.**
Edward Wakin.   New York: William Morrow, 1963. 178p.

A study of Coptic-Muslim relations in modern Egypt based on information
collected by the author during his stay in Egypt in the early 1960s.

Modern Egypt: studies in politics and society.
See item no. 10.

A Fabian in Egypt: Salamah Musa and the rise of the professional classes in Egypt, 1909-1939.
See item no. 496.

The education of Salāma Mūsā.
See item no. 538.

Languages

Arabic

449 **A comprehensive study of Egyptian Arabic.**
Ernest T. Abdel-Massih, A. Fathy Bahig, el-Said M. Badawi,
Carolyn G. Killean, Zaki N. Abdel-Malek, Ernest N.
McCarus. Ann Arbor, Michigan: University of Michigan,
Center for Near Eastern and North African Studies, 1978-79.
4 vols.

The most comprehensive work on modern Egyptian Arabic, this is an
indispensable tool for anyone who wants to learn the language. Volume one
comprises conversations, cultural texts and socio-linguistic notes; volume two
covers proverbs and metaphoric expressions; volume three is a reference grammar
of Egyptian Arabic; and volume four consists of a lexicon, both Arabic-English
and English-Arabic.

450 **An introduction to Egyptian Arabic.**
Ernest T. Abdel-Massih. Ann Arbor, Michigan: University of
Michigan, Center for Near Eastern and North African Studies,
1983. 7th impression. 405p.

Written by a well-known Egyptian linguist, this book comprises six parts which
respectively present the following: phonology; an introductory unit and twenty
basic units; twenty-five texts; one hundred proverbs; word lists (twenty lists); and
an Egyptian Arabic-English lexicon. Includes many drills.

451 **Colloquial Arabic of Egypt.**
     Russell H. McGuirk.   London; Boston, Massachusetts: Routledge
     & Kegan Paul, 1986. 193p.

This book consists of an introduction and sections on pronunciation, the Arabic
alphabet, root letters and grammatical patterns, followed by sixteen lessons,
proverbs, readings, a key to exercises and Arabic-English and English-Arabic
glossaries.

452 **An introduction to Egyptian colloquial Arabic.**
     T. F. Mitchell.   London: Oxford University Press, 1956. 285p.

The author presents his description of Egyptian colloquial Arabic in the form of
lessons with exercises and texts, accompanied by grammatical guidance and a
practical glossary. The book provides as good a guide to learners of the spoken
language as the printed page can give them. The reading transcription, though not
a rigid system of spelling, is thoroughly Arabic and is designed to help the student
to acquire early fluency in speaking and comprehension.

453 **Spoken Arabic of Cairo.**
     Maurice B. Salib.   Cairo: American University in Cairo Press,
     1981. 385p.

The author provides in this book a comprehensive elementary course in Egyptian
colloquial Arabic as spoken in the capital, Cairo. The speech of Cairo, though
different in some respects from the speech found in other regions of the country,
particularly Upper Egypt, is widely understood and implicitly accepted as
standard throughout the country. Thanks to radio broadcasts, films, and the fact
that a large number of Egyptians work as educators, doctors, and in other
professions in other Arab countries, this dialect is also generally understood
throughout the Arab world.

454 **An Arabic-English dictionary of the colloquial Arabic of Egypt,
     containing the vernacular idioms and expressions, slang phrases,
     vocables, etc., used by native Egyptians.**
     Socrates Spiro.   Beirut: Librairie du Liban, 1980. New
     impression. 659p.

The only available dictionary of its kind, originally published in London, 1895.

455 **A transformational grammar of spoken Egyptian Arabic.**
     Hilary Wise.   Oxford, England: Basil Blackwell for the
     Philosophical Society, 1975. 197p. bibliog. (Publications of the
     Philosophical Society, 26).

A partial description of colloquial Egyptian, or rather Cairene, Arabic. Good
reading for a linguist.

Coptic

456 **A Coptic dictionary.**
Compiled, with the help of many scholars, by W.E. Crum. Oxford, England: Clarendon Press, 1939. 953p.

The standard Coptic dictionary, and a milestone in Coptic studes. Has indexes in English, Greek and Arabic.

457 **Introduction to Sahidic Coptic.**
Thomas O. Lambdin. Macon, Georgia: Mercer University Press, 1983. 377p.

An elaborate up-to-date grammar, with exercises, chrestomathy and vocabulary. The grammatical explanations are substantial, making the book perhaps easier than others to use in the absence of a teacher. Many aspects of the language are introduced stage by stage, and the book is not so convenient as a reference grammar: for this purpose, many students, even with little German, use *Koptische Grammatik (Saïdischer Dialekt) mit Bibliographie, Lesestücken und Wörterverzeichnissen* by Walter C. Till (Leipzig, GDR: VEB Verlag Enzyklopädie, 1961. 2nd improved ed. All editions since the second are simply reprints).

458 **An introductory Coptic grammar (Sahidic dialect).**
J. Martin Plumley. London: Home & van Thal, 1948. 192p.

The Sahidic dialect is chosen in this book, not because of any theory about its age, but for the practical reason that it is the dialect which holds pride of place in Crum's *Coptic dictionary*. In addition, there exists a wide variety of texts in this dialect for the student to read. The examples, all of which are actual quotations from texts, are drawn for the most part from the Bible.

459 **A concise Coptic-English lexicon.**
Compiled by Richard Smith. Grand Rapids, Michigan: William B. Eerdmans, 1983. 81p.

This small Coptic lexicon has its origin in a word list compiled for students at Fuller Theological Seminary. The unavailability of a student dictionary had presented an obstacle to the teaching of the language, and the work thus grew out of a classroom setting. It is intended primarily for beginners.

460 **An elementary Coptic grammar of the Sahidic dialect.**
C. C. Walters. Oxford, England: B. H. Blackwell, 1972. 81p.

A succinct teaching grammar, with exercises and vocabularies.

Egyptian (Ancient)

461 Notes on late Egyptian grammar: a Semitic approach.
A. M. Bakir. Warminster, England: Aris & Phillips, 1983. 134p. bibliog.

In this work and in his *Notes on Middle Egyptian grammar*, the author, an eminent Arabic-speaking Egyptologist, explores the possibilities for a better understanding of Egyptian if its affinities to the Semitic languages are stressed.

462 Notes on Middle Egyptian grammar.
A. M. Bakir. Warminster, England: Aris & Phillips. 2nd revised ed. 1984. 174p.

See preceding annotation.

463 An Egyptian hieroglyphic dictionary.
Sir E. A. Wallis Budge. London: Murray, 1920. 1356p.

This dictionary has an index of English words, a king list, and a geographical list with indexes, a list of hieroglyphic characters, and Coptic and Semitic alphabets. It is now of purely historical interest. The standard hieroglyphic dictionary is A. Erman and H. Grapow, *Wörterbuch der Aegyptischen Sprache*, the main five text volumes of which were published in Leipzig in 1926-31. The entire work, 7 vols. in 13, Leipzig (and Berlin), 1926-63, has been reprinted (Berlin, GDR: Akademie Verlag, 1971). The only modern dictionary in English is the concise dictionary by Faulkner (item no. 467).

464 Egyptian language: easy lessons in Egyptian hieroglyphics with sign list.
Sir E. A. Wallis Budge. London: Routledge & Kegan Paul, 1963. 8th ed. 246p.

This book is intended to form an easy introduction to the study of Egyptian hieroglyphic inscriptions. It contains a short account of the decipherment of the Egyptian hieroglyphs, and a sketch of hieroglyphic systems of writing. The grammatical side of the book is in many respects severely outdated. An excellent account of the decipherment appeared in the author's (otherwise also largely outdated) *The mummy: a handbook of Egyptian funerary archaeology*, second edition, revised and greatly enlarged, published in Cambridge in 1925 (reprinted London, New York: KPI, 1987).

465 The Rosetta Stone.
Sir E. A. Wallis Budge. London: British Museum, 1983. Reprint ed. 8p.

A brief account of the Rosetta Stone, first published in 1950, which deals with its discovery, its arrival in England, its earliest decipherers, the method of its decipherment, and its contents.

466 **Egyptian hieroglyphs.**
W. V. Davies. London: British Museum Publications, 1987. 64p.

An excellent brief introduction for the non-specialist to the language and scripts of Ancient Egypt. The reader is shown how to begin to read a hieroglyphic text and offered 'a little grammar'. There is an account of the decipherment, and of the scripts which borrowed from those of Egypt. The illustrations are well chosen from British Museum material.

467 **A concise dictionary of Middle Egyptian.**
R. O. Faulkner. Oxford, England: Griffith Institute, Ashmolean Museum, 1981. 327p.

Middle Egyptian is the phase of the language which has the widest general application, and this dictionary is addressed primarily to the student, providing him with suitable translations of words as they occur in the most widely read range of texts, to which numerous references are given.

468 **Ancient Egyptian calligraphy: a beginner's guide to writing hieroglyphs.**
Henry George Fischer. New York: Metropolitan Museum of Art, 1979. 63p. bibliog.

This book is both a practical introduction, designed to guide the student in the acquisition of a good hieroglyphic hand, and also a contribution to the study of the hieroglyphs as representations of real objects, noting numerous details and variations in the form of signs. In its second aspect, it in effect supplements the 'sign-list' of Gardiner's *Egyptian grammar* (see item no. 469).

469 **Egyptian grammar; being an introduction to the study of hieroglyphs.**
Sir Alan Gardiner. London: Published on behalf of the Griffith Institute, Ashmolean Museum, Oxford by Oxford University Press, 1957. 3rd rev. ed. 646p.

The first edition of this work appeared in 1927. (Allusions to a 'fourth edition' are in fact mistaken references to reprints.) Apart from being a reference grammar, it includes a series of exercises, to which Gardiner 'attached the greatest possible importance'. Egyptian–English and English–Egyptian vocabularies are provided. The elaborate sign-list remains the standard listing. The hieroglyphic types specially prepared for this work remain an ideal, and are now available for laser-setting. Although the work had already in 1957 been overtaken by research, particularly on syntax and the verbal system, it remains widely used in teaching, and has no obvious successor. In any case, it is difficult to improve on the wealth of examples provided.

470 **Papyrus and tablet.**
Edited by A. Kirk Grayson, Donald B. Redford. Englewood Cliffs, New Jersey: Prentice-Hall, 1973. 178p. bibliog.

This book does not aim to provide a representative sampling of all the various kinds of written documents from Ancient Egypt and Mesopotamia, rather it takes twelve topics and presents documents in translation to illustrate them. The topics were chosen either because they are an outstanding feature of ancient culture or because they are particularly relevant to our modern world. The six topics relating to Egypt are the Egyptian state, Egyptian imperialism, Egyptian revolution, the Egyptian autobiography, Egyptian narrative and the Egyptian wit.

471 **Hieroglyphs: the writing of ancient Egypt.**
Norma Jean Katan, with Barbara Mertz.   London: British
Museum Publications, 1985. Revised ed. 80p.
After a short introduction, the chapters of this book cover in turn hieroglyphs and magic, the craft of the scribe, reading the hieroglyphs, and some important rulers and their dynasties.

472 **An Egyptian grammar with chrestomathy and glossary.**
Samuel A. B. Mercer.   New York: Frederick Ungar, 1961. 184p.
A textbook intended for beginners. Both simple and supplied with exercises, it is intended to provide one academic year's work on the basis of three hours' study per week.

473 **The relationship of the Semitic and Egyptian verbal systems.**
T. W. Thacker.   Oxford, England: Clarendon Press, 1954. 341p.
This study is the result of three lines of research: an investigation into various problems presented by the Semitic verbal system, a study of the verb in the Egyptian Pyramid Texts, and a study of the relationship of Egyptian to the Semitic language. It addresses questions of morphology and syntax in Egyptian. The book was unfortunate in appearing at a time when many scholars were enthusiastically following up the insights into the verbal system offered by the work of H. J. Polotsky, and many of the Thacker's points have only slowly been taken up.

474 **Introducing Egyptian hieroglyphs.**
Barbara Watterson.   Edinburgh: Scottish Academic Press, 1981.
152p. bibliog.
This book consists of two parts. In part one the author covers Napoleon's expedition to Egypt and the decipherment of hieroglyphs by Young, Champollion and others, how writing in Egypt began, the principles of the Egyptian system of picture writing, hieroglyphs, hieratic, demotic, the scribes, changes in the spoken language, and the Copts and Coptic. Part two comprises eleven lessons on grammar, with exercises. Lists of hieroglyphic signs and of Egyptian-English and English-Egyptian vocabulary are included.

475 **More about Egyptian hieroglyphs: a simplified grammar of Middle Egyptian.**
Barbara Watterson.   Edinburgh: Scottish Academic Press, 1986.
195p.

This book is a sequel to the author's *Introducing Egyptian hieroglyphs* (see previous entry), and represents an attempt to bring a simplified grammar of the Ancient Egyptian language to the student in the form of a practical manual which covers the main aspects of the language in twenty chapters.

Literature

Ancient Egyptian Literature

476 **The book of the dead, or Going forth by day: ideas of the ancient Egyptians concerning the hereafter as expressed in their own terms.**
Translated by Thomas George Allen, prepared for publication by Elizabeth Blaisdell Hanset. Chicago, Illinois: University of Chicago Press, 1974. 306p. (Oriental Institute of the University of Chicago, Studies in Ancient Oriental Civilization, no. 37).

An authoritative eclectic translation of the Book of the Dead, based on an exhaustive study of the numerous versions.

477 **Egyptian tales and romances, pagan, Christian and Muslim.**
Sir E. A. Wallis Budge. London: Thornton Butterworth, 1931. 424p.

The Egyptian tales and stories included in this volume are intended to illustrate the fiction and historical romances of the Egyptians from the early dynastic period to the present. These tales were translated from Egyptian, including Demotic, Coptic and Arabic texts. Although our understanding of the texts has progressed since Budge's time, his translations are notable for their style, and he often sensed the true meaning of a passage, even if he virtually offers a paraphrase rather than a translation.

478 **The triumph of Horus: an Ancient Egyptian sacred drama.**
Translated and edited by H. W. Fairman, with a chapter by Derek Newton and Derek Poole. Berkeley, California; London: University of California Press, 1974. 150p.

This drama was first published in English translation accompanied by a detailed commentary by the late Professor A. M. Blackman and H. W. Fairman.

Nevertheless, the form in which the play appears in this book is entirely new, as Fairman explains in his preface. The play was acted annually at Edfu on the twenty-first day of the second month of winter and on each of the following four days. It formed part of the annual Festival of Victory and commemorated the wars between Horus and Seth, the victory of Horus and his coronation as king of a united Egypt, the dismemberment of the body of his defeated enemy, and his final triumph or justification.

479 **The ancient Egyptian pyramid texts.**
Translated into English by R. O. Faulkner. Oxford, England: Clarendon Press, 1969. 2 vols.

A briefly annotated translation of the texts inscribed within the various royal pyramids of the late fifth and of the sixth Dynasties, based upon a combination of the surviving versions. The second volume comprises a 'Supplement of hieroglyphic texts': essentially additional material available since K. Sethe's edition *Die altaegyptischen Pyramidentexte* of 1908-10.

480 **The ancient Egyptian coffin texts.**
R. O. Faulkner. Warminster, England: Aris and Phillips, 1973-78. 3 vols.

A complete, briefly annotated translation of the corpus of funerary texts found chiefly on coffins of the Middle Kingdom, sharing material both with the earlier pyramid texts, and with the later Book of the Dead.

481 **Love songs of the New Kingdom.**
Translated from the Ancient Egyptian by John L. Foster. New York: Charles Scribner's Sons, 1974. 120p.

The love songs contained in this volume are almost all that remains to us of the genre. The book is illustrated with hieroglyphs drawn by the translator and with paintings by Nina M. Davies reproducing those in Egyptian tombs.

482 **The Ancient Egyptian Book of Two Ways.**
Leonard H. Lesko. Berkeley, California; London: University of California Press, 1972. 148p.

The Book of Two Ways was copied onto the inside bottom of the coffins of nobles, probably so that the dead would have this guide at their feet when waking in the underworld. The book received its name from the two zigzag paths that form a kind of map for the use of the deceased. It is divided into nine sections, which include a number of different gods, goals and spells.

483 **Ancient Egyptian literature.**
Miriam Lichtheim. Berkeley, California; London: University of California Press, 1973-80. 3 vols.

Provides, in up-to-date translation, a representative selection of Ancient Egyptian literature in a chronological arrangement designed to bring out the evolution of literary forms. Presented in a convenient and inexpensive format, this work is meant to serve several kinds of readers. Volume I covers the Old and Middle Kingdoms, volume II the New Kingdom, and volume III the late period. The selection of texts is notable for including a number of inscriptions with some claim to be considered as literature (although no purely documentary texts), and, in volume 3, demotic material.

484 **Popular stories of Ancient Egypt.**
Gaston Maspero, translated by A. S. Johns, revised by Gaston Maspero, new foreword to this edition by Aziz S. Atiya. New Hyde Park, New York: University Books, 1967. 316p.

Maspero's translation of narrative texts is still worth consulting, because of his sympathy with the material, and his many revealing comments, not all of which were taken note of by later translators.

485 **The literature of Ancient Egypt: an anthology of stories, instructions and poetry.**
Edited with an introduction by William Kelly Simpson, with translations by R. O. Faulkner, Edward F. Wente, Jr., William Kelly Simpson. New Haven, Connecticut; London: Yale University Press, 1972. 328p. bibliog.

This book is divided into four parts which present respectively: Narratives and tales of Middle Egyptian literature; Late Egyptian stories; Instructions, lamentations and dialogues; and Songs, poetry, and hymns. A revised edition appeared in 1973.

Arabic Literature and Translations

486 **My life: the autobiography of an Egyptian scholar, writer and cultural leader.**
Aḥmad Amīn, translated from the Arabic with an introduction by Issa J. Boullata. Leiden, The Netherlands: E. J. Brill, 1978. 242p.

Amīn (1886-1954) was one of the foremost Egyptian scholars and writers of the second quarter of the 20th century and played a leading role in modern Arab culture. His autobiography, published towards the end of his life, is an honest portrayal of himself as well as an important document that captures the anguish, the hopes, and the frustrations of a period of transition in which Egypt and the Arab world moved towards modernity.

487 **Orient and occident.**
Aḥmad Amīn, translated from the Arabic by Wolfgang H.
Behn. Berlin, FRG: Adiyok, 1984. 76p.

A personal account of the scientific and cultural interaction between east and west. The author, a well-known Egyptian writer, expresses in this book his deep respect for many aspects of Western civilization: constitutionalism, individual rights, universal education, rationality, technical and scientific achievements, and national independence.

488 **A critical introduction to modern Arabic poetry.**
M. M. Badawi. Cambridge, England: Cambridge University
Press, 1975. 289p.

This book covers among other Arab poets the Egyptian poets Mahmud Sami al-Barudi, Ahmad Shawqi, Hafiz Ibrahim, the Diwan Group (Abd al-Rahman Shukri, Abd al-Qadir al-Mazini, Abbas Mahmud al-'Aqqad), Abu Shadi and the Apollo Group, Naji and Mahmūd Taha.

489 **The style of the modern Arabic short story.**
Jan Beyerli. Prague: Department of Asian and African Studies,
Faculty of Philosophy, Charles University, 1971. 134p. bibliog.
(Studia Orientalia Pragensia, III).

A linguistic study.

490 **The house of power.**
Sami Bindari, translated from the Arabic by Sami Bindari and
Mona St. Leger. Boston, Massachusetts: Houghton Mifflin, 1980.
216p.

This novel, entitled *al-Sarāyah* in the Arabic original, concerns Egyptian rural life and focuses on a young man's experiences in life vis-à-vis his family, the village, and the world beyond. The translation is by the author himself and retains the impassioned tone against official oppressions and personal jealousies which gave this first novel some notoriety on its publication in Cairo in 1971.

491 **An introduction to the history of modern Arabic literature in Egypt.**
J. Brugman. Leiden, The Netherlands: E. J. Brill, 1984. 439p.
bibliog. (Studies in Arabic Literature, vol. 10).

After providing an introduction on the last representatives of the post-classical age in Egypt, this book deals with modern poetry from the middle of the 19th century to the beginning of the 1950s, and this is followed by discussions of neo-classical prose, the novel, the short story, and the development of literary criticism. Brief biographies and bibliographies of the most important authors are included.

492 **Arabic proverbs, or the manners and customs of the modern Egyptians illustrated from their proverbial sayings current at Cairo.**
John Lewis Burckhardt, introduction by C. E. Bosworth.
London: Curzon Press; Totowa, New Jersey: Rowman & Littlefield, 1972. 283p.

An alphabetical list of 782 Egyptian proverbs, with an English translation and an explanation for each proverb, collected in the early 19th century.

493 **Ṭāhā Ḥusayn: his place in the Egyptian literary renaissance.**
Pierre Cachia. London: Luzac & Co., 1956. 260p. bibliog.

In part one of this book the author covers the background of the Egyptian literary renaissance, while part two includes a biography of Hussein and a chapter on his character. Part three presents Hussein's philosophical views about modernism, the social order and education, part four is devoted to Hussein as a man of letters, and parts five and six contain evaluations of his works. Summaries of his novels are included in an appendix.

494 **Yaḥyā Ḥaqqī as critic and nationalist.**
Miriam Cooke. *International Journal of Middle East Studies*, vol. 13, no. 2 (May 1981), p. 21-34.

An excellent article about an Egyptian writer and literary critic who believes that the critic should have a socio-political vision which should guide his literary criticism.

495 **The anatomy of an Egyptian intellectual: Yahya Haqqi.**
Miriam Cooke. Washington, DC: Three Continents Press, 1984. 188p. bibliog.

A scholarly study of Yahya Haqqi, a 20th-century Egyptian novelist, writer, and diplomat.

496 **A Fabian in Egypt: Salamah Musa and the rise of the professional classes in Egypt, 1909-1939.**
Vernon Egger. Lanham, New York; London: University Press of America, 1986. 255p. bibliog.

An account of a prominent Coptic writer who achieved a position of leadership between 1909 and 1939, although his influence lasted long after that date. Musa's advocacy of anticolonialism, democracy, industrialization and secularism is covered fully.

497 **Tradition and change: Egyptian intellectuals and linguistic reform 1919-1939.**
Giora Eliraz. *Asian and African Studies* (Haifa), vol. 20, no. 2 (July 1986), p. 233-62.

The impact of the encounter between the west and the Muslim world led to a growing awareness of the gap between literary Arabic and the contemporary needs of the modern world among Egyptian intellectuals belonging to what the author defines as the 'mainstream'. Mainstream intellectuals followed a course somewhere in the middle between tradition and change, between the defence of the foundation of their cultural language and the acceptance of ways to meet the challenge of the new situation.

498   **Three pioneering Egyptian novels.**
Translated from the Arabic with a critical introduction by Saad el-Gabalawy.   Fredericton, New Brunswick: York Press, 1986. 120p.

The three novellas included in this volume are *The Maiden of Dinshway* by Mahmud Tahir Haggi (1906), *Eve Without Adam*, by the same author (1934), and *Ulysses's Hallucinations or the Like* by Saad El-Khadem (1985).

499   **Between Ottomanism and Egyptianism: the evolution of 'national sentiment' in the Cairene middle class as reflected in Najīb Maḥfuẓ's *Bayn al-Qaṣrayn*.**
Israel Gershoni.   *Asian and African Studies*, vol. 17 (1983), p. 227-63.

As a result of the 1919 revolution, new classes emerged in Egyptian society to challenge the dominance of the Ottomanism of upper-class Egyptians. This essay is a study of the topic as portrayed by Mahfuz in his novel *Bayn al-Qaṣrayn*.

500   **The man who lost his shadow.**
Fathy Ghanem, translated from the Arabic by Desmond Stewart.   Boston, Massachusetts: Houghton Mifflin; Cambridge, England: Riverside Press, 1966. 352p.

This story portrays the rise of a young and ambitious Cairo journalist. The author, an Egyptian writer born in Cairo in 1924, enjoys a considerable reputation throughout the Arab world for his careful and conscientious craftsmanship and for his ability to evoke the mood of his characters and a sense of place. Desmond Stewart, the translator, is a well-known British journalist and author who has spent three decades in the Middle East, and his translation is in a very readable style. Reprinted in 1980 (London: Heinemann; Washington, DC: Three Continents Press. Arab Authors, 14).

501   **Maze of justice.**
Tewfik el Hakim, translated from the Arabic by A. S. Eban.   London: Harvill Press, 1947. 122p.

In this fictional diary of an Egyptian deputy public prosecutor, the author gives a series of vivid pictures of rural Egyptian society, humorously and mercilessly portraying both the governing (the petty officials and government employees), and the governed. The poor peasants are forcefully described with both compassion and observation. The original *Yaumīyāt nā'ib fī al-aryāf* was published in the 1940s, and in a preface to a 1974 French translation, Tawfiq al-Hakim wrote that nothing had changed since 1940, when the events described in the book took place.

502   **The tree climber: a play in two acts.**
Tewfik al-Hakim, translated from the Arabic by Denys Johnson-Davies.   London: Oxford University Press, 1966. 87p.
A play of murder and philosophy which takes place in a suburb of modern Cairo. It contains some nicely timed surprises and some wry humour.

503   **Bird of the east.**
Taufik al-Hakim, translated from the Arabic with an introduction by R. Bayly Winder.   Beirut: Khayats, 1966. 169p.
This novel is an autobiographically-inspired tale in which Muhsin, the young Egyptian student who is the protagonist, relives the author's own student days in Paris. The major theme of the work is the similarities and differences between Western and Near Eastern culture.

504   **Fate of a cockroach: four plays of freedom.**
Tawfiq al-Hakim, selected and translated from the Arabic by Denys Johnson-Davies.   London: Heinemann, 1973. 184p. (Arab Authors, 1).
These four plays, by the undisputed pioneer of dramatic writing in Arabic, are: *Fate of a Cockroach*, *The Song of Death*, *The Sultan's Dilemma*, and *Not a Thing Out of Place*.

505   **Plays, prefaces and postscripts of Tawfiq al-Hakim.**
Tawfiq Al-Hakim, translated from the Arabic by William M. Hutchins with A. I. Abdulai, M. B. Lawani.   Washington, DC: Three Continents Press, 1984. 350p. bibliog.
This volume brings together six plays from Tawfiq al-Hakim's later period. They are all concerned with the role and plight of the individual in local and world society.

506   **A new Egyptian: the autobiography of a young Arab.**
Sayed Hegab, translated by the author with the assistance of Marie-Hélène Tawil.   New York: Praeger, 1971. 160p.
The author writes: 'The story stops when I am twenty-four years old. I am now thirty. Many things have happened in the past six years, but I cannot write about them yet, because I am still living them or living through their aftermath. As a poet, I became more and more committed to oppressed peoples. I married and, with my friends, lived through much conflict. Together we went to prison for political reasons. Some betrayed our cause. A new war broke out in 1967. Our generation experienced another defeat. Now I write for radio, television, and cinema. Some people condemn what I write, others bless it. Many things have changed in my life. Perhaps one day, when all the changes are behind me, I may write about them.'

507 **The eye with an iron lid.**
Sherif Hetata, translated from the Arabic by the author. London:
Onyx Press, 1982. 409p.

First published in Arabic in two volumes, *The eye with an iron lid* in 1974, and
Two wings to the wind in 1976, this book is written in the first person as 'a story
which I lived', in which political activity leads to a gaol sentence. Hetata's novel
The net, originally published in Arabic in 1982, has also been translated into
English (London: Zed Books, 1986).

508 **City of wrong: a Friday in Jerusalem.**
Muhammad Kamel Hussein, translated from the Arabic with an
introduction by Kenneth Cragg. London: Geoffrey Bles, 1959.
225p.

This book, by a famous Egyptian Muslim surgeon, scholar and writer about the
crucifixion of Christ, explores the human emotions that surrounded that great
historical event. It is a masterpiece that was translated into several other
languages.

509 **The hallowed valley: a Muslim philosophy of religion.**
Muhammad Kamel Hussein, translated and with an introduction by
Kenneth Cragg. Cairo: American University in Cairo Press, 1977.
120p.

The author reflects in this book on the nature of human personality and explores
the meaning of religious faith. 'The hallowed valley' is a Quranic phrase referring
to the setting in which life recognizes its true dimensions under God and on behalf
of truth. The author draws widely on metaphors from medicine to illuminate what
mediaeval writers called 'the wound of absence' – the condition of faithlessness,
of man being separated from truth.

510 **An Egyptian childhood.**
Taha Hussein, translated from the Arabic by E. H. Paxton.
Washington, DC: Three Continents Press, 1981. Reprint ed. 85p.
(Arab Authors, 16).

Taha Hussein (1899-1973) was a leader of modernism in Egypt and a widely read
and respected scholar. In this first part of his three-part autobiography, he
chronicles specific remembered events from his early youth and offers his mature
reflections on how his past formed his adult character. The telescopic, distant
quality of the writing is heightened by the use of the third person. Originally
publised in 1932 (London: Routledge).

511   **The stream of days: a student at the Azhar.**
Taha Hussein, translated from the Arabic by Hilary
Wayment.   Cairo: Al-Maaref Printing and Publishing House,
1943. 210p.

The second volume of Hussein's autobiography, one of the acknowledged masterpieces of contemporary Arabic literature. In this volume Hussein describes the years of his adolescence at al-Azhar. A second, revised edition was published in London in 1948.

512   **A passage to France.**
Ṭāhā Ḥusaîn, translated from the Arabic by Kenneth Cragg.
Leiden, The Netherlands: E. J. Brill, 1976. 165p. (Arabic
Translations Series of the Journal of Arabic Literature, vol. 4).

This third volume of Hussein's autobiography was published in Arabic in 1973. It carries his story into the academic liberation afforded by the beginning of modern university life in Egypt and, thence, to his final attainment of a doctorate at the Sorbonne. The narrative, in the view of the translator, constitutes a personal saga of tenacity and perseverance in the face of daunting odds – blindness, the demands of French academic disciplines, the acquisition of new languages, the vicissitudes of the First World War, and the oscillating hopes and fears of a strenuous and sensitive ambition.

513   **The dreams of Scheherazade.**
Taha Hussein, translated from the Arabic by Magdi Wahba. Cairo:
General Egyptian Book Organization, 1974. 108p.

A novel by a renowned Egyptian writer based on the *Tales from the Thousand and One Nights*.

514   **The call of the curlew.**
Ṭāhā Ḥusaîn, translated from the Arabic by A. B. As-Safi.
Leiden, The Netherlands: E. J. Brill, 1980. 130p. (Arabic
Translations Series of the Journal of Arabic Literature, vol. 5).

A unique work of fiction in modern Egyptian literature. Critics agree that this novel can almost be seen as a piece of poetry, and this judgement applies both to its romantic theme of the triumph of love over revenge, and also to its highly elevated style.

515   **In the eye of the beholder: tales of Egyptian life from the writings of Yusuf Idris.**
Yusuf Idris, edited by Roger Allen, illustrations by Kamal
Boullata.   Minneapolis, Minnesota; Chicago: Bibliotheca
Islamica, 1978. 198p. (Studies in Middle Eastern Literatures,
no. 10).

Fourteen short stories translated by various hands, preceded by an introduction by the editor about Yusuf Idris.

123

Literature. Arabic Literature and Translations

516 The cheapest nights and other stories.
Yusuf Idris, translated from the Arabic with an introduction by
Wadida Wassef.   London: Heinemann; Washington, DC; Three
Continents Press, 1978. 196p.

A collection of fifteen short stories, all except for 'The Cheapest Nights' selected at the request of the author from five other collections of short stories.

517 Rings of burnished brass.
Yusuf Idris, translated from the Arabic by Catherine
Cobham.   London: Heinemann; Washington, D.C.: Three
Continents Press, 1984. 142p. (Arab Authors, 21).

A collection of four longer short stories: 'The Stranger' (1961) tells the story of a young boy's relationship with an outlaw and murderer in the Egyptian countryside during the Second World War; 'The Black Policeman' (1962) is a sombre tale of a torturer employed by the political police in the late 1940s; 'The Siren' (1969) is the drama of the surrender of a peasant woman to the 'Man in the Suit', urban civilization and Cairo; and 'Rings of Burnished Brass' (1969) tells of an encounter between a well-off middle-aged mother and a poor boy of eighteen.

518 Egyptian one-act plays.
Translated from the Arabic by Denys Johnson-Davies.
Washington, DC: Three Continents Press, 1981. 118p.

Contains *The Interrogation* by Farid Kamil, *The Trap* by Alfred Farag, *Marital Bliss* by Abdel-Moneim Selim, *The Wheat Well* by Ali Salem, and *The Donkey Market* by Tewfik al-Hakim. This five-play anthology is representative of the new drama emerging from Egypt. Most of such work constitutes serious commentary on the country's character and history.

519 Taha Hussein.
Marsden Jones, Hamdi Sakkut.   Cairo: American University in
Cairo Press, 1975. 342p. bibliog. In Arabic. (Leaders in
Contemporary Egyptian Literature Series, no. 1).

This volume contains an authoritative critical assessment and a full-scale bibliography covering not only Hussein's complete works but also the entire body of criticism in French, English, German and Italian as well as Arabic, amounting to over 2,000 entries in all.

520 History of the Egyptian novel: its rise and early beginning.
Saad el-Khadem.   Fredericton, New Brunswick: York Press, 1985.
77p. bibliog.

A brief study of the development of the Egyptian novel in the 19th and early 20th centuries. The author covers early narrative forms, translations, imitations, and 'novelistic efforts and serious novelistic attempts'.

521 **Poetry and the making of modern Egypt (1882-1922).**
Mounah A. Khouri. Leiden, The Netherlands: E. J. Brill, 1971.
210p. bibliog. (Studies in Arabic Literature, vol. 1).
This book investigates the work of Mahmud Sami al-Barudi, Ahmad Shawqi, Hafiz Ibrahim, Khalil Mutran, 'Abd al-Rahman Shukri, 'Abbas Mahmud al-'Aqqad, Ibrahim 'Abd al-Qadir al-Mazini, Ali al-Ghayati, and a number of other leading Egyptian poets of the period of British occupation, assessing the aesthetic value of their poetry, but laying principal emphasis on the importance of this poetry as a source for the study of the social and intellectual trends of the time.

522 **The development of early Arabic drama, 1847-1900.**
Mohamed A. al-Khozai. London; New York: Longman, 1983.
183p.
A study of the development of Arabic drama in the 19th and 20th centuries, with special reference to Egypt.

523 **The modern Egyptian novel: a study in social criticism.**
Hilary Kilpatrick. London: Ithaca Press, 1974. 250p. bibliog. (St. Antony's Middle East Monographs, no. 1).
A study of social criticism in the work of Egyptian novelists, covering the period from 1911 to the present.

524 **The short stories of Yusuf Idris, a modern Egyptian author.**
P. M. Kurpershoek. Leiden, The Netherlands: E. J. Brill, 1981.
222p. bibliog. (Studies in Arabic Literature. Supplements to the Journal of Arabic Literature, no. 7).
The most comprehensive study of Yusuf Idris's works; it includes both a biography of Idris and a comprehensive list of works by him and on him.

525 **Tawfiq al-Hakim: playwright of Egypt.**
Richard Long. London: Ithaca Press, 1979. 235p. bibliog.
An in-depth and well-documented study of the most famous Egyptian playwright. The volume includes a list of all the plays written by him in Arabic and a list of the foreign editions of these plays.

526 **God's world: an anthology of short stories.**
Nagib Mahfuz, translated with an introduction by Akef Abadir, Roger Allen. Minneapolis, Minnesota: Bibliotheca Islamica, 1973. 240p. (Studies in Middle Eastern Literatures, 2).
Includes an introduction about Mahfuz's works, a short biography of him and a brief descriptive survey of his novels.

527 **Midaq Alley.**
Naguib Mahfuz, translated from the Arabic by Trevor
LeGassick. Washington, DC: Three Continents Press, 1975.
246p.

First published in 1947, *Midaq Alley* represents Egypt's foremost novelist in his
realist phase and tells the story, in rich sociological detail, of a girl who becomes a
prostitute. This is a corrected edition of the translation first published in 1966
(Beirut: Khayats). To this period also belongs another novel set in Cairo, *The
Beginning and the End*, written in 1942-43 and published in 1944. A translation by
Ramses Hanna Awad was published in 1985 (Cairo: American University in Cairo
Press).

528 **Mirrors.**
Nagib Mahfuz, translated from the Arabic by Roger
Allen. Minneapolis, Minnesota; Chicago, Illinois: Bibliotheca
Islamica, 1977. 277p. (Studies in Middle Eastern Literatures, 8).

A novel first published in serial form in the Arabic magazine *Radio and Television*
in 1971, and then in book form in 1972. It presents to the reader a series of 55
Egyptian characters, who are introduced by a narrator who frequently intrudes his
own views and affairs into the story. During the course of this long series of
vignettes, a great deal of Egyptian history and many historic events of the 20th
century are discussed.

529 **Miramar.**
Naguib Mahfouz, translated from the Arabic by Fatma Mousa-
Mahmoud, edited and revised by Maged el Kommos, John
Rodenbeck, introduction by John Fowles. London: Heinemann,
in association with the American University in Cairo Press, 1978.
141p. (Arab Authors, 9).

Though this novel is set in Alexandria it is essentially about Egypt itself and the
conflicts – both public and personal – that have arising during the successive
revolutions of the late 19th and 20th centuries. Miramar, the heroine, is
determined to emancipate herself, which the men about her either admire or
resent, and they are perhaps best defined by their varying reactions to her, since
she stands for Egypt itself.

530 **Children of Gebalawi.**
Naguib Mahfouz, translated with an introduction by Philip
Steward. London: Heinemann; Washington, DC: Three
Continents Press, 1981. 355p. (Arab Authors, 15).

This novel by Mahfuz portrays the successive heroes of his imaginary Cairo alley
who relive unknowingly the lives of Adam, Moses, Jesus and Muhammad and
their aged ancestor, Gebalawi, who represents God or rather 'not God, but a
certain idea of God that men have made'. The story caused great uproar when it
was first published in the newspaper *al-Ahram* in 1959 under the title *Awlād
Hāratinā*.

531 Wedding song.

Naguib Mahfouz, translated from the Arabic by Olive E. Kenny, edited and revised by Mursi Saad el Din, John Rodenbeck.   Cairo: American University in Cairo Press, 1984. 99p.

A translation of the Arabic *Afrāḥ al-Qubbah*, first published in 1981, which is a tale of Cairo life and is an example of a new phase in the development of Mahfuz' writing. The novel may be regarded as showing the impact of the passing of time of the four principal characters, who each tell their own story in the first person.

532 Arabic writing today: drama.

Edited by Mahmoud Manzalaoui.   Cairo: American Research Center in Egypt, 1977. 648p. bibliog.

The largest and most representative anthology of Egyptian theatre currently available, this collection ranges from historical drama to farce and includes works by many Egyptian playwrights. The editor contributes a lengthy introduction in which he traces the development of Egyptian theatre from its beginnings in 1847 to the present.

533 Ibrahim the writer.

Ibrahim Abdel Qadir al-Mazini, translated from the Arabic by Magdi Wahba, revised by Marsden Jones.   Cairo: General Egyptian Book Organization, 1976. 344p.

A novel which is a work of autobiographical fiction, and recounts the hero's three flawed romances. For its time, the novel was considered daring both in its structure and themes. The author was a leading literary innovator in poetry, novel and essay writing.

534 Al-Mazini's Egypt.

Ibrahim Abd al-Qadir al-Mazini, translation and introduction by William Hutchins.   Washington, DC: Three Continents Press, 1983. 185p. bibliog. (Unesco Collection of Representative Works, Arabic Series).

Three short stories by the Egyptian humourist, essayist and critic Ibrahim Abd al-Qadir al-Mazini (1889–1949). al-Mazini's vision of Egypt forms an essential part of all three, which are entitled 'Midu and his Accomplices', 'Return to a Beginning', and 'The Fugitive'.

535 The origins of modern Arabic fiction.

Matti Moosa.   Washington, DC: Three Continents Press, 1983. 250p. bibliog.

Egypt is the cradle of modern Arabic fiction, and this book attempts to trace the genesis and analyse the development of Arabic fiction in the 19th century and the early part of the 20th century. The author presents a social and literary history rather than simply an exercise in literary criticism. Most of the pioneers, and the translators of Western fiction into Arabic during the period such as Salim al-Bustani and Jurji Zayden, lived and worked in Egypt.

536   **Seeds of corruption.**
      Sabri Moussa, translated from the Arabic by Mona
      Mikhail.   Boston, Massachusetts: Houghton Mifflin, 1980. 169p.

This novel, entitled *Fasad al-amkinah* in the Arabic original, is the story of an Egyptian engineer's life working in the eastern desert region beside the Red Sea. The imagery and metaphorical tone of the desert, its simplicity and naturalness contrasted with the corrupting qualities and deviousness of the town, make the tale memorable. The author is a well-known journalist.

537   **The Arabic novel in Egypt (1914-1970).**
      Fatma Moussa-Mahmoud.   Cairo: Egyptian General Book
      Organization, 1973. 162p. bibliog.

The chapters of this book were originally prepared as a series of radio talks. The material is presented in a form suitable for the reader with little or no previous knowledge of the subject. Although the major novels of the period are discussed in relation to their social and literary background, they are mainly considered as works of art and points of technique are stressed throughout.

538   **The education of Salāma Mūsā.**
      Salāma Mūsā, translated from the Arabic by L. O.
      Schuman.   Leiden, The Netherlands: Brill, 1961. 248p.

A translation into English of the autobiography of Salāma Mūsā, who was born into a Coptic family at the end of the 19th century. He became influential in the liberal movement of Arabic literature in Egypt before independence in 1922. He studied in France and England before the First World War and returned to Egypt a staunch modernizer and westernizer. He is one of the important Egyptian writers of the early 20th century.

539   **Religion, my own: the literary works of Najīb Maḥfūẓ.**
      Mattityahu Peled.   New Brunswick, New Jersey; London:
      Transaction Books, 1983. 247p. bibliog.

A study of the literary production of one who is regarded by many Arab critics as the greatest living Arabic writer. His prolific output has encompassed several phases of development. This study deals with three phases of Mahfūz' writing – the historical works, the realist period, and the later 'neo-realist' stage.

540   **War in the land of Egypt.**
      Yusuf al-Qa'id, translated from the Arabic by Olive and Lorne
      Kenny, Christopher Tingley.   London: Al-Saqi, 1986. 183p.

On the eve of the 1973 war, a young man is drafted into the army. His father, the village elder, persuades a poor night watchman to send his own son as a stand-in, but the impersonation goes horribly wrong. Qa'id's tragi-comic tale of this fiasco parodies outrageous corruption and ludicrous bureaucracy. It was originally published in Arabic in 1978.

541 **Distant view of a minaret and other stories.**
Alia Rifaat, translated by Denys Johnson-Davies. London:
Quartet, 1983. 116p.

A collection of short stories written by an Egyptian woman in her early fifties who has spent most of her married life in various parts of provincial Egypt, which provide the setting for many of her stories. She convincingly portrays what it means to be a woman in a traditional Muslim society.

542 **Woman at point zero.**
Nawal El Saadawi, translated from the Arabic by Sherif Hetata.
London: Zed Books, 1983. 106p.

This novel is by a renowned Egyptian feminist, novelist and psychiatrist, and tells the story of Firdaus, a woman condemned to death for killing a pimp. Firdaus's observations evoke for the reader her village childhood, her distasteful marriage in Cairo, her life of prostitution and her experience of love. In the end she kills a pimp and welcomes death as the only means of achieving freedom. Other novels by Nawal el Sa'adawi which are available in translation are *God dies by the Nile*, translated by Sherif Hetata and published in 1985 (London: Zed Books), which is set in rural Egypt, and *Two women in one*, set in Cairo, and published in a translation by Osman Nusairi and Jana Gough in 1985 (London: Al Saqi).

543 **Hidden face of eve: women in the Arab world.**
Nawal El Saadawi, translated from the Arabic by Sherif Hetata.
London: Zed Press, 1980. 212p.

In this work, the author draws on her own experience as an Egyptian woman, and her work as a doctor in Egypt, to provide a graphic and vivid account of the realities of women's lives in Egypt today, and the cultural traditions and values that surround and constrain them.

544 **A bridge through time: a memoir.**
Laila Said. New York: Summit Books, 1985. 282p.

The memoirs of a living Egyptian woman writer, teacher, theatre producer and director, and feminist.

545 **The Egyptian novel and its main trends from 1913 to 1952.**
Hamdi Sakkut. Cairo: American University in Cairo Press, 1971.
166p.

The author aims to demonstrate the main trends in the development of the Egyptian novel from 1913 to 1952; he examines thirty-one novels by twenty writers representing three types of writing: the romantic, the historical and the realistic.

546 **Abbas Mahmud al-Aqqad.**
Hamdi Sakkut. Cairo: American University in Cairo Press, 1983.
2 vols. In Arabic. (Leaders in Contemporary Egyptian Literature
Series, no. 5).

This comprehensive study of a famous Egyptian writer consists of firstly, a
biography and an account of his works, his poetic theory and criticism, and his
status among his contemporaries; secondly, a complete bibliography of his books,
articles, translations and poetry; and thirdly, a bibliography of works about him in
both Arabic and Western languages.

547 **The Egyptian novel.**
Angele B. Samaan. New York; London: Longman, 1984. 160p.

A study of the nature and genesis of the Egyptian novel. The author believes that
there is a direct relationship between the novel and the social conditions
prevailing in the novelist's time.

548 **Nehad Gad: an Egyptian playwright.**
Angele B. Samaan. *Prism: Quarterly of Egyptian Culture*,
vol. 11 (January-March 1985), p. 24-9.

A portrait of a leading Egyptian woman playwright with a sample of her writing,
The Man Who Did Not See the Next Day, or Sitt Adila: A Monodrama.

549 **The cobbler and other stories.**
Youssef el-Sebai. Cairo: Atlas Press for the Permanent Bureau
of Afro-Asian Writers, 1973. 339p. (Afro-Asian Literature Series,
no. 4).

A collection of 20 short stories translated from the Arabic by various translators.
A list of the writer's other works and a biographical summary are also included.

550 **Folktales of Egypt.**
Edited and translated from the Arabic by Hasan el-Shamy.
Chicago: Chicago University Press, 1980. 348p.

A collection of Egyptian folktales with accompanying notes. The editor presents
nine fantasy tales, sixteen realistic and philosophical tales, six tales based on
religious themes, six etiological belief narratives, eleven tales of axes, saints and
cultural heroes, seven local belief legends, seven animal and formula tales and
seventeen narratives and jokes. This is the most important compilation of
folktales of Egypt after Edward William Lane's *Account of manners and customs
of the modern Egyptians*, which was first published in London in 1836.

551 **Egyptian earth.**
A. R. Sharkawi, translated from the Arabic by Desmond
Stewart. London: Heinemann, 1962. 250p.

This is Sharkawi's masterpiece, dealing with peasant life and the problems of land
in rural Egypt.

552 **Egyptian one-act plays.**
Edited by David Woodman.   Cairo: American University in Cairo
Press, 1974. 224p.

Twelve modern plays which represent a wide range of playwriting techniques,
theatrical possibilities and social and environmental insights. The original Arabic
edition of this collection was edited by Hamdi Sakkut (Cairo: American
University in Cairo Press, 1973).

Modern Egypt: studies in politics and society.
See item no. 10.

**Society in the mirror: representations of social cohesion in Egyptian
fiction.**
See item no. 596.

Social Conditions

553 **Egyptian marriage advertisements: microcosm of a changing society.**
Janet Abu-Lughod. *Marriage and Family Living*, vol. 23 (May 1961) p. 127-36.
The author here explores the nature of the social situation which leads individuals to advertise for marriage partners. The advertisements in a leading Egyptian weekly magazine, *Rose el-Yousef*, are seen as indicative of a changing culture at the time of writing.

554 **Growing up in an Egyptian village: Silwa, Province of Aswan.**
Hamed Ammar. London: Routledge & Kegan Paul, 1966.
Reprint ed. 299p. bibliog.
Originally published in 1954, this book describes village life and social structure and, in particular, the impact of a modern system of schooling on the outlook and activities of the villagers.

555 **Khul-Khaal: five Egyptian women tell their stories.**
Nayra Atiya, foreword by Andrea Rugh. Syracuse, New York: Syracuse University Press, 1982. 216p.
These self-portraits provide a rare glimpse into contemporary Egyptian life from a woman's perspective. The five women who tell their stories are: a gatekeeper's wife, a charity worker, a housekeeper, a fisherwoman and Dunya, who tells the story of her marriages and her struggle with her family.

556 **The Egyptian peasant.**
Henry Habib Ayrout, S.J., translated from the French by John
Alden Williams, introduction by Morroe Berger. Boston,
Massachusetts: Beacon Press, 1968. 167p. maps.
A realistic and accurate view of the daily life and customs of the Egyptian
peasantry, first published in French in 1938 under the title *Moeurs et coutumes des
fellahs.*

557 **The fellāhīn of Upper Egypt: their religious, social and industrial
life today with special reference to survivals from ancient times.**
Winifred S. Blackman. London: Harrap & Co, 1927. 316p.
A classic and detailed study of the life of the peasants, their customs and
traditions in the 1920s.

558 **The Egyptian élite under Cromer, 1882-1907.**
Jeffrey G. Collins. Berlin, FRG: Klaus Schwarz Verlag, 1984.
389p. bibliog. (Islamkundliche Untersuchungen, 99).
A study of Egyptian society during the first twenty-five years of the British
occupation, with special reference to the Egyptian élite. This book analyses the
political and economic structures of Egypt and the social transformations which
took place as a result of changes in the political and economic relationships.

559 **The women of Egypt.**
Elizabeth Cooper. London: Hurst and Blackett, 1914. 376p.
A detailed and sympathetic description of the lives of Egyptian women of all
classes and walks of life, both urban and rural, in the early 20th century. The local
traditions, and the changes being brought about by the introduction of schooling
and the nascent feminist movement, are portrayed.

560 **Income distribution and basic needs in urban Egypt.**
Amr Mohie el-Din. Cairo: American University in Cairo Press,
1982. 112p. (Cairo Papers in Social Science, Vol. 5, Monograph 3).
Discusses the structure of the urban sector in Egypt, and the factors influencing
income distribution in it, including the provision of basic needs, especially services
such as education, health, water, and electricity. Chapter three contains income
distribution estimates.

561 **Youth and women's emancipation in the United Arab Republic.**
Peter C. Dodd. *Middle East Journal*, vol. 22 (Spring 1968),
p. 159-72.
The author surveys a sample of Egyptian youth in order to examine the extent of
male opposition to women's emancipation in Egypt. He feels that modernization
has brought with it a gradual change in sex roles, and provides examples and
tables which support the proposition that the mother's education influences the
son's attitudes.

562 **The resettlement of Egyptian Nubians: a case study in developmental change.**
Hussein Mohamed Fahim.   PhD thesis, University of California, Berkeley, 1968. 124p. maps. bibliog. (Available from University Microfilms, Ann Arbor, Michigan, order no. 69-14880).

A case study of the resettlement of the Egyptian Nubians which resulted from the building of the Aswan High Dam, by an anthropologist who specializes in the study of social development and change.

563 **Kafr el-Elow: an Egyptian village in transition.**
Hani Fakhouri.   New York: Holt, Rinehart & Winston, 1972. 126p. bibliog.

An anthropological study of a peasant community some eighteen miles south of Cairo, undertaken in 1964. The study is concerned with the manner in which industrialization and urbanization have affected social institutions in the village.

564 **Architecture for the poor: an experiment in rural Egypt.**
Hassan Fathy.   Chicago, Illinois: University of Chicago Press, 1973. 231p.

This book attempts to solve the problem of providing low-cost housing for the poor in Egypt which is suited to their cultural traditions and community life, and within their financial reach. Hassan Fathy is well-known for his innovative use of modern mud-brick architecture. A total of 132 illustrations are appended to the text.

565 **Nubians in Egypt: peaceful people.**
Robert Fernea, Georg Gerster, with architectural drawings and notes by Horst Jaritz.   Austin, Texas: University of Texas Press, 1973. 146p. map. bibliog.

Fernea, an anthropologist, and Gerster, a photographer, spent four years in Old Nubia before the land was flooded by the backwaters of the Aswan High Dam in the early 1960s. They recorded the life of the Nubians in their native land and later visited them in the resettlement area near Kom Ombo. In this volume they present a unique portrait of a centuries-old way of life which no longer exists. Includes over a hundred plates, both colour and black and white.

566 **Cairo's Nubian families.**
Peter Geiser.   Cairo: American University in Cairo Press, 1981. 83p. bibliog. (Cairo Papers in Social Science, Vol. 4, Monograph 1).

Presents the results of field research conducted to study the life of the Nubian urban family in Cairo.

567 Real estate rights in urban Egypt: the changing sociopolitical winds.
Milad M. Hanna. In: *Property, social structure, and law in the modern Middle East*. Edited by Ann Elizabeth Mayer. Albany, New York: State University of New York Press, 1985, p. 189-211.

The housing problem in urban Egypt is multidimensional and complex and this essay is by an Egyptian expert on the subject. The author examines the housing situation in urban Egypt, and especially in Cairo, and its effect on the social and economic fields from before the Second World War to the time of Sadat's assassination.

568 Polemics on the modesty and segregation of women in contemporary Egypt.
Valerie J. Hoffman-Ladd. *International Journal of Middle East Studies*, vol. 19, no. 1 (February 1987), p. 23-50.

A well-documented paper on the arguments about women's status and role in Egyptian society in the 1980s. These arguments occur between two major groups, the Islamic fundamentalists and the modernists. There are indications that the liberal modernists are losing to the very conservative religious group. The modesty and segregation of women is one of the most important and controversial issues in Egypt today.

569 The role of women in social reform in Egypt.
Aziza Hussein. *Middle East Journal*, vol. 7, no. 4 (1954), p. 440-50.

The author discusses social reform in Egypt with reference to the status of women. She claims that the movement for women's rights was part of a larger movement for political and civil rights at all levels.

570 Status of women and family planning in a developing country, Egypt.
Aziza Hussein.In: *Egypt: population problems and prospects*. Edited by Abdel Rahim Omran. Chapel Hill, North Carolina: Carolina Population Center, 1973, p. 181-9.

This paper discusses the relationship of family planning to the status of women, traditional and modern roles of Egyptian women, the feminist movement in Egypt, and women and voluntary associations.

571 Class conflict in Egypt, 1945-1970.
Mahmoud Hussein, translated by Michel and Susanne Chirman, Alfred Ehrenfeld, Kathy Brown. New York; London: Monthly Review Press, 1973. 379p.

Originally published under the title *La Lutte de classe en Egypte de 1945 à 1968* (Paris: François Maspero). The author's aim was to present a systematic challenge to the bourgeois conceptual apparatus which, he argued, Nasserism used to justify itself and to protect itself against the growing consciousness on the part of the

Social Conditions

working masses of the regime's class nature. In other words, the author aimed to 'reevaluate the Nasser regime within a proletarian, revolutionary conceptual framework, i.e., from the point of view of the masses and their aspirations toward an anti-imperialist and democratic people's revolution'.

572 **An analytic index of survey research in Egypt.**
Compiled by Madiha el Safty, Monte Palmer, Mark Kennedy.
Cairo: American University in Cairo, 1985. 282p. (Cairo Papers in Social Science, Vol. 8, Monographs 1 & 2).
Aims to provide planners and scholars with an analytical summary of some of the most important survey research projects that have been completed in Egypt over the course of the past twenty years.

573 **Distributing disposable income and the impact of eliminating food subsidies in Egypt.**
Karima Korayem.   Cairo: American University in Cairo Press, 1982. 99p. bibliog. (Cairo Papers in Social Science, Vol. 5, Monograph 2).
This volume includes two papers which discuss factors relating to the standard of living of the Egyptian population. The paper on income distribution shows that a large proportion of the population falls into the relatively low-income brackets; the second paper shows how important food subsidies are in keeping down the cost of living for the low-income urban population.

574 **Urban research strategies for Egypt.**
Edited by Richard Lobban.   Cairo: American University in Cairo Press, 1983. 125p. (Cairo Papers in Social Science, Vol. 6, Monograph 2).
The various papers in this volume discuss the problem of governing Cairo, and the housing situation within it, the problem of urban conservation, an urban-rural comparison of Egyptian youth and justice systems, urban employment and its problems, and production as a focus for urban studies.

575 *Ibn al-Balad:* **a concept of Egyptian identity.**
Sawsan el-Messiri.   Leiden, The Netherlands: E.J. Brill, 1978. 116p. (Social, Economic and Political Studies of the Middle East, Vol. XXIV).
An essay on the concept of the *Ibn al-Balad* (native son) in Egyptian society and culture. The author examines the social manifestations of the groups associated with the concept in both historical and contemporary times.

576 **The legal status of women among Awlad Ali.**
Safia K. Mohsen. *Anthropological Quarterly*, vol. 40, no. 3 (July 1967), p. 153-66.

The author describes the legal and social status of women in the tribal community of Awlad Ali in Egypt's Western Desert. Generally, women are considered inferior in every respect to men and hence the absolute authority of men over women in the community.

577 **The Egyptian woman: between modernity and tradition.**
Safia K. Mohsen. In: *Many sisters*. Edited by Carolyn J. Matthiasson. New York: Free Press, 1974, p. 37-58.

The author argues that reformers who support women's rights have concentrated on legal reform and neglected cultural practices and attitudes, resulting in the continued influence of traditional values. In support of her view, she examines family laws, sexual attitudes, education, and legal reform.

578 **The poor man's model of development. Development potential at low levels of living in Egypt.**
C. A. O. van Nieuwenhuijze, M. Fathalla al-Khatib, Adel Azer. Leiden, The Netherlands: Brill, 1985. 206p. (Social, Economic & Political Studies of the Middle East, vol. 40).

This is a study of the process of development and the methods by which the living conditions of the poor can be improved, within the constraints imposed by their low level of living, their communities, and the economic and political environment in which they operate. Cases of community services and private initiatives are examined and the reasons for success and failure analysed.

579 **Population and food dynamics: a caloric measurement in Egypt.**
Manoucher Parvin, Louis Putterman. *International Journal of Middle East Studies*, vol. 12, no. 1 (August 1980), p. 81-100.

The difficulties Egypt encounters in feeding its population are part of a matrix of internal problems which significantly influence its foreign policy. The resource/ population imbalance has had repercussions on a number of international issues: Egypt's repeated advances towards and retreats from political union with neighbours (for example, Syria, Libya, the Sudan); its continuing aspiration to a major political and economic position in the Arab world; and its relationships with the main powers. While this paper is limited to a study of Egyptian agriculture and population as an internal issue, such wider implications add to the importance of the topic, and the findings are relevant to an understanding of the broader issues as well.

580 **Programme of reconstruction and development.**
Cairo: Ministry of Housing and Reconstruction, 1976. 100p.

A government programme which aims at solving the housing problems of overpopulated Cairo.

581 **Peasant differentiation and politics in contemporary Egypt.**
Alan Richards. *Peasant Studies*, vol. 9, no. 3 (Spring 1982),
p. 145-61.

Between 1952 and 1982 the rich peasantry benefited from Nasser's land reform law and continued to consolidate their position. The poorer peasants continued to be poor because of market, political and demographic forces. It is the author's view that the open door policy has increased the role of the private sector, thereby restricting the upward mobility of the lower middle class.

582 **Coping with poverty in a Cairo community.**
Andrea B. Rugh. Cairo: American University in Cairo Press,
1979. 100p. (Cairo Papers in Social Science, Vol. 2, Monograph 1).

A study of Bulaq in Cairo, focusing on the housing and cramped living conditions prevalent there, with the attendant strain on people's lives and family relationships. This volume considers the various strategies to which people resort to deal with their problems, and the constraints their poverty imposes on them.

583 **Family in contemporary Egypt.**
Andrea B. Rugh. Syracuse, New York: Syracuse University
Press, 1984. 296p. bibliog.

This study focuses mainly on lower and middle class urban families and their adjustments to the demands of contemporary city life. The author discusses the family as a social institution, its role and definitions, and marriage in theory and in actual practice. The role of religion and traditional obligations to family and kin, and the extent of change dictated by the new conditions of city life, are also examined.

584 **Harem years: the memoirs of an Egyptian feminist (1879-1924).**
Huda Shaarawi, translated from the Arabic and introduced by
Margot Badran. London: Virago, 1986. 152p.

This is an edition and translation of the memoirs of Huda Shaarawi's early years, written towards the end of her life. She was born into an upper-class family and was one of the last Egyptian women to live in seclusion. She became an active nationalist and she is famous as the leading Egyptian feminist of her time. She remained head of the Egyptian Feminist Union until her death in 1947.

585 **Basic needs, inflation and the poor of Egypt, 1970-1980.**
Myrette Ahmed el-Sokkari. Cairo: American University in Cairo
Press, 1984. 103p. maps. bibliog. (Cairo Papers in Social Science,
Vol. 7, Monograph 2).

The main aim of this study was to establish how the poor fared during the 1970s and to evaluate whether their welfare improved or worsened. The results of the study show that while income has grown even at the lower income levels, a significant proportion of the population is still unable to obtain its very basic needs, whether privately obtained or provided by the government. The author recommends that planning policies for economic growth and development should explicitly aim at raising the standards of living of these specific income groups.

586   **Migration and the selectivity of change: Egyptian peasant women in Iraq.**
Camillia Fawzi el-Solh. *Peuples Méditerranéens*, no. 31-32 (April-September 1985), p. 243-58.

In 1975, the governments of Iraq and Egypt signed a bilateral agreement by which Egyptian peasant families would be resettled permanently in Iraq. One hundred settlers and their families from Lower, Middle and Upper Egypt arrived a year later to live at Khalsa settlement, built for them by the Iraqis some 36 miles south of Baghdad. The majority of families took advantage of economic opportunities offered to them and came to enjoy a higher standard of living than they had in Egypt. The study found that post-resettlement changes in the Egyptian peasant families' social attitudes and economic behaviour are to a large extent directed by traditional norms and values.

587   **Family, power and politics in Egypt: Sayed Bey Marei – his clan, clients, and cohorts.**
Robert Springborg.   Philadelphia, Pennsylvania: University of Pennsylvania Press, 1982. 297p.

Focusing upon the family and career of the prominent Egyptian politician Sayed Bey Marei, this book provides a valuable picture of the political life and social network of the élite in Egypt from the 1920s to the Sadat era.

588   **Women in Egyptian public life.**
Earl L. Sullivan.   Syracuse, New York: Syracuse University Press, 1986. 223p. bibliog.

This book studies the public role of women in modern Egypt. It demonstrates clearly and unambiguously that a growing number of Egyptian women are important in politics and business and are seen to be so. The author concentrates on women in parliament, the wives of Egypt's presidents, women in the political opposition, and women in business.

589   **Social identity and class in a Cairo neighbourhood.**
Nadia Adel Taher.   Cairo: American University in Cairo Press, 1986. 119p. (Cairo Papers in Social Science, Vol. 9, Monograph 4).

An empirical study carried out in 1982 in a district of Cairo, which identified a division between the original inhabitants and 'newcomers'.

590   **Egyptian migration and peasant wives.**
Elizabeth Taylor. *MERIP Reports*, vol. 14, no. 5, issue no. 124 (June 1984), p. 3-10.

Studies the impact of temporary migration of male peasants from the Egyptian village of Dahahur (in Giza Province). Although peasant wives have control over the remittances sent by their husbands, no change in the patriarchal family structure is discerned. Migration does not affect the development of capitalist farming owing to land and labour constraints.

591 **The situation of Egyptian women in the first half of the 19th century.**
Nada Tomiche. In: *Beginnings of modernization in the Middle East. The nineteenth century.* Edited by William Polk, Richard L. Chambers. Chicago, Illinois: University of Chicago Press, 1968, p. 171-84.

The author believes that Muhammad Ali's reign was a revolutionary period for women in Egypt. Before and after that period traditional customs dominated the status of women.

592 **Women in nineteenth-century Egypt.**
Judith E. Tucker. Cambridge, England: Cambridge University Press, 1985. 264p. bibliog.

The author explores the position and power of peasant and urban lower-class Egyptian women between 1800 and 1914 in relation to their access to power, their position in the family unit, their participation in social production, and the prevailing ideological definitions of their roles.

593 **Three centuries: family chronicles of Turkey and Egypt.**
Emine Foat Tugay, with a foreword by the Dowager Marchioness of Reading. London: Oxford University Press, 1963. 324p. bibliog.

Very little had been written about upper-class family life in the Ottoman Empire during the 19th and early 20th centuries, and this book was an attempt to fill the gap. It contains details of Muhammad Ali's family life.

594 **Life among the poor in Cairo.**
Unni Wikan, translated by Ann Henning. London: Tavistock Publications, 1980. 167p. bibliog.

An important book which describes the crucial effect of extreme material deprivation on interhuman relations. Women's experiences of poverty, their means of coping with it, and its effect on their lives, marriages, relations with their families and neighbours are described in detail.

595 **Living conditions among Cairo's poor: a view from below.**
Unni Wikan. *Middle East Journal*, vol. 39, no. 1 (Winter 1985), p. 7-26.

Using well-established criteria for measurement, the author concludes that living conditions among Cairo's poor have improved significantly between 1969 and 1984, partly through the efforts of the poor themselves.

596 **Society in the mirror: representations of social cohesion in Egyptian fiction.**
Rivka Yadlin. *Asian and African Studies*, vol. 17, nos. 1-3 (Nov. 1983), p. 207-25.
A study of social cohesion among Egyptians as portrayed in fiction and short stories by modern Egyptian writers, based on an analysis of a sample of short stories published between 1948 and 1976.

Shahhat: an Egyptian.
See item no. 3.

Themes in the economy of the Bedouin of South Sinai in the nineteenth and twentieth centuries.
See item no. 116.

Memoirs from the women's prison.
See item no. 341.

Egyptian Nubians: resettlement and years of coping.
See item no. 432.

The Egyptian Nubian: a study in social symbiosis.
See item no. 434.

Maze of justice.
See item no. 501.

The effects of the Egyptian food ration and subsidy system on income distribution and consumption.
See item no. 755.

An annotated research bibliography of studies in Arabic, English and French of the *fellah* of the Egyptian Nile, 1798-1955.
See item no. 959.

Women in the Middle East and North Africa: an annotated bibliography.
See item no. 987.

The modern Arab woman: a bibliography.
See item no. 988.

Social Services, Health and Welfare

597 **Child development in Egypt.**
Edited by Nicholas V. Ciaccio.   Cairo: American University in
Cairo Press, 1979. 91p. bibliog. (Cairo Papers in Social Science,
Vol. 3, Monograph 2).

This monograph includes a variety of articles dealing with the children of Egypt
and their families. Each article has a research base in the real world of Egyptian
childhood and each in its own way suggests directions for further work at both the
research and applied levels in child development. The articles are: 'Planning
recommendations for children and youth in Egypt: a working paper presented for
the International Year of the Child', by Nicholas V. Ciaccio; 'Women in
development: the integrated care project for primary school children', by Saneya
A.W. Saleh, Suzanne H. Moubarek; 'Psychiatric clinics for Egyptian school
children; focus: the Garden City Psychiatric Clinic of Cairo', by Claire Fahim
Gobrial; 'Changing women in a changing society: the study of emergent
consciousness of young women in the city of Akhmim in Upper Egypt', by Hoda
Youssef Fahmy; 'Child mental health in Egypt', by Nahed Waines; and
'Children's reports of child-rearing practices: a preliminary study', by Maissa el-
Mofty.

598 **Supplementary feeding in rural Egypt: the health system in action.**
John Osgood Field, Robert Burkhardt, George Ropes.   *Food
Policy*, vol. 6, no. 3 (August 1981), p. 163-72.

Describes the Egyptian Ministry of Health's efforts to make food supplements
available to rural children suffering from malnutrition. The Ministry's experiment
highlights the importance of management issues in health care delivery.

599 **The influence of the health system on the recorded incidence of infant mortality and birth rates in rural Egypt.**
John Osgood Field, George Ropes. *L'Egypte Contemporaine*, vol. 73, no. 387 (January 1982), p. 25-59.
A study of the influence of the expansion of health services in Egypt on birth and infant mortality statistics. It was found that underrecording of infant deaths is extensive. Health services are being extended to areas of greater need and the more they expand, the more infant deaths are recorded, so that any decrease in infant death rate is not detected. Birth statistics were found to be unaffected by the expansion of health services.

600 **Public assistance in Egypt: an ideological analysis.**
Jean L. Garrison. *Middle East Journal*, vol. 32, no. 3 (Summer 1978), p. 279-306.
A review of the philosophy and regulations of public assistance in Egypt since the 1940s. The author found that the changing rhetoric about public assistance in the absence of substantive programmatic changes indicates that the primary function of public assistance has been to justify and legitimize the regime.

601 **Adjustment to Egypt: somatopsychic health guide.**
Teresa el-Mehairy. Cairo: American University in Cairo Press, 1975. 56p.
A handbook for newcomers to Egypt, describing how to remain healthy and happy while coping with children, servants, pets and household chores as well as the Cairene environment.

602 **Medical doctors: a study of role concept and job satisfaction – the Egyptian case.**
Theresa el-Mehairy. Leiden, The Netherlands: Brill, 1984. 208p. map. (Social, Economic & Political Studies of the Middle East, vol. 33).
This book developed out of a pilot study carried out in Menoufia Governorate at rural health units in which doctors function as unit administrators, because of the pressing need to improve Egypt's health services. The study describes the health care system, medical education in Egypt, and the operation of Egypt's present health care delivery system.

603 **Providing affordable medical care in a third world country: the case of Egypt.**
Gita Meier. *Inquiry*, vol. 19 (Winter 1982), p. 346-56.
A study of the twenty-year history of the Health Insurance Organization in Egypt, which provides comprehensive medical care for 20 per cent of the urban population. HIO services are funded by contributions from employers and employees and are available only to working people. The autonomous governing board of HIO attempts to maintain basic standards, inspect facilities, and employ and train specialists to improve services.

604 **Social insurance in the Arab Republic of Egypt.**
Ministry of Social Insurance, Arab Republic of Egypt. *International Social Security Review* (Geneva), vol. 37, no. 4 (1984), p. 424-40.

An official statement explaining the Egyptian social insurance system, 1954-1984, and providing details of the coverage and benefits provided by the social insurance laws. These laws cover civil servants, public and private sector workers, employers, the self-employed, casual workers, and Egyptians working abroad; they provide pensions, unemployment compensation, sickness and maternity benefits and injury compensation.

605 **Mother and child welfare studies: a critical review.**
Wedad Soliman Morcos. Cairo: Population and Family Planning Board, Research Office, 1981. 53p. bibliog. (Research Monographs Series, No. 1).

A critical analysis of previous studies dealing with the topic of women and children in Egypt, with reference to subjects, methods and conclusions. These studies fall into two groups: those concerned with family social status, its evaluation and the extent of its influence on children's upbringing; and those concerned with the social status of childhood, particularly as regards health, education and work.

606 **Rural health care in Egypt.**
Nawal el Messiri Nadim. Ottawa, Canada: International Development Research Centre, 1980. 40p. (Publication IDRC-TS15e).

A monograph on the interrelationship between the formal health service and traditional medicine in rural communities of Egypt, which describes the traditional practitioners of medicine and presents some case studies.

607 **Women, health and development.**
Prepared and edited by Cynthia Nelson. Cairo: American University in Cairo Press, 1977. 82p. (Cairo Papers in Social Science, Vol. 1, Monograph 1).

This volume contains the following papers presented at the 1976 Open University seminar on health care in Egypt: 'Reconceptualizing health care', by Cynthia Nelson; 'Styles and sources of social change: women's movements as critiques of health care systems', by Virginia Olesen; 'Nutrition: facts, fallacies and implications for women concerned with development', by Anne M.S. Coles; 'Education for women – for what?' by Wafik Hassouna; 'Current problems in gynecology and obstetrics and their effects on patient attitudes', by Samira el-Mallah; and 'Health, development and women', by Earl L. (Tim) Sullivan.

608 **Social security and the family in Egypt.**
Helmi R. Tadros.   Cairo: American University in Cairo Press,
1984. 87p. bibliog. (Cairo Papers in Social Science, Vol. 7,
Monograph 1).

Presents the results of a study which set out firstly, to identify arrangements and
plans for economic and social security in old age, and during disability and long-
term illness; secondly, to identify attitudes, expectations and plans relating to
both formal and informal support; and thirdly, to establish the implications of
these mutual influences for policies and programmes addressed to family
planning, social and economic security and community development in Egypt.

609 **Folk medicine in modern Egypt; being the relevant parts of the *Tibb
al-rukka* or old wives' medicine of 'Abd al-Raḥmān Ismā'īl.**
John Walker.   London: Luzac & Co., 1934. 128p.

A translation of a book published in Cairo in 1892 by an Egyptian doctor, 'Abd
al-Rahmān Effendi Ismā'īl, under the title of *Tibb al-rukka*, meaning the
medicine of old women or folk medicine.

Politics and
Government

610   **The student movement and national politics in Egypt, 1923-1973.**
      Ahmed Abdalla.   London: Al Saqi Books, 1985. 281p. (Distri-
      buted by Zed Books.)

An invaluable study of the role of Egyptian students in politics by someone who
was a student activist himself. Useful reading for all students and observers of the
Egyptian political scene. Contains a postscript on student activism from 1974 to
1984.

611   **Egypt: military society – the army regime, the Left, and social
      change under Nasser.**
      Anouar Abdel-Malek, translated from the French by Charles Lam
      Markmann.   New York: Random House, 1968. 458p. bibliog.

An analysis of Nasser's regime and ideology as perceived by a leftist Egyptian
scholar who actively opposed Nasser's policies. Originally published in French in
1962 (Paris: Editions du Seuil).

612   **The intellectual origins of Egyptian nationalism.**
      J. M. Ahmed.   Oxford, England: Oxford University Press, 1960.
      135p. (Middle Eastern Monographs, no. 3).

Published under the auspices of the Royal Institute of International Affairs, this
remains the basic work on the development of Egyptian nationalist thought.

613   **The Islamic militants in Egyptian politics.**
      Hamied N. Ansari.   *International Journal of Middle East Studies*,
      vol. 16, no. 1 (March 1984), p. 123-44.

Sociological studies of the militant phenomenon before Sadat's assassination
correctly diagnosed religious extremism as the product of conditions of alienation.

146

These conditions come about as a consequence of the breakdown of traditional solidarities and communal ties under the impact of urbanization or rural migration into the cities. The object of this essay is not only to substantiate these earlier conclusions, with the support of empirically grounded research, but also to advance our knowledge of the phenomenon by mapping out the social context and areas of concentration where the Islamic militants had most appeal.

614 Sectarian conflict in Egypt and the political expediency of religion.
Hamied Ansari. *Middle East Journal*, vol. 38, no. 3 (Summer 1984), p. 397-418.

An excellent paper by an objective observer who is a professor of Middle Eastern politics. Sadat abandoned the Nasserite formula of political mobilization based on secular ideals and adopted instead a formula which was designed to win the support of the traditional and conservative elements in his struggle with the Left. Sadat's formula had two disastrous consequences for the stability of the political system. Firstly, it alienated the Coptic minority and forced the traditionally acquiescent Coptic church to take a militant stand; and secondly, the politically expedient appeal to religion had the unintended consequence of arousing Islamic militancy.

615 Bureaucracy and politics in contemporary Egypt.
Nazih N.M. Ayubi. London: Ithaca Press, 1980. 547p. bibliog. (St. Antony's Middle East Monographs, No. 10).

Analyses the politics of bureaucracy during the two decades which followed Nasser's revolution, the attempt to transform the bureaucracy, the creation of a new élite, and the bureaucratization of politics which in fact took place.

616 Stateness and ideology in contemporary Egyptian politics.
Gabriel Ben-Dor. In: *Islam, nationalism and radicalism in Egypt and the Sudan.* Edited by Gabriel R. Warburg and Uri M. Kupferschmidt. New York: Praeger, 1983, p. 73-96.

An analysis of the relationship between the political ideology prevailing in Egyptian society and the actual political situation Egypt has faced during the last thirty years.

617 The ideological revolution in the Middle East.
Leonard Binder. New York: John Wiley, 1964. 287p.

The author devotes three chapters of this book to the study of the ideological foundations of Egyptian-Arab nationalism, Nasserism, which he describes as the protest movement of the Middle East, and Egypt's positive neutrality as advocated by Nasser's regime.

618 **In a moment of enthusiasm: political power and the second stratum in Egypt.**
Leonard Binder. Chicago, Illinois: University of Chicago Press, 1978. 437p.

The two goals of this study are firstly, to provide as thorough an empirical description of the political size and power of the rural middle class as may be allowed by available data; and secondly, to offer an interpretation of the Egyptian political system – under Nasser and thereafter – that takes account of these empirical constraints as well as the course of Egyptian political history as seen from various ideological perspectives.

619 **Egypt: about the political culture, political groups, political structures, political leadership, political policies and major political events in Egypt.**
Bruce Maynard Borthwick   In: *Comparative politics of the Middle East, an introduction.* Englewood Cliffs, New Jersey: Prentice-Hall, 1980, p. 148-84.

620 **The Egyptian communist movement in perspective.**
Selma Botman. *Journal of South Asian and Middle Eastern Studies*, vol. 10, no. 3 (Spring 1987), p. 78-94.

There have been three distinct periods during the 20th century when Egyptian communism has operated as an active oppositional ideology: during the early 1920s; during the Second World War until the fall of the monarchy in 1952; and during Nasser's rule in the 1950s and 1960s. At each particular historical moment, the prevailing political environment determined, to a large extent, the character and content of left-wing radical activity.

621 **Local politics and development in the Middle East.**
Edited by Louis J. Cantori, Iliya Harik.   Boulder, Colorado; London: Westview Press, 1984. 258p. bibliog.

The authors of this book concentrate on how local politics influence development in the Middle East; their aim is to encourage more appropriate – and thus more effective – assistance programmes. They discuss general policy issues and the nature of centre/periphery relations in Middle East countries and delve into specific problems encountered in Egypt, Jordan, Lebanon, Syria, Iraq, Turkey, Tunisia, and North Yemen, showing how information about local political schemes can aid administrators of development programmes in providing assistance that is acceptable – and accepted – at the local level. Four of the ten papers are about the Egyptian case.

622 **The impact of the Egyptian Muslim Brotherhood's political Islam since the 1950s.**
Olivier Carre. In: *Islam, nationalism and radicalism in Egypt and the Sudan.* Edited by Gabriel R. Warburg and Uri M. Kupferschmidt. New York: Praeger, 1983, p. 262-80.
An exploration of how the Muslim Brothers' political ideas have affected the politics of Nasser and Sadat and other political situations in the Arab world.

623 **The demilitarization of the Egyptian cabinet.**
Mark N. Cooper. *International Journal of Middle East Studies,* vol. 14, no. 2 (May 1982), p. 203-25.
A study of the process of political liberalization in Egypt from 1952 to 1982. The author chose the Egyptian cabinet as his case study of that aspect of the country's political life, and found that whereas in 1967 65.5% of the cabinet had a military background, this had dropped to 9.7% by 1977. He speculates that the liberal civilian approach to politics has not achieved stability, and that this may lead to the reestablishment of the role of the military in government.

624 **Party politics in Egypt: the Wafd and its rivals, 1919-1939.**
Marius Deeb. London: Ithaca Press, 1979. 452p. bibliog. (St. Antony's Middle East Monographs, No. 9).
A comprehensive analysis of the relationship between political and socioeconomic change in Egypt between the First and Second World Wars. At the centre of this process stood the Wafd, a mass nationalist movement which gradually became an ordinary political party. Using a wealth of new material from Egyptian and British archives, the author examines the nature of the Wafdist organization, its ideology and social structure, and details its complex and weakening struggle with the British, the Royal Palace, and a growing number of local rivals for the control of Egypt.

625 **Democracy in Egypt: problems and prospects.**
Ali E. Hillal Dessouki. Cairo: American University in Cairo, 1978. 90p. (Cairo Papers in Social Science, Vol. 1, Monograph 2).
This monograph is the outcome of a symposium which was held in Cairo, 8-11 December 1976. The seven papers included in it represent, essentially, the testimony of a number of Egyptian intellectuals and their accumulated perceptions of the problems that democracy faces in their country. The appendix includes 23 documents relating to the development of constitutional and parliamentary life in Egypt between 1952 and 1977.

626 **The emergence of Pan-Arabism in Egypt.**
Israel Gershoni. Tel Aviv, Israel: Shiloah Center for Middle Eastern and African Studies, Tel Aviv University, 1981. 142p. bibliog.
This book studies the question of how and when Pan-Arabism first appeared as a major ideological force in the consciousness of the cultural and political élite in

Egypt. In a detailed and comprehensive analysis, the author concludes that the years 1936-1940 formed the crucial period of its development. The concluding chapter deals briefly with the waning of Pan-Arabism in the 1970s under Sadat.

627 Tinker, tailor, and textile worker: class and politics in Egypt, 1930-1952.

Ellis Goldberg. Berkeley; Los Angeles; London: University of California Press, 1986. 220p. maps. bibliog.

A study of workers and politics: an examination of the course of Communist Party activity among Egyptian workers, and of rival ideologies such as that of the Muslim Brothers. In 1952, the whole political landscape of Egypt was changed by the Free Officers' coup.

628 The return of consciousness.

Tawfiq al-Hakim, translated from the Arabic by Bayly Winder. London: Macmillan, 1985. 83p.

A translation of the second Arabic edition, published in December 1974, of a work which is described as the intellectual forerunner of 'Sadatism'. It marks the first public, published repudiation of 'Nasserism' to emerge from the upper-class, liberal, westernized intelligentsia in Egyptian society. As a published document, it broke Egypt's group solidarity and created a sensation, claiming that the Egyptians had been taken in by the promise of the 1952 revolution.

629 Arab socialism: a documentary survey.

Sami A. Hanna, George H. Gardner, with contributions by Sherif Mardin, Fayez Sayegh, foreword by Aziz S. Atiya. Salt Lake City, Utah: University of Utah Press, 1969. 418p. bibliog.

This volume presents materials relating to Arab socialism which are designed to promote understanding of the inner movements of Arab society. The authors consulted a vast amount of the basic source material of the socialist movement in the Arab world, especially in Egypt.

630 The political mobilization of peasants: a study of an Egyptian community.

Iliya Harik. Bloomington, Indiana: Indiana University Press, 1974. 291p. bibliog. (Studies in Development, 8).

A study of a village near Damanhur in Beheira Province which portrays the response of the villagers to the revolution and the operation of the new political structures at the local level.

631 The legal left in Egypt.

Bertus Hendriks. *Arab Studies Quarterly*, vol. 5, no. 3 (Summer 1983), p. 260-75.

An historical review of Egypt's National Progressive Unionist Grouping, with details of its formation in 1976 and its activities. As the party increased its opposition to government policies, it gained more support.

632 **Egypt's elections, Mubarak's bind.**
Bertus Hendriks. *MERIP Reports, Middle East Research and Information Project*, vol. 14, no. 1, issue no. 129 (January 1985), p. 11-18.

An excellent report of the May 1984 general elections in Egypt, with details of the role of each party which participated.

633 **Children of the élite: political attitudes of the westernized bourgeoisie in contemporary Egypt.**
Raymond A. Hinnebusch. *Middle East Journal*, vol. 36, no. 4 (Autumn 1982), p. 535-61.

An examination of the political ideology of the westernized wing of the Egyptian bourgeoisie through a study of the attitudes of its children. The author found that internally, the bourgeoisie prefers a secular liberal democratic capitalist approach, and dislikes authoritarianism; externally, the bourgeoisie advocates political alignment with the West and economic integration into world capitalist markets.

634 **The reemergence of the Wafd party: glimpses of the liberal opposition in Egypt.**
Raymond A. Hinnebusch. *International Journal of Middle East Studies*, vol. 16, no. 1 (March 1984), p. 99-121.

After an introduction on the rise and eclipse of the old Wafd, the oldest and largest political party in Egypt, the author studies the reemergence of the new Wafd in 1978. He presents a sociological analysis of its leadership, its ideology and attitudes, and an analysis of its programme. He concludes with an analysis of the new Wafd and the Sadat regime with special reference to the dilemmas of liberalism in the developing world. For a longer and more detailed study of Egyptian politics, see by the same author *Egyptian politics under Sadat: the post-populist development of an authoritarian-modernizing state*, published in 1985 (Cambridge, England: Cambridge University Press).

635 **Ibn Arabi in the People's Assembly: religion, press, and politics in Sadat's Egypt.**
Th. Emil Homerin. *Middle East Journal*, vol. 40, no. 3 (Summer 1986), p. 462-78.

A discussion of the banning of the books of the Arab mystic Ibn Arabi (1165-1240 AD) by the People's Assembly on 15 February 1979 leads to a consideration of the role of religion in Egyptian politics and the growing role of religious conservatism in Egyptian society. The author also describes how Sadat's government used this situation to further its own interests.

Politics and Government

636 **Egypt: politics and society 1945-1984.**
Derek Hopwood. London; Boston, Massachusetts: Allen &
Unwin, 1985. 2nd rev. ed. 203p. bibliog.

A comprehensive survey of Egyptian politics and society in all its aspects from
1945. The author includes chapters on the political ideologies of Nasser and
Sadat, on the economic problems of Egypt, on Egyptian culture and literature,
and on the life of the ordinary Egyptian.

637 **The Arab left.**
Tareq Y. Ismael. Syracuse, New York: Syracuse University
Press, 1976. 204p.

This concise volume is a primer of Arab leftist and neo-leftist parties and
organizations, clarifying their origins and ideologies. It includes sections on
Nasserism, Arab nationalism, and Egyptian socialism.

638 **Egypt's young rebels: 'Young Egypt', 1933-1952.**
James P. Jankowski. Stanford, California: Hoover Institution
Press, 1975. 154p. bibliog.

A study of the Young Egypt Society, 1933-1936, and its successors of various, but
similar names, which continued to operate until the revolution of 1952.

639 **Protest movements and religious undercurrents in Egypt: past and
present.**
Afaf Lutfi al-Sayyid Marsot. Washington, DC: Center for
Contemporary Arab Studies, Georgetown University, 1984. 10p.
(Occasional Papers Series).

The author offers a brief summary of the social, political and economic
dislocations that often precede and give rise to protest movements. She examines
three periods in Egypt's history as illustrations: the last decades of the 18th
century, the 1930s, and the last few years of Sadat's regime.

640 **Religion or opposition? Urban protest movements in Egypt.**
Afaf Lutfi al-Sayyid Marsot. *International Journal of Middle
East Studies*, vol. 16, no. 4 (November 1984), p. 541-52.

The major theme of this paper is that movements of protest in Egypt take on a
religious colouring when all channels of discourse are closed to the population;
when autocracy reigns, supported and encouraged by outside forces which are
seen to manipulate local society for their own political and economic ends; and
when political leaders possessing charisma and popular appeal are absent.

641 **Rural politics in Nasser's Egypt: a quest for legitimacy.**
James B. Mayfield. Austin, Texas: University of Texas Press,
1971. 270p. bibliog.

Describes and analyses the functioning of an Egyptian village as a political
community embracing three interlocking organizations: the local branch of the

Arab Socialist Union (ASU); the centrally appointed administrative officials; and the village council. This book examines the way the local elements of the central government function, and the extent to which they are successful in promoting government policies and maintaining control, and providing communication between the political leadership and the village leadership.

642 **Aḥmad Amīn (Cairo 1887-1954): advocate of social and literary reform in Egypt.**
   A. M. H. Mayzad.   Leiden, The Netherlands: Brill, 1963. 107p.

A biography and discussion of the works of Ahmad Amin, who was one of the intellectuals whose influence over many years largely helped to prepare Egyptians for the age of reform introduced by the revolution of 1952. This book discusses his essays on social problems and reform, and on literature and language.

643 **Political parties in Egypt.**
   Fauzi M. Najjar.   *Arab Perspectives*, vol. 4 (October 1983), p. 5-11.

A study of political parties in Egypt during the period from 1970 to 1981. In 1976 Sadat transformed the platforms he created in 1974 into political parties, but remained sensitive to opposition; hence his contradictory policies of restrictions and liberalization.

644 **Egypt in search of political community: an analysis of the intellectual and political evolution of Egypt, 1804-1952.**
   Nadav Safran.   Cambridge, Massachusetts: Harvard University Press, 1961. 298p. bibliog.

Discusses the roles played by traditional and reformist Islamic ideologies, liberal nationalism and the traditionalist reaction to it in forming modern Egyptian political culture.

645 **The Wafd 1919-1952: cornerstone of Egyptian political power.**
   Janice J. Terry.   London: Third World Centre for Research & Publishing, 1982. 315p. bibliog.

A study of the rise and fall of the Wafd party. Part 1 covers the years 1914-1927 and the achievement of independence, while part 2 deals with the period 1928-1952 – the second generation and their confrontation with the British and the king in the 1930s and 1940s, until the revolution of 1952 put an end to the Wafd government.

646 **The Egyptian army in politics: pattern for new nations.**
   P.J. Vatikiotis.   Bloomington, Indiana: Indiana University Press, 1961. 261p. bibliog.

This book can be seen as a preliminary attempt to understand the conditions that brought military groups into political eminence in the Middle East and the early evolution of their political behaviour, with particular reference to Egypt as a case study. Reprinted in 1971 with a new preface.

Politics and Government

647 **The evolution of the Egyptian national image from its origins to Aḥmad Luṭfī al-Sayyid.**
Charles Wendell.   Berkeley, California: University of California Press, 1972. 313p. bibliog.
After a general description of the Islamic *umma* or political community, this book discusses the difficult and contradictory concepts of the Islamic world view which conceived of one joint *umma*, and the incipient nationalist concept of a separate Egyptian nation state. The struggle between these two ideas underlies a series of social, political and intellectual crises in the Near East from the 19th century onwards. Chapters 4 and 5 discuss the influence of the most prominent Egyptian writers and thinkers.

648 **The Middle East political dictionary.**
Laurence Ziring.   Santa Barbara, California; Oxford, England: ABC-CLIO Information Services, 1984. 416p. maps. bibliog.
This dictionary contains about thirty entries on Egypt under such headings as Arab Socialist Union (p. 181-4), British occupation (p. 356) and Camp David (p. 315-17).

Modern Egypt: studies in politics and society.
See item no. 10.

Memoirs from the women's prison.
See item no. 341.

Religious and political trends in modern Egypt.
See item no. 395.

A Fabian in Egypt: Salamah Musa and the rise of the professional classes in Egypt, 1909-1939.
See item no. 496.

Constitution, Legal System and Administration

649 Constitutions of African states.
Prepared by the Secretariat of the Asian–African Legal
Consultative Committee, New Delhi.   New York: Oceana
Publications, 1972. 2 vols. bibliog.

A summary of constitutional development in Egypt is included in volume 2,
commencing on p. 1691.

650 Bureaucracy and society in modern Egypt: a study of the higher civil service.
Morroe Berger.   New York: Russell & Russell, 1969. 231p.
Reprint ed. (Princeton Oriental Studies, Social Science, No. 1).

Originally published in 1957 by Princeton University Press, this book describes
the structure and functioning of Egypt's public bureaucracy and its historical
development from the time of Muhammad Ali to independence.

651 The Mixed Courts of Egypt.
Jasper Yeates Brinton.   New Haven, Connecticut; London: Yale
University Press, 1968. 2nd ed. 297p.

The Mixed Courts held the supreme judicial authority in Egypt for about a
quarter of a century until they were closed in 1949. Any litigation involving
foreigners came before them, and they were the dominating judicial institution in
the country. This book is a detailed description of their history and functioning.

652 **Business law in Egypt.**
Michael H. Davies, Deventer, The Netherlands: Kluwer Law
and Taxation Publishers, 1984. 387p.

An important reference source for any businessman who wants to do business in
Egypt, this book covers the laws and regulations governing the private sector and
foreign business activities in Egypt. Translations of certain laws and ministerial
decisions are contained both in the main body of the book and in appendices.

653 **Women in Muslim family law.**
John L. Esposito. Syracuse, New York: Syracuse University
Press, 1982. 155p. bibliog.

Surveys women and the family in pre-Islamic and Islamic Arabia, and reviews and
criticizes efforts at reform in Egypt and Pakistan.

654 **Executive regulations: law no. 43 of 1974 as amended.**
Cairo: The General Authority for Investment and Free Zones,
[n.d.]. 48p.

Text of the decree of the Minister of Economy and Economic Cooperation
no. 375 of 1977 regarding the executive regulations for the law concerning Arab
and foreign investment and free zones.

655 **Mahkama!: studies on the Egyptian legal system. Courts and
crimes; law and society.**
Enid Hill. London: Ithaca Press, 1979. 198p. maps. bibliog.

This book describes the operation of the country's legal system, using case studies
to illustrate its essentially Egyptian character.

656 **al-Sanhuri and Islamic law: the place and significance of Islamic law
in the life and work of 'Abd al-Razzaq Ahmad al-Sanhuri, Egyptian
jurist and scholar, 1895-1971.**
Enid Hill. Cairo: American University in Cairo Press, 1987.
140p. (Cairo Papers in Social Science, vol. 10, monograph 1).

A study of the life, work and significance of the jurist, al-Sanhuri, whose
achievement lay in the Islamization of Egyptian law. The revision of the Egyptian
Civil Code in 1948 was essentially his work.

657 **Law no. 43 of 1974 concerning the investment of Arab and foreign
funds and the Free Zones as amended by law no. 32 of
1977.**
Cairo: The General Authority for Investment and Free Zones,
[n.d.]. 31p.

The text of law no. 43 of 1974 regulating the activities of foreign capital in Egypt,
published together with the amendment of 1977.

658 **Apathy, values, incentives and development: the case of the
Egyptian bureaucracy.**
Ali Leila, el-Sayed Yassin, Monte Palmer. *Middle East Journal*,
vol. 39, no. 3 (Summer 1985), p. 341-62.
The objectives of this paper are as follows: to assess the magnitude of the apathy
problem in the Egyptian bureaucracy; to explore the various reasons for the
existence of the apathy problem to the extent that it does, indeed, exist; to
examine the incentive values of Egyptian bureaucrats; to place the incentive
values of Egyptian bureaucrats in comparative and theoretical perspective; and to
suggest possible alternative or supplementary incentives that might be used in
place of or in addition to monetary incentives as a means of increasing the
productivity of government employees.

659 **Dustur (Constitution). In: *Encyclopaedia of Islam.***
Edited by B. Lewis, C. Pellat, J. Schacht. Leiden, The
Netherlands: E. J. Brill, 1965, vol. II, p. 647-9. bibliog.
A very brief review of constitutional developments in Egypt from the Council of
Representatives in 1869 to the National Charter of 1962.

660 **The Egyptian bureaucracy: a sociological analysis.**
Ragai N. Makar. *Arab Journal of the Social Sciences*, vol. 2,
no. 1 (April 1987), p. 37-53.
A sociological analysis of the Egyptian public bureaucracy, with reference to its
origins, development and problems. The author's basic assumption is that the
socio-political and power structures of a society are the major sources for any
bureaucracy's identifying characteristics; he explains the basic differences between
the public bureaucracy of a democratic society and that of a non-democratic
society.

661 **Return to Islamic legislation in Egypt.**
M. Martin, R.M. Ma'ad. In: *Islamic law and change in Arab
society*. Beirut: Dar el-Mashreq Publishers, for the Centre for the
Study of the Modern Arab World, Saint Joseph University, 1976,
p. 47-81. (CEMAM Reports, vol. 4).
Describes the attempts of Egyptian Muslim fundamentalists since the 1940s to
impose Islamic *shari'a* as the only source of law for all Egyptians, among whom
15 per cent are Christians. An excellent chronological review of how these
fundamentalists have been pressing relentlessly to revise the law.

662 **Law and social change in contemporary Egypt.**
Edited by Cynthia Nelson, Klaus Friedrich Koch. Cairo:
American University Press, 1979. 177p. (Cairo Papers in Social
Science, vol. 2, monograph 4).
A wide variety of topics are covered in this volume: 'Law and social change: an
overview and assessment' by Ahmed Khalifa; 'An anthropological note on law
and development' by Klaus Koch; 'Lawyers and scientists in search of a role in

Constitution, Legal System and Administration

societal development' by Mark Kennedy; 'Law as an instrument of social change: the case of population policy' by Adel Azer; 'Changing the law on personal status within a liberal interpretation of the *sharia*' by Mohammed Nowaihi; 'Change and continuity in an Egyptian judicial institution: the *niyāba*' by Enid Hill; 'Law and the Egyptian cultural heritage: the pyramids plateau project' by Neamat Fouad; 'The pyramids plateau project' by Ahmed Gami.

663   **Islam in the new Egyptian constitution: some discussions in Al-Ahrām.**
Joseph P. O'Kane.   *Middle East Journal*, vol. 26, no. 2 (Spring 1972), p. 137-48.

An accurate, although brief, summary of discussions in the newspaper *Al-Ahram* in 1971 concerning the drawing up and enacting of the new Egyptian constitution and the inclusion of *shari'a* (Islamic law) as the principal source, the only source, or just one source of legislation. The discussions also covered the text to be adopted regarding the status of women.

664   **Constitutions of nations.**
Amos J. Peaslee, Dorothy Peaslee Xydis.   The Hague: Martinus Nijhoff, 1965-70. 3rd rev. ed. 4 vols.

The Egyptian constitution of 25 March 1964 is included in volume 1, p. 988-1008.

665   **Lawyers and politics in the Arab World, 1880-1960.**
Donald Reid.   Chicago, Illinois: Bibliotheca Islamica, 1981. 435p. bibliog.

An excellent study of the rise of lawyers as a professional class and of their role in Arab society, especially in Egypt. A detailed account of the Egyptian experience is presented.

666   **The law affecting foreigners in Egypt, as the result of the capitulations, with an account of their origin and development.**
James Henry Scott.   Edinburgh: William Green, 1907. 385p.

A considerable historical introduction discusses the history of the Ottoman capitulations, the Tanzimat reforms, and the Ottoman law of protection and nationality, the land laws of Turkey and Egypt, the Firmans and British occupation, the privileges of the capitulations, the privileges of jurisdiction and legislation before the institution of the Mixed Courts of Egypt, and changes since the reform of 1876.

667 **Lawyers, the rule of law and liberalism in modern Egypt.**
Farhat J. Ziadeh.   Stanford, California : Stanford University
Press, 1968. 165p. bibliog. (Hoover Institution on War, Revolution
and Peace).

By the nature of their profession, lawyers became public figures, addressing themselves to public issues, and they started by participating in nationalist action for Egypt's complete independence and the development of constitutional government. This book discusses the secularization of state and law, the growth of a modern legal system, the development of the legal profession, laywers' nationalist action, lawyers as a liberal force, and lawyers and legal reform.

Foreign Relations

General

668   **The foreign policy of Egypt in the post-Sadat era.**
Boutros Boutros-Ghali.   *Foreign Affairs*, vol. 60, no. 4 (Spring
1982), p. 769-88.

A delineation of Egyptian foreign policy by the Egyptian minister of state for foreign affairs, Boutros Boutros-Ghali, following the assassination of President Sadat in October 1981. He envisages that relations with Israel should be maintained as part of a continuous Egyptian effort for Palestinian rights and a comprehensive peace, and hopes that other Arab states will join in the peace process; non-alignment and African affairs will remain keystones of Egypt's foreign policy.

669   **Egypt and the United Nations: report of a study group set up by the Egyptian Society of International Law.**
New York: Manhattan Publishing Company, 1957. 197p.

A report prepared for the Carnegie Endowment for International Peace. The first part is devoted to Egypt's preparation for participation in the United Nations and covers the Egyptian delegation's activities at the San Francisco Conference and the state of Egyptian public opinion at the time of the ratification of the Charter. The second part is an analysis of Egypt's position within the United Nations during the first eight years of its existence.

670   **Turkish-Egyptian relations 1952-1957.**
Baruch Gilead.   *Middle Eastern Affairs*, vol. 10 (Nov. 1959),
p. 356-66.

Explores the rivalry between Egypt and Turkey for the position of political leadership in the Middle East.

671 **The Islamic Pact, an obvious trick.**
Cairo: under the auspices of the Supreme Council for Islamic
Affairs, 1966. 170p.
Contains speeches and statements by Nasser and Egyptian religious leaders
against an alliance of Islamic states led by Saudi Arabia and Iran.

672 **The U.A.R. in Africa: Egypt's policy under Nasser.**
Tareq Y. Ismael. Evanston, Illinois: Northwestern University
Press, 1971. 258p. maps.
Egypt's policy towards Africa has evolved out of continuous reassessment of
Egypt's interests on the continent, and this is here examined with particular
reference to two case studies which detail Egypt's relations with the Sudan and
the Congo, principally during the period 1952-1969.

673 **Arab-Chinese relations, 1950-71.**
Mon'im Nasser-Eddine. Beirut: Arab Institute for Research and
Publishing, [n.d.]. 322p. bibliog.
Despite its title, this book studies only the case of Egyptian-Chinese relations.
The author traces these from their origins and concentrates on relations between
the two nations in the 1950s and 1960s. He aims to clarify and detail the scope of
Egyptian-Chinese relations in order that any ambiguities about Chinese
communist influence may be more clearly defined.

674 **The international status of the Suez Canal.**
Joseph A. Obieta. The Hague: Martinus Nijhoff, 1970. 2nd ed.
154p. bibliog.
A legal discussion of the question of whether the world has free right to use the
Suez Canal in time of peace. The author argues that the concession of 1856, seen
in its diplomatic context, imposes on Egypt a duty to afford free passage to the
merchant ships of all nations in time of peace.

675 **The Middle East and the Western Alliance.**
Edited by Steven L. Spiegel. London; Boston, Massachusetts:
Allen & Unwin, 1982. 256p.
This book provides a comprehensive analysis of problems jointly affecting the
interests of the Western Alliance (the North Americans, the Europeans and the
Japanese), the states of the Middle East and the Soviet Union. The author
discusses such central issues as the Arab-Israeli conflict, the dynamics of the
energy crisis and the effect of growing Middle Eastern instability on the interests
of individual allies.

676   **Egypt's regional policy from Muhammad Ali to Muhammad Anwar al-Sadat.**
       Gabriel R. Warburg.   In: *The contemporary Mediterranean world.* Edited by Carl F. Pinkele and Adamantia Pollis.   New York: Praeger, 1983, p. 124-50.

Outlines Egypt's regional policy in the 19th and 20th centuries with reference to the Sudan, the Red Sea, North Africa and the Middle East.

Arab countries

677   **The Saudi-Egyptian conflict over North Yemen, 1962-1970.**
       Saeed M. Badeeb.   Boulder, Colorado: Westview Press; Washington, DC: American Arab Affairs Council, 1986. 148p. bibliog.

A study of the Yemeni coup d'état of 1962 and the subsequent war between the Republican and Monarchist forces. That war created what the author describes as 'the inevitable partnership' between Saudi Arabia and the Yemen Arab Republic.

678   **The Arabs and the world: Nasser's Arab nationalist policy.**
       Charles D. Cremeans.   New York; London: Praeger for the Council on Foreign Relations. 1963. 324p. map. bibliog.

A detailed study of the early years of Nasser's rule, charting the course of his relations with the other Arab states, the troubled union with Syria, his early dealings and confrontations with Israel, and his Afro–Asian policies.

679   **Intervention in the Yemen: an analysis of Egyptian perceptions and policies.**
       A.I. Dawisha.   *Middle East Journal,* vol. 29, no. 1 (Winter 1975), p. 47-63.

Discusses Egypt's position in the Arab world, how the decision to intervene in Yemen in 1962 was made, and the war in Yemen and its aftermath.

680   **Egypt in the Arab world: the elements of foreign policy.**
       A.I. Dawisha.   London: Macmillan; New York: Wiley, 1976. 234p. bibliog.

A two-part account of Egypt's foreign policy with respect to the states of the Arab Middle East. The first part describes, through the utilization of historical analysis, the development of Egypt's relations with the other Arab states during the period 1952-1970. The second part, which forms the major portion of the book, explores the setting, the actors, the attitudes and the processes involved in Egypt's foreign policy.

681 **Egyptian–Syrian defense pact.**
Middle Eastern Affairs, vol. 6, no. 11 (Nov. 1955), p. 347-8.
Reproduces the thirteen-article Egyptian–Syrian defence pact which bound each
to use its armed forces in support of the other. The pact also provided for the
establishment of a supreme council, war council and joint command, and is
regarded as an important stage leading to the creation of the United Arab
Republic.

682 **The break-up of the United Arab Republic, its effect on inter-Arab
relations, 1961-2.**
Richard Gott. In: *Survey of international affairs, 1962*. Edited by
D. C. Watt.   London; New York: Oxford University Press, 1970,
p. 465-81.
A detailed outline of the causes and consequences of the break-up of the United
Arab Republic in September 1961. The main causes are seen to lie in Nasser's
progressive alienation of all the main currents of Syrian political life, leading to
Syria's secession.

683 **The struggle for the Arab world: Egypt's Nasser and the Arab
League.**
Tawfig Y. Hasou.   London: Kegan Paul, 1985. 228p. bibliog.
In the first two chapters of this book, the author examines the historic
background of the Arab League and considers to what extent Egypt's role was
dominant in its creation. He devotes chapter 3 to a discussion of Egyptian foreign
policy goals under President Nasser, while chapters 4-7 explain how these goals
were advanced. Finally, the author explains how the Arab League was effectively
used by Nasser to promote his goals.

684 **The Arab cold war: Gamal 'Abd al-Nasir and his rivals, 1958-1970.**
Malcolm H. Kerr.   London: Oxford University Press for the
Royal Institute of International Affairs, 1971. 3rd ed. 156p.
bibliog.
Describes Egypt's relations with the other Arab states in Nasser's time in the light
of the confrontation of divergent political interests and ideological outlooks in the
Arab world.

685 **Documents on international affairs, 1958.**
Edited by Gillian King.   London: Oxford University Press, 1962.
605p.
Includes two important documents: the proclamation of the United Arab
Republic on 1 February 1958 and the Constitution of the United Arab States
(United Arab Republic and Yemen).

686 **The economic embargo of Egypt by Arab states: myth and reality.**
Victor Lavy. *Middle East Journal*, vol. 38, no. 3 (1984), p. 419-
32.

This article examines the impact of the post-Camp David Arab embargo on the
Egyptian economy; the analysis uses data obtained from government publications
and Arab newspapers, and focuses on four aspects: Arab aid, tourism, trade in
goods and services, and migration of labour.

687 **A Middle East power, Egypt, mainspring of Arab power.**
Joseph J. Malone, J.E. Peterson. In: *Emerging powers, defense
and security in the third world.* Edited by Rodney W. Jones, Steven
A. Hildreth. New York: Praeger, in cooperation with the Center
for Strategic and International Studies, Georgetown University,
1986, p. 223-66.

The authors consider Egypt the primary regional power on the basis of its Islamic,
cultural and intellectual leadership in the Arab world. The developments in
Egypt's role as such are ably interpreted.

688 **The United Arab Repubic: assessment of its failure.**
Monte Palmer. *Middle East Journal*, vol. 20, no. 1 (Winter 1966),
p. 50-67.

An account of the collapse of Syria's union with Egypt which argues that the
causes of the secession were much more deep-seated than the fact that the
military coup precipitated it, and discusses the focuses of Syrian discontent.

689 **The Egyptian policy in the Arab world. Intervention in Yemen,
1962-1967: case study.**
Ali Abdel Rahman Rahmy. Washington, DC: University Press of
America, 1983. 391p. 5 maps. bibliog.

A detailed study of Egypt's position in the Arab world, its interests and policy in
Yemen, the origins of the Yemeni revolution, and the Egyptian intervention in
Yemen and its ramifications.

690 **The break-up of the United Arab Republic.**
Patrick Seale. *World Today*, vol. 17, no. 11 (Nov. 1961), p. 471-9.

Describes the army coup in Damascus of September 1961 and Syria's secession
from the UAR. The wider causes of the union's failure are explored and Nasser's
reactions to the secession are also discussed.

691 **Syrian break from the United Arab Republic.**
Middle Eastern Affairs, vol. 12, no. 9 (Nov. 1961), p. 269-78.

Reprints statements made by President Nasser and Premier Mamun al-Kuzbari in
September 1961 following Syrian secession from the UAR.

Egypt, Islam and the Arabs: the search for Egyptian nationhood, 1900-1930.
See item no. 271.

Nasser of the Arabs: an Arab assessment.
See item no. 298.

Israel and Palestine

692 **The cold peace.**
Joel Beinin. *MERIP Reports: Middle East Research and Information Project*, vol. 14, no. 1, issue no. 129 (January 1985), p. 3-10.
Describes Egyptian-Israeli relations between 1982 and 1985 and the effects of the Israeli invasion of Lebanon in June 1982 on the normalization of relations between the two countries.

693 **The promise of peace: economic cooperation between Egypt and Israel, a staff paper.**
Henry J. Bruton.   Washington, DC: Brookings Institution, 1981. 29p.
The author argues that direct cooperation between the two countries is needed more than aid programmes, and he believes it is important to try to establish strong informal links between small-scale industrial and agricultural enterpreneurs and between workers in the two countries.

694 **The six day war.**
Randolph S. Churchill, Winston S. Churchill.   London: Heinemann, 1967. 243p. maps.
A good, straightforward account of the course of the war, with a brief sketch of the historical background, and a summing-up of the situation as it appeared at the end of hostilities. Appendix 1 discusses the BBC coverage of the war, and appendix 2, Israel's political parties.

695 **Egypt and Palestine: a millennium of association (868-1948).**
Edited by Amnon Cohen, Gabriel Baer.   New York: St. Martin's Press, 1984. 390p.
This collection of twenty-two studies on Egypt and Palestine is divided into three main sections: the pre-Ottoman period, the Ottoman period, and the 20th century. An outline of the historical setting and of some of the major trends and developments is presented in an introductory paper by David Ayalon.

696 **Elusive victory: the Arab–Israeli wars, 1947-1974.**
Trevor N. Dupuy. London: Macdonald & Jane's, 1978. 633p.
maps. bibliog.
A military history of the wars between Israel and the Arab states, in each of which Egypt played a major part. This account attempts to reconcile the conflicting versions of earlier books and official statements. A lucid and dispassionate account.

697 **The Egyptian-Israeli peace treaty.**
Middle East Journal, vol. 33, no. 3 (Summer 1979), p. 327-47. 3 maps.
Presents the text of the Egyptian-Israeli peace treaty as issued by the White House, Monday, 26 March 1979, under the title 'Treaty of peace between the Arab Republic of Egypt and the State of Israel'. The treaty consists of a preamble and nine articles, followed by Annex I, 'Protocol concerning Israeli withdrawal and security arrangements', Appendix to Annex I entitled 'Organization of movements in the Sinai', and Annex III, 'Protocol concerning relations of the parties'.

698 **The Egyptian–Israeli treaty: text and selected documents.**
Beirut: Institute for Palestine Studies, 1979. 124p. (Basic Documentary Series, no. 13).
Presents the text of the treaty with three annexes, six letters of agreement accompanying the treaty, and supplementary documents to the treaty. A series of documents and statements follow illustrating the Palestinian response, the Arab response and a selection of responses from the rest of the world.

699 **Negotiating for peace in the Middle East.**
Ismail Fahmy. London: Croom Helm; Baltimore, Maryland: Johns Hopkins University Press, 1983. 321p.
The memoirs of the man who was Egypt's minister of foreign affairs during Sadat's attempts to achieve peace with Israel. He resigned in protest at Sadat's visit to Jerusalem, before the signing of the Camp David agreement.

700 **Middle East mission: the story of a major bid for peace in the time of Nasser and Ben-Gurion.**
Elmore Jackson. New York; London: W.W. Norton, 1983. 115p.
The author of this book claims that Nasser made a major effort to achieve a political settlement with Israel, and presents full details of the story.

701 **Egyptian responses to the Palestine problem in the interwar period.**
James Jankowski. *International Journal of Middle East Studies*, vol. 12, no. 1 (August 1980), p. 1-38.
What were the original 'sentiments' upon which early concern with events in Palestine were based? Who took the lead in organizing the demonstrations over Palestine which began to occur when Nasser was a student? What were the ideas

of Egyptian national interest or strategic involvement which came to overlay 'sentiment' as time passed? These are among the questions which the author addresses in his examination of Egyptian responses to the Palestine problem. Within the two decades covered by the study he concentrates most intensively on the years 1929 and 1930, when events in Palestine provided a focus for the expression of Egyptian opinion on the issue.

702 **Beyond Camp David: emerging alignments and leaders in the Middle East.**
Paul A. Jereidini, R.D. McLaurin.   Syracuse, New York: Syracuse University Press, 1981. 197p. maps. bibliog.

This book examines some of the deeper changes that have taken place since the Camp David Agreements were signed. The authors consider the political and economic forces at work, new patterns of power alignments that have developed, emerging regional leaders and political/social interrelationships. Included are the texts of the Camp David Agreements, the Egyptian-Israeli Peace Treaty, and correspondence on these documents between Carter, Begin and Sadat.

703 **The Camp David Accords: a testimony.**
Mohamed Ibrahim Kamel.   London: Kegan Paul, 1986. 414p. bibliog.

The author was foreign minister of Egypt during the negotiations between Egypt, Israel, and the United States which ended with the signing of the Camp David Agreements – to which 'he was totally opposed'. For an account from the Israeli side, see Moshe Dayan, *Breakthrough: a personal account of the Egypt–Israel peace negotiations*, published in 1981 (London: Weidenfeld & Nicolson), and from the American side see William B. Quandt, *Camp David: peacemaking and politics*, published in 1986 (Washington, DC: Brookings Institution).

704 **The road to war 1967: the origins of the Arab–Israel conflict.**
Walter Laqueur.   London: Weidenfeld & Nicolson, 1968. 352p. map. bibliog.

Traces the history of Israel's confrontation with the Arab states from 1948, concentrating on the build-up to war from 1966. Eleven appendices contain important documents and speeches relating to the outbreak of war.

705 **Egypt and the Palestine question, 1936-1945.**
Thomas Mayer.   Berlin, GFR: Klaus Schwarz Verlag, 1983. 391p. bibliog. (Islamkundliche Untersuchungen, 77).

The creation of the Arab League in 1945 was a confirmation of the Egyptian government's Pan-Arabism and its support for the Palestinian cause. This work is a well-documented and careful description and analysis of the political and diplomatic process which led to the adoption of this policy during that period.

Foreign Relations. Israel and Palestine

706 **Egypt and the Palestinian cause: benefit and burden.**
Aaron David Miller. In: *The Arab States and the Palestine question: between ideology and self-interest.* New York: Praeger Scientific, with the Center for Strategic and International Studies, Georgetown University, Washington, DC, 1986, p. 53-67. (The Washington Papers, No. 120).

A study of the role of Egypt in the Palestine question. For geopolitical and historical reasons Egypt has been more flexible and detached with regard to the Palestinian problem than either Jordan or Syria could afford to be.

707 **Camp David and after: foreign policy in an interdependent environment.**
Salua Nour, Carl F. Pinkele. In: *The Contemporary Mediterranean World.* Edited by Carl F. Pinkele and Adamantia Pollis. New York: Praeger, 1983, p. 257-75.

An evaluative review of the Camp David Agreements with reference to how they were achieved, the personalities involved, and the results which followed.

708 **The third Arab–Israeli war.**
Edgar O'Ballance. London: Faber & Faber, 1972. 279p. map.

A straightforward, factual military account of the course of the 1967 war.

709 **The struggle for peace in the Middle East.**
Mahmoud Riad. London: Quartet Books, 1981. 365p. map.

The author was Egypt's foreign minister from 1964 to 1971 and secretary-general of the Arab League from 1972 to 1979. He here describes the peace efforts relating to the Arab-Israeli conflict on the basis of his own experience as an Egyptian official.

710 **Egypt and Israel.**
Howard M. Sachar. New York: Richard Marek Publishers, 1981. 384p. 14 maps. bibliog.

An account of the history and development of relations between Egypt and Israel from 1936 to the conclusion of the peace treaty at Camp David, 26 March 1979. The text of that treaty is included in the appendix.

711 **Self-views in historical perspective in Egypt and Israel: proceedings of an Israeli-Egyptian colloquium held at the Tel-Aviv University, April 15, 1980.**
Edited by Shimon Shamir. Tel Aviv, Israel: Tel Aviv University, 1981. 132p.

This colloquium took place one year after the signing of the peace treaty between the two countries, and can be seen as a landmark in the process of normalization, for it was the first intellectual dialogue between members of the two societies. Five papers deal with Egyptian 'self-views' and three with 'reflections on parallels' between Jews and Muslims and Israelis and Egyptians.

168

712 **Israel and the Arabs: the October 1973 war.**
Edited by Lester A. Sobel. New York: Facts on File, 1974. 185p.

This book is a record of the war of October 1973, of the events that led to it, of the negotiations that produced the ceasefire, of the aftermath of the war, and of the various developments in Israel, in the Arab countries and in other parts of the world related to the conflict. The material consists largely of the printed records compiled by Facts on File for its weekly reports on world events.

713 **Camp David: a new Balfour Declaration.**
Edited by Faith Zeadey. Detroit, Michigan: Association of Arab-American University Graduates, 1979. 90p. (Special Report No. 3).

A collection of eight papers about the Camp David peace agreement between Egypt and Israel. The papers all express views critical of that agreement.

The October War: documents, personalities, analyses and maps.
See item no. 299.

The Israeli–Egyptian war of attrition 1969-1970.
See item no. 303.

The making of a war: the Middle East from 1967 to 1973.
See item no. 304.

Sadat and his statecraft.
See item no. 307.

Sadat and Begin: the domestic politics of peacemaking.
See item no. 308.

The road to Ramadan.
See item no. 313.

The war of atonement.
See item no. 315.

The Yom Kippur War.
See item no. 319.

Egypt and the West: salient facts behind the Suez crisis.
See item no. 327.

The electronic war in the Middle East 1968-70.
See item no. 337.

Return to Sinai: the Arab–Israeli war, 1973.
See item no. 338.

The crossing of the Suez.
See item no. 347.

The multinational force and observers in the Sinai: organization, structure and function.
See item no. 351.

The economic impact of the Six-Day War: Israel, the occupied territories, Egypt, Jordan.
See item no. 769.

The institutionalization of Palestinian identity in Egypt.
See item no. 430.

Crisis: the inside story of the Suez conspiracy.
See item no. 729.

The Sudan

714 **The Egyptian Soudan: its loss and recovery.**
Henry S.L. Alford, W. Dennistoun Sword.   New York: Negro
Universities Press, 1969. Reprint ed. 336p. bibliog.

Originally published in 1898 (London: Macmillan). Describes the events in the Egyptian Sudan which led up to the rise and subsequent downfall of the Dervishes (Mahdists). The authors include a rapid sketch of the history of the Sudan, an account of the Dongola expedition of 1896, and full details of the Nile expedition of 1897-98. Includes service records of the officers involved, and portraits.

715 **Sudanese-Egyptian relations: a chronological and analytical study.**
Abd el-Fattah Ibrahim el-Sayed Baddour.   The Hague: Martinus
Nijhoff, 1960. 250p. bibliog.

An excellent, well-documented historical review of relations between Egypt and the Sudan from the time of the pharaohs to the coup d'état of 17 November 1958. It consists of four major parts. Part I covers relations before the modern period, and includes a study of Arab treaties; part II deals with the unification of the Nile Valley in the 19th century and the origin of the Anglo-Egyptian agreements of 1899 in regard to the Sudan; part III examines the agreements of 1899 in the light of international law; and part IV considers relations as influenced by the Egyptian revolution and Sudanese independence.

716 **Egypt and the Sudan.**
Robert O. Collins, Robert L. Tignor. Englewood Cliffs, New
Jersey: Prentice Hall, 1967. 180p. map. bibliog. (The Modern
Nations in Historical Perspective).
A study of the two major countries of the Nile Valley, describing the land and the
people, the beginnings of modernization, the Nile Valley, and Nasser's Egypt and
independent Sudan.

717 **The Sudan in Anglo-Egyptian relations: a case study in power
politics, 1800-1956.**
L.A. Fabunmi. Westport, Connecticut: Greenwood Press, 1973.
Reprint ed. 466p. maps. bibliog.
A well-documented study by a Nigerian scholar, first published in 1960 (London:
Longman). Part I examines the historical background and foundations of the
Anglo-Egyptian dispute; part II covers the factors causing Anglo-Egyptian
tension; part III describes the Second World War and post-war developments in
the dispute; part IV considers the final stages of the dispute and the reemergence
of the Sudanese, 1948-56; part V contains the summary and conclusions. The
author believes that his study of the Sudan aids an understanding of similar
problems in other parts of the world.

718 **Suakin and Massawa under Egyptian rule, 1865-1885.**
Ghada H. Talhami. Washington, DC: University Press of
America, 1979. 309p. bibliog.
A study of Egyptian influence in the eastern province of the Sudan (Red Sea
region) from 1865 to 1885, its administration there, and its struggles with the
Ethiopians and, later, the British.

719 **Trade between Egypt and Bilad As-Sudan, 1700-1820.**
Terence Walz. Cairo: Institut Français d'Archéologie Orientale,
1978. 297p. 4 maps. bibliog. (Textes Arabes et Etudes Islamiques,
Vol. VIII).
The facts of geography firmly point to Egypt's place in the African continent, yet
her relationships with African states to her south have always been obscure. This
study examines one aspect of Egypt's contact with Black Africa, long distance
trade.

720 **Egypt and the Sudan: studies in history and politics.**
Gabriel R. Warburg. London: Frank Cass, 1985. 253p. map.
bibliog.
A well-documented work which examines certain aspects of the history of Egypt
and the Sudan from 1882 to the present day. Until Israel appeared as a political
threat, Egypt's overriding foreign policy concerns were British rule and control of
the Sudan.

171

Great Britain

721 **Great Britain and Egypt, 1914-1951.**
London: Royal Institute of International Affairs, 1952. 210p. map.
bibliog. (Information Papers, No. 19).

This book presents an account of the political and economic evolution of Anglo-Egyptian relations from the outbreak of the First World War to the Egyptian abrogation of the alliance in October 1951. It presents the British point of view because it is based largely on British official documents and the British press and only to a lesser extent on Egyptian sources.

722 **The Suez War.**
Paul Johnson, foreword by Aneurin Bevan.   London: Macgibbon
& Kee, 1957. 145p.

A critical view of the Anglo-French-Israeli attack on Egypt in 1956.

723 **The Suez contractors.**
Sir Norman Kipping, with an introduction by Field Marshal Sir
Richard Hull.   Havant, England: Kenneth Mason Publications,
1969. 80p.

In the years 1954 to 1956, a plan was conceived and executed for the British forces based in the Suez Canal zone to be progressively and completely withdrawn, while the continued maintenance and partial operation of the base was to be carried on by a civilian organization. This is an account of these little-known events.

724 **The Suez Canal settlement: a selection of documents relating to the
settlement of the Suez Canal dispute, the clearance of the Suez
Canal and the settlement of disputes between the United Kingdom,
France and the United Arab Republic, October 1956-March 1959.**
Edited by E. Lauterpacht.   London: Stevens & Sons; New York:
Praeger, 1960. 80p. bibliog.

A collection of texts of documents published under the auspices of the British Institute of International and Comparative Law.

725 **The British in Egypt.**
Peter Mansfield.   London: Weidenfeld & Nicolson; New York:
Holt, Rinehart and Winston, 1971. 351p. bibliog.

A good and straightforward account of the British occupation of Egypt from 1882 to 1954, which the author believes 'is in many ways neither a happy one nor one of which Englishmen can be especially proud'.

726 **Anglo-Egyptian relations (1800-1956).**
John Marlowe. London: Frank Cass, 1965. 2nd ed. 432p. bibliog.
Covers the history of relations between Egypt and Great Britain from the French Campaign of 1798 to the Suez War of 1956. The author discusses relations between Britain and Muhammad Ali, the international control of the Suez Canal, the Egyptian-British rule of the Sudan and the roles of Cromer, Gorst and Kitchener. He makes an assessment of the British occupation (chapter 10) and the 1936 treaty between Britain and Egypt, relations between Egypt and the Arab League, the strategic importance of Egypt, the 1952 revolution and the Suez War.

727 **Warriors at Suez.**
Donald Neff. New York: Simon & Schuster, 1981. 479p. bibliog.
A well-documented history of the Suez War of 1956. The author, an American journalist with vast experience in the reporting of world events, believes that the Suez crisis marked the end of Britain and France as world powers.

728 **No end of a lesson: the story of Suez.**
Anthony Nutting. London: Constable; New York: Clarkson N. Potter, 1967. 205p.
An account of the Suez War of 1956 by a well-informed politician who was a member of the British government and who resigned his posts in protest at the policies adopted by Britain in the dispute. For a view from the Egyptian side, see Mohamed Heikal, *Cutting the lion's tail: Suez through Egyptian eyes*, published in 1987 (London: André Deutsch; New York: Arbor House).

729 **Crisis: the inside story of the Suez conspiracy.**
Terence Robertson. London: Hutchinson, 1965. 339p. bibliog.
A history of the diplomatic intrigue and conspiracy that led to the invasion of 1956, and the events which followed upon it.

Suez: the double war.
See item no. 309.

The real Suez crisis: the end of a great nineteenth century work.
See item no. 310.

Egypt and the West: salient facts behind the Suez crisis.
See item no. 327.

Suez: the twice-fought war.
See item no. 328.

Middle East in crisis: a historical and documentary review.
See item no. 330.

Suez: ten years after – broadcasts from the BBC Third Programme.
See item no. 331.

International crises and the role of law: Suez 1956.
See item no. 340.

The Suez crisis and the containment policy.
See item no. 742.

United States of America

730 **From sideshow to center stage: U.S. policy toward Egypt, 1946-1956.**
Geoffrey Aronson. Boulder, Colorado: Lynne Rienner, 1986. 208p. bibliog.

This well-documented study traces and analyses the development of US policy during the decade following the Second World War. The author attempts to explain the failure of US policy to achieve the goals which it set itself during the period.

731 **The American effort in Egypt: a chapter in diplomatic history in the nineteenth century.**
Jasper Yeates Brinton. Alexandria, Egypt: Imprimerie du Commerce, 1972. 147p.

This history of the early American consuls in Egypt is written by an American judge and diplomat who served in Egypt for fifty years.

732 **Egypt and the United States: collaborators in economic development.**
Donald S. Brown. *Middle East Journal*, vol. 35, no. 1 (Winter 1981), p. 3-14.

The United States is deeply involved in Egypt's economy and is supportive of the key emphases in the process in which Egypt is engaged. The most important aspect of the American role has been its official economic assistance programmes, but trade and investment relationships have also had an important part. Private participation – academic and business exchanges – plays an increasingly important role in Egyptian perceptions of how their economy can develop, but, the author argues, Egypt must resolve many critical issues if the open door economic policy is to bear fruit.

733 **Economic aid and American policy toward Egypt, 1955-1981.**
William J. Burns, with a foreword by Ambassador Hermann
Frederick Eilts. Albany, New York: State University of New
York Press, 1985. 285p. bibliog.

This study shows how the American government attempted to use its economic
aid programme to induce or coerce Egypt to support US interests in the Middle
East in the quarter of a century following the 1955 Czech-Egyptian arms
agreement. The author has analysed recently released government documents and
interviews with former policymakers to throw light on the use of aid as a tool of
American policy towards the Nasser regime. He also offers valuable observations
on the role of the American economic assistance programme in the Sadat era.
The book provides some useful lessons on the objectives, applications, and effects
of aid policy.

734 **Americans in the Egyptian army.**
Pierre Crabitès.   London: George Routledge, 1938. 277p. maps.

This book presents the achievements of some of the high-ranking American
officers hired by Egypt in the 1870s. They included Brigadier-General Charles P.
Stone, Major-General Thaddeus P. Mott, Major Erastus Purdy, Colonel R.E.
Colston and Colonel Chaille-Long among others.

735 **Moslem Egypt and Christian Abyssinia; or military service under
the Khedive, in his provinces and beyond their borders, as
experienced by the American staff.**
William M. Dye.   New York: Negro Universities Press, 1969.
Reprint ed. 500p.

Originally published in 1880 (New York: Atkin & Prout), this book gives an
account of the American officers hired by the Khedive of Egypt to serve in the
Egyptian army. It also portrays something of the character and life of the peoples
with whom they came into contact, from Zanzibar in East Africa to Alexandria in
Egypt. A list of the names and ranks of the officers involved is included.

736 **The blue and the gray on the Nile.**
William B. Hassetine, Hazel C. Wolf.   Chicago, Illinois:
University of Chicago Press; Toronto: University of Toronto Press,
1961. 290p. bibliog.

An account of the American officers who were hired by Khedive Ismail and his
successors in the 1870s to serve in the Egyptian army. Most of these officers were
graduates of West Point and Annapolis who had superior training and experience,
and there were in all some fifty of them.

737 **Egypt and the United States: the formative years.**
Gail F. Meyer.   Teaneck, New Jersey: Fairleigh Dickinson
University Press, 1980. 230p. bibliog.

A history of the fluctuations in relations between Egypt and the United States
between 1952 and 1958.

738 **Egypt and the politics of U.S. economic aid.**
Marvin G. Weinbaum. Boulder, Colorado; London: Westview Press, 1986. 192p. bibliog.

In this study of the origins and consequences of the aid programme, the author describes its scope and identifies the constraints that delayed the limited programme implementation. The author claims that far-reaching reforms could only be attained through major changes in Egypt's political structure.

USSR

739 **The Soviets and the Arabs: 1917-1955.**
Faiz S. Abu-Jaber. *Middle East Forum*, vol. 45, no. 1 (1969), p. 13-44.

The topics discussed in this paper include the pro-Arab Soviet stance, Soviet-Egyptian opposition to the Middle East Defense Organization, Soviet-Egyptian trade, positive neutralism, and Afro-Asian conferences.

740 **The Soviet attitude toward Arab revolutions: Yemen, Egypt, Algeria, Iraq and Palestine.**
Faiz S. Abu-Jaber. *Middle East Forum*, vol. 46, no. 4 (1970), p. 41-65.

The author analyses in this paper the Soviet way of dealing with the different revolutions in the Arab countries.

741 **Soviet foreign policy towards Egypt.**
Karen Dawisha. London: Macmillan, 1979. 271p. bibliog.

An excellent study of the developments and fluctuations in Soviet-Egyptian relations from 1955 to 1978.

742 **The Suez crisis and the containment policy.**
M.A. Fitzsimons. *Review of Politics*, vol. 19 (October 1957), p. 419-45.

Analyses the Eisenhower doctrine and its ramifications for Soviet policy in the Middle East after the 1956 Suez War.

743 **Sphinx and commissar: the rise and fall of Soviet influence in the Arab world.**
Mohamed Heikal.   London: Collins, 1978. 303p.
This is an analysis of the USSR's fluctuating political relationships with several Arab countries, but essentially it tells the story of Nasser's dealings with the Soviet Union. A vivid account by Nasser's closest confidant and friend who was present at many of the events described.

744 **Soviet–Egyptian relations, 1945-1985.**
Mohrez Mahmoud el Hussini.   London: Macmillan Press, 1987. 260p. bibliog.
A study of the evolution and fluctuating fortunes of the relations between the Soviet Union and Egypt before the revolution of 1952, and during the regimes of Nasser, Sadat, and Mubarak, from the viewpoint of the Egyptian navy.

745 **Soviet advances in the Middle East.**
George Lenczowski.   Washington, DC: American Enterprise Institute for Public Policy Research, 1972. 176p.
This book includes a chapter (p. 77-102) on Soviet-Egyptian relations between 1959 and 1972.

746 **New dimensions of big-power rivalry in the Middle East.**
George Lenczowski. In: *The contemporary Mediterranean world.* Edited by Carl F. Pinkele and Adamantia Pollis.   New York: Praeger, 1983, p. 32-49.
In this review of the relationship between the United States, the Soviet Union and the Middle Eastern countries, the author makes many references to Egypt.

747 **Red star on the Nile: the Soviet-Egyptian influence relationship since the June War.**
Alvin Z. Rubenstein.   Princeton, New Jersey: Princeton University Press, 1977. 383p. bibliog.
The main purpose of this study is to contribute an understanding of the Soviet-Egyptian relationship in terms of who influenced whom to do what, when, how, and why, in the period from the June War of 1967 to the time of writing.

748 **U.S. and U.S.S.R. aid to developing countries: a comparative study of India, Turkey and U.A.R.**
Leo Tansky.   New York: Praeger, 1967. 192p. (Special Studies in International Economics and Development).
A comparison of the purpose, content and achievements of American and Soviet economic aid to India, Turkey and Egypt.

Economy and Economic Development

749 **Egypt's absorptive capacity during 1960-1972.**
Nazem Abdalla. *International Journal of Middle East Studies*,
vol. 16, no. 2 (May 1984), p. 177-98.

This paper identifies and examines the factors contributing to Egypt's low absorptive capacity. They are categorized as: availability of efficient personnel; infrastructure; institutional, political, and cultural factors; availability of sound projects; saving, consumption, and government policy; exports and imports; foreign exchange rate; and time period in which capital is to be employed.

750 **The political economy of Nasserism: a study in employment and income distribution policies in urban Egypt, 1952-1972.**
Mahmoud Abdel-Fadil. Cambridge, England: Cambridge
University Press, 1980. 140p. bibliog. (DAE Occasional Papers,
No. 52).

An in-depth analysis of the substantial policy-motivated shifts in the fields of employment, income distribution and social composition in the 1950s and 1960s. The author conducts his analysis within a broad context in an attempt to contribute to an understanding of the basic contours of the political economy of Nasserism.

751 **Planning and development in Egypt.**
Soliman Abdel Hai, and others. *Third World Planning Review*,
vol. 3, no. 2 (May 1981), p. 1-249.

This whole issue of *Third World Planning Review* is devoted to a discussion of planning and development in Egypt. It contains seven articles: 'The Third World view: planning consultancy in the developing world', by S. Abdel Hai; 'Housing in the Suez Canal towns; an introduction'; and 'Port Said: planning for reconstructon and development' by M. Welbank and A. Edwards; 'Ismailia: from

178

master plan to implementation' by F. Davison; 'The development of the city of Suez' by R. Stewart; 'Taming the growth of Cairo: towards a deconcentration of the metropolitan region of Cairo' by B. Jenssen, K. Kunzmann and S. Saad-el Din; 'Planning new development regions in Egypt; settlement planning related to economic development' by A. Beshara.

752 The political economy of income distribution in Egypt.
Edited by Gouda Abdel-Khalek, Robert Tignor. New York; London: Holmes & Meier, 1982. 525p. (Political Economy of Income Distribution in Developing Countries, No. 3).

This volume is concerned with the question of income distribution and equity-related issues in the period 1952-1977. Written by specialists from Egyptian and American universities, it contains fourteen papers.

753 Absorptive capacity of the Egyptian economy: an examination of problems and prospects.
Yusuf J. Ahmad. Paris: Development Centre of the Organisation for Economic Co-operation and Development, 1976. 182p. bibliog.

One of the main aims of this study was to provide a perspective in which the flow of financial resources to the Egyptian economy could be examined. It was in that sense an exercise in the determination of the indirect absorptive capacity generated by surplus oil revenues during 1974 and the first quarter of 1975.

754 Egypt's economic potential.
Roberto Alboni, Ali Hillal Dessouki, Saad Eddin Ibrahim, Giacomo Luciano, Piercarlo Padoan. London: Croom Helm, 1984. 225p. bibliog.

Discusses Egypt's economic and financial structure in detail, with a section on Egypt's social equilibrium and political and international status.

755 The effects of the Egyptian food ration and subsidy system on income distribution and consumption.
Harold Alderman, Joachim von Braun. Washington, DC: International Food Policy Research Institute, 1984. 125p. bibliog. (Research Report, 45).

A comprehensive analysis of the effects of the subsidy system on the distribution of food, how well it succeeds in helping the poorest families to improve their diet, and to what extent the system favours the rich more than it favours the poor. This report also discusses the regressive effects of the system and its burden on the government.

756 **Food supply and economic development (with special reference to Egypt).**
Galal A. Amin. London: Cass, 1966. 125p. bibliog.
A study of the role played by food supply in development and, in particular, an examination of the food problem in Egypt – production, consumption, distribution, etc.

757 **Middle East economies in the 1970s: a comparative approach.**
Hossein Askari, John Thomas Cummings. New York; London: Praeger, 1976. 481p. bibliog. (Praeger Special Studies).
A broad survey of the base upon which the Middle Eastern Arab countries can construct a modern economy and bring to their millions of inhabitants a standard of living approaching that of the West. The book discusses agriculture, industry, manpower, trade, and the role of government. Egypt's case is discussed in almost every chapter.

758 **From state socialism to controlled commercialism: the emergence of Egypt's open door policy.**
Nazih N.M. Ayubi. *Journal of Commonwealth and Comparative Politics*, vol. 20, no. 8 (November 1982), p. 264-85.
An analysis of the social changes in Egypt between 1952 and 1974 which led to the establishment of the open door economic policy by Sadat. Nasser's regime created a new class of state-employed technocrats, many of whom enriched themselves and opened private businesses in direct competition with the state. This class demanded the open door policy (*infitah*) and the privatization of the economy to perpetuate their gains.

759 **Economic development in the United Arab Republic (Egypt).**
Rashed al-Barawy. Cairo: Anglo-Egyptian Bookshop, 1970. 334p. bibliog.
The author of this book is an Egyptian economist who was a principal official of economic planning in the 1950s and 1960s, and his aim is 'to provide the foreign reader with a brief, but objective, account of the UAR's economic development, including policies, techniques and achievements under the impact of the revolution of 1952 up to the present time (1970)'.

760 **Egypt's development in the seventies.**
Henry Bruton. *Economic Development and Cultural Change*, vol. 31, no. 4 (July 1983), p. 679-704.
An evaluation of Egypt's economic development in the 1970s, which indicates that the economic 'state of limbo' was a result of the initiation of the open door policy in 1974. The foreign exchange revenues from oil, the Suez Canal, tourism, workers' remittances and foreign aid improved the economic indicators without increasing development. In the author's opinion the problems of low investment and productivity, tight labour supply and uncontrollable bureaucracy should be solved to accelerate the development process.

761 **Foreign investment and development in Egypt.**
David William Carr.   New York; London: Praeger, 1979. 148p.
bibliog. (Praeger Special Studies).

The first section of this book presents the essential elements of the dynamic view of foreign trade or investment, stressing the contention that high net benefits are most likely to arise when there are vigorous reactions by host entities. The second section analyses in detail the technology transfer mechanism and describes how the various returns from direct investment originate. With the industrial organization approach, the returns are attributable to the transfer and dissemination of the special assets possessed by foreign investors. An outline of the major issues dealt with in this book is presented in the concluding section of the first chapter.

762 **Country report: Egypt.**
London: Economist Intelligence Unit, 1986- , quarterly, with an annual supplement 'Country profile: Egypt'.

These reports are continuations of the *Quarterly Economic Review of Egypt* (1951-) and its annual supplement (the title varies slightly). They contain a useful summary of the current economic situation and a briefing on the political developments, together with tables and statistics.

763 **Planning for economic development: methodology, strategy and effectiveness – a comparative case study of Indian and Egyptian experiences.**
Abd el-Hamid el-Ghazali.   Cairo: Modern Cairo Bookshop, 1971. 540p. bibliog.

Originally a doctoral dissertation submitted to the University of Glasgow Department of International Economic Studies in 1968, this is a quantitative comparative case study in development planning, dealing with India and Egypt during the period 1946-1972. The aim of the study is twofold: firstly, to provide a critical review of the basic features of planning outline and strategy in the two countries; and secondly, to evaluate the two countries' planning exercises against the actual results achieved.

764 **The tripartite relationship: government, foreign investors, and local investors during Egypt's economic opening.**
Kate Gillespie.   New York: Praeger, 1984. 226p. bibliog.

This is a case study of the tripartite relationship existing between the government, foreign investors and local private investors. It examines the way each of the parties interacts with the other two, forming and breaking coalitions, in pursuit of its own perceived self-interest, and describes what happened in Egypt during the policy of 'economic opening' under Sadat.

765 **Egypt's ten year economic plan: 1973-1982.**
Albert L. Gray, Jr. *Middle East Journal*, vol. 30, no. 2 (Winter 1976), p. 36-48.

After reviewing the achievements of the 1960-1970 economic plan and the goals of that of 1973-1982, the author considers the prospects for the latter in terms of savings, investments, balance of payments and employment. He concludes that, with massive foreign assistance, many of the goals of the Second Ten Year Plan could be achieved.

766 **Status of the open-door policy up to December 31, 1981: an investment guide.**
Edited and translated by Shafick S. Hassan. Cairo: Central Agency for Public Mobilization and Statistics, 1982. 204p. (Ref.No. 72-14541-82).

This book illustrates the concept of the open door economic policy, gives the reasons that induced Egypt to adopt that policy, and states the objectives which are expected to be achieved from its implementation.

767 **Egypt in revolution: an economic analysis.**
Charles Issawi. London: Oxford University Press, under the auspices of the Royal Institute of International Affairs, 1963. 3rd rev. ed. 331p. bibliog.

The first edition of this book, entitled *Egypt: an economic and social analysis*, was published in 1947. A second, much revised edition, entitled *Egypt at mid-century: an economic survey*, was published in 1954. This third edition, revised and largely rewritten, presents a detailed economic study of Egypt from 1798 to 1962.

768 **Economic development and planning in Egypt.**
Magdi M. el-Kammash, foreword by Joseph J. Spengler. New York; London: Praeger, 1968. 468p. bibliog.

A study of economic planning and the progress of economic development in Egypt. The author suggests that one or the other or both of two relative shortages retard economic development: a relative shortage of productive factors, or a relative shortage of aggregate demand. It seems clear that a shortage of inputs is overriding, and that Egypt's long-term as well as its short-term economic future depend on whether its population ceases to grow.

769 **The economic impact of the Six-Day War: Israel, the occupied territories, Egypt, Jordan.**
Eliyahu Kanovsky. New York: Praeger, 1970. 451p. bibliog.

Part 3 of this study (p. 205-340) is devoted to Egypt. After a 75-page introduction on the Egyptian economy between 1952 and 1967, the author considers the effect of the war on all aspects of Egyptian economic activity.

770 **The U.A.R. in development: a study in expansionary finance.**
George K. Kardouche.   New York: Praeger, 1966. 170p. bibliog.
(Praeger Special Studies in International Economics and
Development).

The author explains in his preface that the term 'expansionary finance' was chosen
because it seemed to describe best the intent and results of the Egyptian
government's economic programme, which set rapid material development as the
primary policy target. This programme was achieved mainly through governmental investment expenditures, and the attendant problems, which were similar
to those encountered by other developing nations, form the subject of this study.

771 **Rich and poor states in the Middle East: Egypt and the New Arab
Order.**
Edited by Malcolm H. Kerr, el-Sayed Yassin. Boulder,
Colorado: Westview Press; Cairo: American University, 1982.
482p. (Westview Special Studies on the Middle East).

This collection of studies on the economic, social and political relationships
between the rich (i.e. oil-rich) and the poor countries in the Middle East focuses
primarily on Egypt, the largest state in the region. The essays consist firstly of an
introduction, 'Egypt in the shadow of the Gulf', by Malcolm H. Kerr, and this is
followed by two essays on the new Arab social order: 'Oil, migration and the new
Arab social order', by Saad Eddin Ibrahim; and 'Migration and social mobility in
Egypt', by Georges Sabagh. The remaining essays are on the new Arab economic
order: 'The Arab economy and its developing strategy: a new Arab economic
order', by Essam Montasser; 'Arab capital and trilateral ventures in the Middle
East: is three a crowd?' by Jeswald W. Salacuse; 'The predicament of the Arab
Gulf oil states: individual gains and collective losses', by Hazem el-Beblawi;
'Expatriate labor and economic growth: Saudi demand for Egyptian labor', by
Naiem A. Sherbiny and Ismail Serageldin; 'The open door economic policy in
Egypt: its contribution to investment and its equity implications', by Gouda
Abdel-Khalek; 'External factors in the reorientation of Egypt's economic policy',
by Galal Ahmad Amin; 'The new Arab political order: implications for the
1980s', by Ali E. Hillal Dessouki; 'Implementation capability and political
feasibility of the open door policy in Egypt', by Nazih N.M. Ayubi; 'Oil, arms,
and regional diplomacy: strategic dimensions of the Saudi-Egyptian relationship',
by Paul Jabber; and 'Egypt and the Arabs in the future: some scenarios', by
Malcolm H. Kerr.

772 **The Egyptian economy 1952-1972.**
Robert Mabro.   London: Oxford University Press, 1974. 254p.
bibliog.

Chapters 1-3 of this book introduce the economy: the historical background, the
demographic features, and natural resources; chapters 4-7 analyse in detail the
major policies and achievements of the Revolution: the land reform, the Aswan
High Dam, planning and nationalization, and industrialization and social policies.
The final chapters contain an analysis of growth and of structural and
distributional changes.

Economy and Economic Development

773 **Business opportunities in the 1980s: Egypt and Sudan.**
A.P. McHale, A. Carsten. London: Metra Consulting Group, 1983. 390p.

The report on Egypt is by Allan P. McHale, and that on the Sudan by Arnold Carsten. Each report includes, after a chapter of background on the country, chapters on the economy, energy and infrastructure, industry, agriculture, commerce, exporting to and investing in the country.

774 **Growth and structural change in the Egyptian economy.**
Donald C. Mead. Homewood, Illinois: Richard D. Irwin, for the Economic Growth Center of Yale Univesity, 1967. 414p. bibliog.

An economic history of Egypt, covering growth and structural change in agriculture, industry, services, international trade, the financial system, money, prices, consumption, investment, and planning.

775 **Middle East Economic Digest.**
London: MEED, 1957- . weekly.

Contains a regular section of short news items about the Egyptian economy. Commonly cited as *MEED*.

776 **Money and power: the dilemma of the Egyptian *infitah*.**
Clement Henry Moore. *Middle East Journal*, vol. 40, no. 4 (Autumn 1986), p. 634-50.

Considers the *infitah* (open door economic policy) and its ramifications. The author argues that privatization of the economy may be viewed in its initial stages primarily as a political tactic for sustaining authoritarian regimes rather than as a set of reforms for stimulating free enterprise or markets. He concludes that the present regime will either continue toward greater pluralism (if not democracy), paralleling a more liberal economy, or be overcome by forces which will put an end to *infitah* altogether.

777 **The revolution in Egypt's economic system: from private enterprise to socialism, 1952-1965.**
Patrick O'Brien. London; New York: Oxford University Press, 1966. 354p. bibliog.

A detailed study of the changes in Egypt's economic structures, and an evaluation of the regime's attempts to deal with Egypt's economic problems.

778 **Cotton and the Egyptian economy, 1820-1914: a study in trade and development.**
E. R. J. Owen. Oxford, England: Clarendon Press, 1969. 416p.

An economic study of Egypt, covering the period during which the British took over the country, owing largely to the impoverished state of its finances.

779 **The effects of oil price increases on the Egyptian economy.**
David Pearce, Ron Edwards. Geneva: International Labour
Office, 1982. 177p. bibliog. (World Employment Programme
Research Working Paper, WEP 2-22/WP 108).
Egypt's oil reserves are expected to last only until the beginning of the 1990s. Yet,
the domestic prices of oil have been much lower than the international prices, and
economic activity has been planned with little incentive for energy conservation.
The authors examine the extent to which oil prices have affected the Egyptian
economy, including its major sectors, and consider the effects of price increases.

780 **Capital formation in Egyptian industry and agriculture, 1882-1967.**
Samir Radwan. London: Ithaca Press for the Middle East Centre
of St. Antony's College, Oxford, 1974. 314p. map. bibliog.
(St. Antony's Middle East Monographs, No. 2).
This study, originally presented in 1973 as a doctoral dissertation at the University
of London, has two major objectives: firstly, measurement of gross and net fixed
capital formation and capital stock in Egyptian agriculture and industry at current
and constant prices, covering the period 1882-1967; and secondly, an outlining of
the broad historical, institutional and economic factors affecting the rate and
structure of capital accumulation during this period. As such, it can be regarded
as a study in quantitative economic history.

781 **Review of British aid to Egypt.**
M.E.N. Economic Weekly (Cairo), vol. 24, no. 19 (May 1985),
p. 4-8.
A review of joint UK-Egyptian technical projects established under the Technical
Co-operation Agreement of 1974. The British Council in Egypt serves as the
agent for the UK's Overseas Development Administration and cooperates in
carrying out a variety of projects funded by the World Bank and other
international organizations.

782 **The monetary system of Egypt: an inquiry into its history and
present working.**
Mohammed Ali Rifaat. London: Allen & Unwin, 1935. 200p.
A brief introduction describes Egypt's economic development and condition from
the time of Muhammad Ali until the 1930s. The monetary system then in
operation is discussed in terms of the currency standard, the credit institutions
and the credit structure, the National Bank, and the economic renaissance of the
1920s.

783 **The dynamics of economic policy making in Egypt.**
Paul Rivlin. New York: Praeger, 1985. 201p.
The author examines the way in which economic policy was made and
implemented in Egypt between 1970 and 1980, the constraints limiting the policy
makers, the problems encountered, and the effects of attempts to reform the
foreign sector of the economy.

Economy and Economic Development

784   **Egypt: strategies for investment.**
Salah el-Sayed.   Cairo: American University in Cairo Press,
1977. 223p.

The author's aims in this book are: to provide a comprehensive summary of the
basic data and development of the Egyptian economy; to set forth the economic
framework and to analyse its laws, policies and practices; to identify markets and
needs in industrial joint ventures, sales of capital and consumer goods, and
provision of services and know-how; to pinpoint special incentives and
advantages, as well as pitfalls and drawbacks, for foreign investment and business
activity; and to lay out the practical means available and the steps required to
proceed successfully within the constraints of the Egyptian economic system.

785   **Impact of development assistance on Egypt.**
Edited by Earl L. Sullivan.   Cairo: American University in Cairo
Press, 1984. 108p. bibliog. (Cairo Papers in Social Science, Vol. 7,
Monograph 3).

A collection of papers by a group of economists, political scientists, anthropologists and sociologists from the American University in Cairo. The papers
present the different perspectives of scholars and officials concerning foreign aid
to Egypt and its impact on aspects of Egyptian activities. The papers included are
as follows: 'Introduction: the impact of development assistance on Egypt', by Earl
L. Sullivan; 'The perspective of the Egyptian Ministry of the Economy on the
impact of American aid on Egypt', by Mostafa al-Said; 'The UNDP in Egypt', by
Luciana Cappelletti; 'The Ford Foundation in Egypt', by Ann M. Lesch; 'The
U.S. Agency for International Development in Egypt', by Michael Stone; 'The
development of cooperation', by Nicholas S. Hopkins; 'Whose knowledge counts:
discourse and development in an Egyptian rural community', by Cynthia Newson;
'The impacts of Egyptian-American academic research: the Cairo/Massachusetts
Institute of Technology program', by Mohamed el-Sayed Selim; 'Egypt and the
helping hand', by Adel A. Beshai; 'Egypt and the U.S.: an aid or trade
relationship', by Dennis D. Miller; 'Conflicting objectives in the Egyptian-
American aid relationship', by Heba A. Handoussa; and 'Conclusion: foreign aid
and the future of Egypt', by Earl L. Sullivan.

786   **Studies in Egyptian political economy: methodology, theory, and
case studies.**
Edited by Herbert M. Thompson.   Cairo: American University in
Cairo Press, 1979. 130p. (Cairo Papers in Social Science, Vol. 2,
Monograph 3).

This volume presents five papers on the political economy of Egypt. The three
case studies cover the political economy of Egypt in the 18th century, the open
door economic policy, and Egypt's public sector industry. The other two papers
present a theoretical framework to assist an understanding of the dynamics of the
political economy of Egypt.

787 **State, private enterprise and economic change in Egypt, 1918-1952.**
Robert L. Tignor.   Princeton, New Jersey: Princeton University
Press, 1984. 317p. bibliog.

An account of the emergence and development of Egyptian industrial capitalism,
with reference to its political and social role in the development of Egyptian
society between 1918 and 1952.

788 **Hydro-politics of the Nile Valley.**
John Waterbury.   Syracuse, New York: Syracuse University
Press, 1979. 320p. maps.

A thoroughly and meticulously researched study of the political economies of
modern Egypt and the Sudan, which depend completely on the River Nile.

789 **Egypt's *infitah* and the politics of U.S. economic assistance.**
Marvin G. Weinbaum   *Middle Eastern Studies*, vol. 21, no. 2
(April 1985), p. 206-22.

The author believes that a reassessment of *infitah* (the open door economic
policy) as well as the American aid relationship was inevitable under the
presidency of Hosni Mubarak. Sadat had embarked on the open door policy as a
result of both domestic social and economic problems, and foreign political
pressures, and it had led to a more consumption-oriented economy, vulnerable to
exploitation by both home and foreign interests, and the hazards of foreign trade.
Egypt's political estrangement from the Arabs as a result of the Camp David
accords was another cause for concern.

790 **Class, power and foreign capital in Egypt: the rise of the new
bourgeoisie.**
Malak Zaalouk.   London: Zed Books, 1987. 272p.

A study of the commercial agents of foreign firms and their role in the political
economy of contemporary Egypt. The author charts the growth of the influence of
this relatively small group and its distortions of the Egyptian political economy
from 1940 to the 1970s.

The Red Sea touristic zones.
See item no. 55.

The economic embargo of Egypt by Arab states: myth and reality.
See item no. 686.

**Development, income distribution and social change in rural Egypt (1952-
1970): a study in the political economy of agrarian transition.**
See item no. 820.

The informal sector in an intermediate city: a case in Egypt.
See item no. 857.

MEN Economic Weekly.
See item no. 1014.

Trade, Banking and Finance

791 **Insurance development in the Arab world: available domestic retention capacity and demand for international reinsurance.**
Abdul Zahra Abdullah Ali.   London: Graham & Trotman, 1985.
369p.
Contains many references to insurance practices in Egypt, and to the Egyptian General Insurance Organization, and there is a section on the Egyptian Reinsurance Company.

792 **Investing in the Eastern Mediterranean: Greece, Egypt, Cyprus.**
J. Chown, G. Stathopoulos.   London: J.F. Chown; Athens:
G.N. Stathopoulos, 1977. 168p.
Incentives, taxes, sources of local funds and a background analysis are provided.
The section on Egypt is on p. 57-137.

793 **Challenging colonialism: Bank Miṣr and Egyptian industrialization 1920-1941.**
Eric Davis.   Princeton, New Jersey: Princeton University Press,
1983. 272p. (Princeton Studies on the Near East).
This work discusses the Bank Misr's sponsorship of Egypt's first indigenously financed and directed industrialization movement, and develops a model to explain the bank's initial successes, its eventual failure to free Egypt from foreign economic control and its crash in 1939. The book makes use of a wide variety of original sources.

794 **The eastern trade directory, 1985-1986.**
Cairo: 17 Kasr El-Nil Street, 1985. annual.

After a very brief section of information on location, area, population, natural resources, agriculture, mining, energy, transport and communication, this directory provides a list of public and private sector companies with addresses, but not telephone numbers. Other useful trade directories include the *Egyptian trade and industry directory* (Cairo: Middle East Public Relations), which provides a broadly classified directory of industrial companies, banks, construction companies and transport companies, and includes a list of foreign firms represented in Egypt; the *Commercial directory of Egypt* (Cairo: Modern Publishing Company), which presents a classified list of Egyptian business firms and of foreign firms operating in Egypt; *Egyptian who's who for agents and distributors* (Cairo: Middle East Publishing Company), which lists foreign firms represented in Egypt and the Middle East with names of their representatives; *Egyptian trade index* (Cairo: Middle East Publishing Company), which contains detailed information on some 6,000 importers, exporters and manufacturers; and *Lists of American firms, subsidiaries and affiliates operating in Egypt* (New York: World Academy Press). New editions of all these directories appear somewhat irregularly.

795 **Egypt: gateway to the Middle East?**
New York: Business International, 1976. 125p.

An assessment of Egypt in terms of business opportunities, including the meaning of Law 43 of 1974 regarding foreign investment. Gives details of the experiences of some businessmen who have worked under that law.

796 **Egypt's export targets: exports estimated to hike to E.L. 4 billion in 1984-1985.**
M.E.N. Economic Weekly, vol. 23, no. 47 (November 1984), p. 6-16.

The value of commodity exports in the fiscal year 1984-85 is projected to reach L.E. (Egyptian pounds) 3,960 million. Exports in the fiscal year 1983-1984 rose to over L.E. 3,209 million. Agricultural exports increased by 30 per cent to L.E. 495 million, while industrial exports rose from L.E. 393 million to L.E. 448 million. The export target for 1986-87 is L.E. 5,870 million. The National Export Bank will distribute L.E. 120 million in loans to exporters in the public and private sectors by January 1985.

797 **Foreign trade in 1980-81.**
M.E.N. Economic Weekly, vol. 21, no. 13 (26 March 1982), p. 4-7.

A report on trends in Egypt's foreign trade in 1980-81 as compared to 1979-80. In 1980-81 there was a trade deficit of L.E. 2966.2 million, although the proportion of exports to imports went up from 45.7% in 1979-80 to 50.5% in 1980-81. A breakdown of imports and exports is included.

798 **Winning business in Egypt.**
Dennis E. Frith. London: Graham & Trotman, 1978. 98p.
A report on the business opportunities available in Egypt. Appendix I includes 18
tables of statistics; Appendix II is a list of useful names and addresses.

799 **Foreign trade regimes and economic development: Egypt.**
Bent Hansen, Karim Nashashibi. New York: Columbia
University Press, 1975. 358p. (National Bureau of Economic
Research. Special Conference Series on Foreign Trade Regimes
and Economic Development, No. 4).
A study of foreign trade regimes in Egypt (1946-1969) with reference to
protection, controls and competitiveness in Egyptian agriculture and industry.

800 **Hints to businessmen visiting the Arab Republic of Egypt.**
London: British Overseas Trade Board, Export Services and
Promotion Division, 1977. 51p.
A guide to businessmen who want to do business in Egypt, periodically updated.

801 **Developing business in the Middle East and North Africa: Egypt.**
Youssef M. Ibrahim. New York: Chase World Information
Corporation, 1977. 344p. maps.
A study that provides guidelines for initiating and implementing high-potential
operations. Contents include: executive summary; the economy; doing business in
Egypt; tourism; industry; infrastructure; oil, gas and petrochemicals; agriculture;
Egypt: land, people, government; and visiting and living in Egypt.

802 **Investment guide in Egypt, 1977: analytical study of investment
laws, foreign trade, currency and labour laws, bilateral agreements
for capital protection.**
Cairo; Alexandria: Middle East Observer, 1977. 162p.
Consists of explanatory chapters on Law 43 of 1974 as follows: Part I, Projects
and invested capital; Part II, Some special cases elaborated (land acquisition,
tourism projects, contractors' activities, financial firms and foreign trade); Part
III, Other laws referred to in the investment law (taxation law, company law,
labour law, etc.); Part IV, Free Zones; Part VI, The General Authority for Arab
and Foreign Investments and Free Zones; Part VII, Bilateral agreements for
capital protection.

803 **Public insurance in Egypt.**
International Insurance Monitor, vol. 35, no. 6 (June 1981), p.5-9.
A report on public insurance in Egypt based on the 1979 government report on
the subject. Includes detailed tables of life and non-life insurance, reinsurance,
consolidated accounts and joint venture company activities. While there was
growth in all sectors, the Arab International Insurance Company experienced an
increase in profits of 147.6%.

804 **Business directory for Egypt, October 1985.**
Prepared by the United States and Foreign Commercial Service
(USFCS). Cairo: United States Embassy; Alexandria: American
Consulate-General, 1986. 259p.

This directory is largely a compilation of documents and business information
frequently requested by the American and Egyptian clients of USFCS at the US
Embassy in Cairo and the Consulate-General in Alexandria. It must be used in
conjunction with the advice and publications provided by the other commercial
organizations listed in the directory and elsewhere.

805 **Banking and finance in the Arab Middle East.**
Rodney Wilson. London: Macmillan; New York: St. Martin's
Press, 1983. 208p.

The second chapter of this book, 'Emergence of modern banking', is about the
National Bank of Egypt, the start and spread of indigenous banking, and Bank
Misr as a development institution. Egypt is also covered in the other chapters of
the book.

806 **Egypt's export diversification: benefits and constraints.**
Rodney J.A. Wilson. *The Developing Economies*, vol. 22, no. 1
(March 1984), p. 86-101.

Analyses export diversification in Egypt from 1965 to 1980. The country is
diversifying its exports in manufactured cotton goods and agricultural products
such as potatoes, oranges, and rice. The benefits of diversification are calculated
on the basis of export price trends, price stability and export constraints, and it is
found that exporting finished goods is better than exporting raw materials.

Industrialization and trade patterns in Egypt.
See item no. 811.

Industry

807 **Egypt: all set to go nuclear.**
Magda Abu-Fadil. *Middle East* (London), no. 125 (March 1985), p. 35-6.

An interview with the Egyptian minister for electricity and energy about nuclear power plants in Egypt.

808 **The challenge of industrialization: Egypt.**
Kasim Alrimawi. Beirut: United Publishers, 1974. 318p. bibliog.

Industrialization is the primary means of achieving economic development, and it has been an aim of the Egyptian government since the first days of the revolution in July 1952. This book sets out to answer the questions of how to meet the challenge posed by industrialization, when to meet it, and who will meet it.

809 **The growth, location and structure of industry in Egypt.**
K.M. Barbour. New York: Praeger, 1972. 222p.(Praeger Special Studies in International Economics and Development).

In addition to an introduction and a conclusion, this volume includes the following chapters: 'Sources for the study of Egyptian industry', 'Historical introduction to the structure and location of industry in Egypt up to 1882', 'Historical introduction to the structure and location of industry in Egypt from 1882 to the present', 'The distribution of industry in Egypt', 'Industrial pattern, structure and concentration', and 'Population, industry and urbanization: the growth poles'.

810   **Energy policy in Egypt.**
Nazli Choucri, Mohamed Zaki Shafei. *L'Egypte Contemporaine*,
no. 395 (January 1984), p. 5-24.

A study of the role of petroleum and natural gas in the Egyptian economy,
focusing on their production, end uses and substitution possibilities. The authors
find that rising domestic consumption and uncertainty about Egypt's reserves will
necessitate certain policy changes. Models and graphs are used to project Egypt's
oil production and exports for the future.

811   **Industrialization and trade patterns in Egypt.**
Maurice Girgis.   Tübingen, FRG: Mohr, 1977. 247p. (Kieler
Studien, no. 143).

Reviews the role of the public sector and its influence on the pattern of industrial
growth from 1950 to 1970, the effects of import and export policy, the changing
pattern of foreign trade, and the reasons for Egypt's relatively poor export
performance.

812   **The industrialization of Egypt, 1939-1973: policy and performance.**
Robert Mabro, Samir M. Radwan.   Oxford: Clarendon Press,
1976. 279p. bibliog.

An in-depth evaluative analysis of the policies and achievements of the Egyptian
industrialization movement during and after the Second World War and up to
1970. The book examines the historical, economic and policy background, and the
growth and structural changes in the manufacturing industry in Egypt. The factors
affecting production, including labour and capital, and the relationship between
industrialization and trade, are also discussed.

813   **Small industries in Egypt: an exploration of the economics of small
furniture producers.**
Donald C. Mead.   *International Journal of Middle East Studies*,
vol. 14, no. 2 (May 1982), p. 159-71.

The author examines the contention that small enterprises play an important role
in the economic activities of the population as supplementary sources of income
in both the rural and urban areas, using the furniture industry as an example. He
comes to the conclusion that it is difficult to generalize about small industries and
that 'small is far from being beautiful, one might say small is backward', contrary
to what is often stated in the literature about development.

814   **The private sector: a dynamic element in the textile industry of
Egypt.**
M.E.N. Economic Weekly, vol. 23, no. 47 (November 1984),
p. 11-14.

Describes the development of Egypt's textile industry, which was first established
by the National Spinning Company in 1911 and was developed by the Misr
Spinning and Weaving Company founded by Bank Misr in 1930. The industry

flourished during the Second World War, when foreign imports ceased, and was nationalized in 1961, but since 1968 the government has encouraged the private sector to play a greater role in production.

815 **Management development in Egypt.**
Edited by Salah el-Sayed.   Cairo: American University in Cairo Press, 1979. 470p. bibliog.

Egypt has a shortage of qualified managers, yet must develop its economy as fast as possible, and this book studies the ways and means by which management development could be carried out effectively in terms of quantity, quality and time.

816 **Workers' participation in management: the Egyptian experience.**
Salah el-Sayed.   Cairo: American University in Cairo Press, 1978. 142p.

This study attempts to estimate the success of the Egyptian worker participation programme by measuring the responses to it of workers themselves, their elected representatives on directorial boards, union officials, middle- and upper-level management, and government spokesmen, during a crucial period that includes the events of 1967 and 1973 as well as the beginnings of economic reliberalization. The book has therefore both a theoretical and a practical value for economists, sociologists, management consultants, and potential investors.

817 **Cases in management (Egypt and Sudan).**
Salah el-Sayed.   Cairo: American University in Cairo Press, 1980. 188p.

This volume presents twenty case studies in management representing different management situations and the underlying decision-making processes. Nine of the case studies concern Egypt, principally in the field of high-level public administration. The book can be used in the teaching of management studies.

818 **Strategic features of development of the industry sector (1981-82).**
M.E.N. Economic Weekly, vol. 21, no. 39 (24 September 1982), p. 11-15.

Investments in industry in the year 1981-82 by the Egyptian Ministry of Industry totaled L.E. 481 million. The value of industrial output for 1981-82 was L.E. 7,345.5 million and the value added was about L.E. 2,232 million.

819   **12 years of industrial development, 1952-1964.**
       Cairo: Government Printing Office, 1964. 342p.

A government report on the development of Egyptian industry over the twelve
years after the revolution. The book includes chapters on the features and details
of industrial development, the third industrialization programme, industry under
socialism, industry and society, industry and export, and new factories
constructed during the twelve years.

Industrialization and population dynamics and characteristics.
See item no. 418.

Images of development: Egyptian engineers in search of industry.
See item no. 889.

Agriculture and
Agrarian Reform

820 **Development, income distribution and social change in rural Egypt**
(1952-1970): a study in the political economy of agrarian transition.
Mahmoud Abdel-Fadil. Cambridge, England: Cambridge
University Press, 1975. 236p. bibliog. (University of Cambridge
Department of Applied Economics, Occasional Paper, 45).

Discusses land reforms and the transformation of the agrarian structure, agrarian
classes and the differentiation of the peasantry, changes in the distribution of
agricultural income, changes in consumption patterns in rural Egypt, the
movement in agricultural terms of trade and the disposal of agricultural surplus.

821 **Development and social change in rural Egypt.**
Richard H. Adams, Jr. Syracuse, New York: Syracuse University
Press, 1986. 231p. bibliog.

A field study of rural development in modern Egypt, including the study of
control and management in the Egyptian countryside, agricultural cooperatives,
land reform, and rural poverty among other topics.

822 **Technological change and surplus labour in Egyptian agriculture,**
1952-1972.
Youssef Hassan Ali, Richard Grabowski. *Journal of Agricultural
Economics*, vol. 35, no. 1 (January 1984), p. 109-16.

According to this analysis of Egypt's agricultural sector from 1952 to 1972, labour
grew by 54 per cent and land by 17 per cent. Output grew by only 48 per cent
while output by male agricultural labour declined. The researchers found that
labour-using technical innovations had appeared only very slowly.

823 **A history of landownership in modern Egypt, 1800-1950.**
Gabriel Baer. London: Oxford University Press, 1962. 252p.
maps. bibliog. (Middle Eastern Monographs).

This socio-economic study of landownership covers the following topics: the development of private ownership of land, land distribution in the 19th and 20th centuries, *waqf* land, state domain and public domain, and views on land reform before the 1952 revolution.

824 **The effects of food price and subsidy policies on Egyptian agriculture.**
Joachim von Braun, Hartwig De Haen. Washington, DC: International Food Policy Research Institute, 1983. 93p. (Research Report No. 42).

A research report on the effects on agriculture of the rapid growth in Egyptian consumer subsidies in the 1970s. The subsidies led to an increase in food imports. Producers' incomes were balanced by the growth in input subsidies and depressed food prices. Subsidies were not at the cost of agriculture as price distortions existed before the subsidy system. To overcome inefficiencies in Egyptian agriculture, the authors recommend reducing these price distortions.

825 **The state and agricultural development in Egypt since 1973.**
Simon Commander. London: Ithaca Press for the Overseas Development Institute, 1987. 301p. bibliog.

A study of three sample villages in the Delta, examining the nature of shifts in the labour market, employment patterns, agricultural production and mechanization, and the bases and possibilities for rural incomes over the last decade.

826 **Egypt.**
New York: Chase World Information Corporation, 1977. 404p.
bibliog. (Chase World Information Series on Agribusiness Potential in the Middle East and North Africa).

A broadly based examination of the possibilities for business ventures in Egyptian land and water resource development and conservation, crop and livestock production, and agribusiness and agroindustry. The report presents the business opportunities within the context of the economic, social, and political setting as it affects the Egyptian agricultural sector.

827 **Land reform in relation to social development: Egypt.**
Saad M. Gadalla. Columbia, Missouri: University of Missouri Press, 1962. 133p. map. bibliog.

An evaluation of Egypt's land reform of 1952, giving a succinct description of the situation before reform, and the effects of reform on rural communities and rural families.

828 **Distribution of land, employment and income in rural Egypt.**
Iliya Harik, Susan Randolph. Ithaca, New York: Cornell
University, Center for International Studies, 1979. 166p. (Special
Series on Landlessness and Near-landlessness).

After an introductory chapter on agrarian reform and rural development strategy,
1952-1967, the authors study the rural population and access to land, the rural
labour force, numbers and activities, and stratification by income.

829 **Continuity and change in local development policies in Egypt: from
Nasser to Sadat.**
Iliya Harik. *International Journal of Middle East Studies*, vol. 16,
no. 1 (1984), p. 43-66.

A study of the rural development strategy of the Nasser and Sadat regimes. The
author points out the obstacles to rural progress, the changes in the cooperative
system, the effects of the agrarian reform laws on local government, and the
structure and leadership of municipal councils. He also explains how resources
were allocated under Sadat's regime, which had no comprehensive strategy for
facing the problems of the countryside.

830 **The social impact of mechanization.**
Nicholas S. Hopkins. In: *Migration, mechanization and
agricultural labor markets in Egypt.* Edited by Alan Richards,
Philip L. Martin. Boulder, Colorado: Westview Press; Cairo:
American University in Cairo Press, 1983, p. 181-97.

An analysis of the impact of agricultural mechanization on the organization of
work and the migration of agricultural labour in rural Egypt, which shows that the
household is still the basic unit for organizing labour. Musha, a village in Upper
Egypt, is used as a case study.

831 **Technical efficiency in production of Egyptian corn: some
econometric comparisons.**
Hassan Aly Khedr. *L'Egypte Contemporaine*, vol. 73, no. 387
(January 1982), p. 17-24.

An econometric analysis of maize production in Egypt from 1970 to 1980. A
mathematical model incorporating such variables as cultivated area, labour costs,
use of machinery and animals, and fertilizer input is used in the analysis. Lower
Egypt receives more output for inputs than do Middle and Upper Egypt.

832 **Land reform law: full text.**
Cairo: H.C.A.R., Press Department, 1955. 31p.

The text of the land reform law issued on 4 December 1954 by the Nasser
government limiting land ownership to 200 acres.

833   **Agrarian reform in Egypt.**
Sayed Marei.   Cairo: Institut Français d'Archéologie Orientale,
1957. 467p. bibliog.

A description, by Egypt's minister of state for agrarian reform, of details of the
land reform law, land distribution, agrarian reform co-operatives, the regulation of
landowner-tenant relationships, agricultural and co-operative credit, the problem
of fragmented holdings, new projects to increase peasants' incomes, the effect of
agrarian reform on economic and social development, and Egypt's population and
land resources problems.

834   **Irrigation and society in rural Egypt.**
Sohair Mehanna, Richard Huntington, Rachad Antonius.
Cairo: American University in Cairo, 1984. 146p. bibliog. (Cairo
Papers in Social Science, Vol. 7, Monograph 4).

This study describes and analyses the local organization of water allocation as it
most directly affects the patterns of cooperation and conflict among farmers and
as it most strongly influences their receptivity to planned changes in the system
and technology.

835   **Agrarian reform and rural poverty; Egypt, 1952-1975.**
Samir Radwan.   Geneva: International Labour Office, 1977. 91p.

The author aims to investigate the alternative organizational forms within which
agricultural developments can be pursued without leading to polarization of
income and wealth and increasing poverty. To this end he studies a wide variety
of experiences ranging from systems of communal land use to egalitarian agrarian
reform in the contexts of private enterprise and the 'intermediate' experiences of
cooperatives. Each experience is assessed in terms of its contribution to reducing
poverty, generating surplus, and creating production and employment. Egypt is
seen as typical of the intermediate variety of experience.

836   **Agrarian change in Egypt: an anatomy of rural poverty.**
Samir Radwan, Eddy Lee.   London: Croom Helm, 1986. 167p.

Based on a survey of eighteen villages in Egypt carried out in 1977, this book
investigates the relationships between poverty, land tenure, and sources of
income, and analyses the dynamics of agrarian change in Egypt over the last three
decades. After a brief historical background study on the evolution of Egypt's
agrarian system and the agrarian question in the 1970s, the authors proceed to
study the following: The generation and distribution of income; The structure of
asset ownership; Poverty, consumption and basic needs; Employment and the
labour market; Efficiency and equity in the 1980s.

837   **Agricultural mechanization in Egypt: hopes and fears.**
Alan Richards.   *International Journal of Middle East Studies*,
vol. 13, no. 4 (November 1981), p. 409-25.

The author argues that there are considerable grounds for scepticism about the
net social benefits of agricultural mechanization in Egypt, and that the following

questions must be asked: if all agricultural operations are to be mechanized by 1990, where will the people displaced by such mechanization be employed? Where will the capital come from to create their new jobs? What will happen if the overseas migrants return? Where will all of these people live?

838 **Egypt's agricultural development, 1800-1980: technical and social change.**
Alan Richards. Boulder, Colorado: Westview Press, 1982. 296p. bibliog.

This book describes and interprets the transformation of Egyptian agriculture from the beginning of cotton cultivation in the early 19th century to the recent changes under Sadat. The author uses both microeconomic theory and social and political analysis to show how the interaction of social classes, technical change, government policy and the international and state systems have shaped Egypt's agricultural development. Arguing that these forces are bound up in a complex web of reciprocal causation, he places the current dilemmas of Egyptian agriculture in historical perspective.

839 **Migration, mechanization and agricultural labor markets in Egypt.**
Edited by Alan Richards, Philip L. Martin. Boulder, Colorado: Westview Press; Cairo: American University in Cairo Press, 1983. 288p.

An excellent study of changes in agricultural labour markets and farm technology in Egypt during the period from 1973 to 1983, which focuses especially on the social consequences and long-term prospects of mechanization. The volume includes the following studies: 'Introduction', by Alan Richards, Philip L. Martin; 'Labour shortages in Egyptian agriculture, by Alan Richards, Philip L. Martin, Rifaat Nagaar; 'Livestock and small farmer labor supply', by James B. Fitch, Ibrahim A. Soliman; '*Tarahil* laborers in Egypt', by Sawsan el-Messiri; 'Who is migrating where? An overview of international labor migration in the Arab world', by J.S. Birks, I. Serageldin, C.A. Sinclair, J.A. Socknat; 'The demand for Egyptian labor abroad', by J.S. Birks, C.A. Sinclair, J.A. Socknat; 'Socio-economic impact of emigration from a Giza village', by Fatma Khafagi; 'Mechanization decisions in Egyptian agriculture', by Wayne N. Dyer, Shawky Imam; 'The social impact of mechanization', by Nicholas S. Hopkins; 'Public policy and the demand for mechanization in Egyptian agriculture', by Wayne N. Dyer, Carl H. Gotsch; 'Agricultural prices, farm mechanization, and the demand for labor', by William Cuddihy; 'Wages, prices, and farm mechanization in Egypt: the need for an integrated policy', by Alain de Janvry, K. Subbarao; and 'Mechanical technology in Egyptian, Indian, and Pakistani agriculture: an induced innovation perspective', by Carl H. Gotsch.

840 **The agricultural policy of Muḥammad 'Alī in Egypt.**
Helen Anne B. Rivlin. Cambridge, Massachusetts: Harvard University Press, 1961. 393p. maps. bibliog.

This excellent study describes land tenure and the changes introduced between 1798 and 1815, the reform after 1815, and the failure of the Egyptian administrative system. Egypt's agricultural and irrigation practices are described. This study concludes that insofar as Muhammad Ali had an agricultural policy, it was merely one aspect of his fiscal policy and inseparable from it.

841 The Egyptian agrarian reform 1952-1962.
Gabriel S. Saab.   London: Oxford University Pres, 1967. 221p. maps. bibliog.

A detailed study of the agrarian reform, the various laws and measures, and the immediate effects. The author discusses the technical aspects of the reform – the distribution of expropriated estates, the co-operative organizations, etc., and the economic, social and financial aspects of the land distribution programme. Part 3 considers agrarian policies and the second agrarian reform.

842 Irrigation water distribution along branch canals in Egypt: economic effects.
Melvin D. Skold, Shinnawi Abdel Atty el-Shinnawi, M. Lotfy Nasr.   *Economic Development and Cultural Change*, vol. 32, no. 3 (April 1984), p. 547-67.

An evaluation of some of the economic costs of inadequate facilities and systems for the distribution of water along the reaches of a branch canal in Egypt. Some remedies are prescribed.

843 U.A.R. desert development and land reclamation projects.
Cairo: General Desert Development Organization, 1961. 55p. maps.

Presents brief reports on desert development and land reclamation projects begun since 1952 in the Nile Valley; these included, in 1961, the New Valley, Natroun Valley, the north-east coast, Mariout and East Canal.

844 Egyptian land reclamation since the revolution.
Sarah P. Voll.   *Middle East Journal*, vol. 34, no. 2 (Spring 1980), p. 127-48.

This paper surveys the history of land reclamation since 1952, and addresses some of the issues which that effort has raised. Any economic evaluation is certain to raise doubts concerning the value of the undertaking.

Rural resettlement in Egypt's reclaimed lands: an evaluation of a case study in the northwestern Nile delta.
See item no. 423.

Under-employment in Egyptian agriculture.
See item no. 860.

Transport

845 Egyptian railways in 125 years, 1852-1977.
Cairo: Egyptian Railways Press, 1977. 271p. map.

An historical survey of the various stages of development of the Egyptian railways from their beginnings in 1852 until 1977. The book describes the construction operations, the progress achieved in spite of unfavourable economic circumstances, and the plans made for both the immediate and long-term future.

846 Middle East railways.
Hugh Hughes. Harrow, England: Continental Railway Circle, 1981. 128p.

After an introductory chapter, covering the Middle East as a whole, the railways of each major region are dealt with in turn and a special section is devoted to the military activities of 1939-45, which affected all the countries of the area. Egyptian railways are well covered.

847 Asymmetrical development and transport in Egypt, 1800-1914.
Charles Issawi. In: *Beginnings of modernization in the Middle East. The nineteenth century*. Edited by William R. Polk, Richard L. Chambers. Chicago, Illinois; London: University of Chicago Press, 1968, p. 383-400.

The history of Egypt during the period 1800-1914 shows a marked asymmetry between economic and social development. The purpose of this paper is to discuss some aspects of this asymmetry, to attempt a general explanation in the light of experience in other regions of the world and in other Middle Eastern countries, and to explore in more detail one of its particular aspects, the development of transport.

848 **A methodology for intercity transportation planning in Egypt.**
Fred Moavenzadeh, Michael J. Markow, Brian Brademeyer,
Kamal Nabil Ali Safwat. *Transportation Research*, vol. 17, no. 6
(November 1983), p. 481-90.

A description of the development of the Egypt Intercity Transportation Model.
The model was developed to explore alternative policies of transportation
investment, maintenance, operation and pricing, and to predict the cost impacts
and performance of the transportation system as a result of the pursuit of
different policies.

Employment, Manpower and Labour Movements

849 **The Egyptian 'brain drain': a multidimensional problem.**
Nazih Ayubi. *International Journal of Middle East Studies*, vol. 15, no. 4 (November 1983), p. 431-50.

An analysis of the emigration of qualified professional university graduates from Egypt. The author discusses its extent, the incentives that exist, and the advantages and disadvantages.

850 **Egyptian guilds in modern times.**
Gabriel Baer.   Jerusalem: Israel Oriental Society, 1964. 149p. bibliog. (Oriental Notes and Studies, No. 8).

The author considers in turn the guilds in Ottoman Egypt; guilds in modern Egypt; the structure of the guilds; the functions of the guilds and their sheikhs; and the decline and disappearance of the guilds. A list of Egyptian guilds is included.

851 **The corporatization of the Egyptian labor movement.**
Robert Bianchi.   *Middle East Journal*, vol. 40, no. 3 (Summer 1986), p. 429-44.

The author seeks to illustrate three important aspects of the development of the Egyptian labour movement and its changing relations with the state. Firstly, Egypt's governments have gradually restructured the union movement from pluralist to corporatist forms of organization. Secondly, the long-term consequences of corporatist policies have been to strengthen and selectively coopt working class organizations rather than to exclude them from the policy-making process. Thirdly, this process of corporatization has already generated new tensions throughout the union hierarchy which may help to promote the re-emergence of pluralism both in the labour movement and in the political system as a whole.

204

852 **Egypt: a frustrated labor exporter?**
J.S. Birks, C.A. Sinclair. *Middle East Journal*, vol. 33, no. 3
(Summer 1979), p. 288-303.
An analysis of Egypt's situation as a labour exporter to the oil-rich Arab
countries. The authors believe that the period of marked expansion in the export
of Egyptian manpower is over, and they predict that by 1985 there will be less
than one million Egyptians working abroad. Subsequently their forecast has
proved to be correct.

853 **Labour and politics in Egypt, 1919-1939.**
Marius Deeb. *International Journal of Middle East Studies*,
vol. 10, no. 2 (August 1979), p. 187-203.
The author analyses the rise and development of a new labour movement in
Egypt between the two world wars. As the history of the movement was
inextricably linked to the Wafd as well as to the competing political forces in
Egypt at the time, he examines the extent to which the various political parties
and personalities were able to hamper the development of an independent trade
union movement during those years. He also discusses the factors which assisted
or hindered, at different times, the promulgation of labour laws, and views the
achievements of the trade union movement (in different sub-periods) in terms of
its success in satisfying the demands of workers, which were opposed by the
predominantly foreign local bourgeoisie.

854 **Facts and figures on investments and employment.**
M.E.N. Economic Weekly, vol. 23, no. 50 (December 1984),
p. 10-14.
Actual public sector investment spending for 1983-84 totalled L.E. 5.3 billion
while private sector investment totalled L.E. 1.45 billion. Tables show investments and employment by sector and project.

855 **Employment opportunities and equity in a changing economy:**
Egypt in the 1980s: a labour market approach.
Bent Hansen, Samir Radwan. Geneva: International Labour
Office, 1982. 293p.
This volume is the report of an inter-agency team financed by the United Nations
Development Programme and organized by the International Labour Office. The
tasks assigned to the team are covered in the following chapters of the report:
Employment and demographic trends – chapters 3,4,5,7,9, and 12; Education and
training – chapters 4,10,11, and 13; Sectoral analysis – chapters 4, 9 and 10;
Export promotion – chapters 8 and 9; Income distribution, poverty and basic
needs – chapters 6, 9. and 14; and Policy analysis – chapters 9 and 14.

856 **Employment planning in Egypt: an insurance policy for the future.**
Bent Hansen, Samir Radwan. *International Labour Review*,
vol. 121, no. 5 (September 1982), p. 535-51.
A survey and analysis of the labour market in Egypt in 1982 with specialist
recommendations for future planning.

857 **The informal sector in an intermediate city: a case in Egypt.**
Michael Hofmann. *Economic Development and Cultural Change*,
vol. 34, no. 2 (1986), p. 263-77.

Discusses the informal sector in Faiyum, the labour force, and the service
industries which form an important part of this economy.

858 **Egyptian labor abroad: mass participation and modest returns.**
Robert J. Latowsky. *MERIP Reports*, vol. 14, no. 4, issue no. 123
(May 1984), p. 11-18.

In 1978 Egypt's labour force abroad represented 11.5% of the Egyptian labour
force, a total of 2.1 million people, 1.3 million of whom were in the Middle East.
They worked primarily in the construction industry. As a result of their
emigration there were sharp increases in wages in the construction industry and
agriculture and manpower shortages in the woodworking industry.

859 **Export of Egyptian schoolteachers to Saudi Arabia and Kuwait: a
cost benefit analysis.**
Suzanne A. Messiha. Cairo: American University in Cairo Press,
1980. 91p. (Cairo Papers in Social Science, Vol. 3, Monograph 4).

An evaluation of the costs and benefits to Egypt of the migration of large
numbers of teachers to the Gulf states. Teachers currently working in the two
states were surveyed to ascertain their reasons for migration, and a model of the
pattern of emigration was drawn up and tested against the results.

860 **Under-employment in Egyptian agriculture.**
Amir Mohie-Eldin. In: *Manpower and employment in Arab
countries: some critical issues.* Geneva: International Labour
Office, 1975, p. 110-39.

This well-documented paper, from a volume of selected papers and reports of an
ILO/ECWA seminar on manpower and employment planning in Arab countries,
held in Beirut, May 1975, is devoted to an examination in quantitative terms of
whether under-employment exists in Egyptian agriculture and on what scale, and
to an investigation of the factors lying behind this phenomenon.

861 **Labor force and employment in Egypt: a demographic and socio-
economic analysis.**
Mostafa H. Nagi, foreword by Edward G. Stockwell. New York;
London: Praeger, 1971. 285p. bibliog. (Praeger Special Studies in
International Economics and Development).

A study of the impact of population trends, especially since the end of the Second
World War, on the size and structure of the labour force and on the employment
situation in Egypt. The author is an Egyptian sociologist and population
specialist.

862   **The Egyptian labor force: its dimensions and changing structure, 1907-1960.**
Abdel-Fattah Nassef.   Philadelphia, Pennsylvania: Population Studies Center, 1970. 339p. bibliog. (Analytical and Technical Reports, 9).

A study of the size, growth, composition, structure, and extent of utilization of the Egyptian labour force. Dependent primarily on data provided by population censuses, which for Egypt are available over a period of many decades, the analysis emphasizes degrees of comparison in relation to the factors of population growth, economic development, and social change.

863   **The brain drain in Egypt.**
Saneya Abdel Wahab Saleh.   Cairo: American University in Cairo Press, 1983. 2nd ed. 136p. bibliog. (Cairo Papers in Social Science, Vol. II, Monograph 5).

A study of the attitudinal and social structural aspects of the brain drain as represented by the Egyptian case, concentrating especially on the reasons behind crucial decisions.

Migration and the selectivity of change: Egyptian peasant women in Iraq.
See item no. 586.

Rich and poor states in the Middle East: Egypt and the New Arab Order.
See item no. 771.

University education and the labour market in the Arab Republic of Egypt.
See item no. 883.

Statistics

864 **Annuaire statistique. Al-kitāb al-sanawī al-'āmm (Statistical yearbook).**
Cairo: Ministère des Finances, Département de la Statistique et du Recensement, 1909-64. annual, but irregular.

Exact title varies. It was published in Arabic and French until it was succeeded by the *Statistical yearbook* (q.v.) which was first published in an Arabic-only edition in 1961. The *Annuaire* contains data on climate, population, health, education, libraries and museums, law, agriculture, health, transport and communications, trade, national income and expenditure, and municipalities.

865 **Statistical abstract of the Arab Republic of Egypt.**
Cairo: Central Agency for Mobilisation and Statistics, 1967/68-1971/72- . annual.

This is a shortened version of the statistical yearbook. The first English edition, entitled *Statistical abstract of the United Arab Republic 1951/52-1967/68*, was published in 1969. Data are presented for several recent years, together with a comparison year of 1952, on the following subjects: population, health, social affairs, education, housing, and various sectors of the economy. Data concern only Egypt, even during the years of the UAR.

866 **Statistical yearbook, Arab Republic of Egypt.**
Cairo: Central Agency for Public Mobilisation and Statistics, 1961- . annual.

This is an English translation of *Al-kitāb al-iḥṣā'ī al-sanawī*, which contains data for recent years and the comparison year 1952. Statistics are presented on population, agriculture, industry and oil, transport and communication, health, social affairs, housing, education, information, tourism and economy. The title varies – it was published as *Statistical handbook* from 1964 to 1972. Data concern only Egypt, even during the years of the union with Syria.

208

867   **Statistical yearbook, Arab Republic of Egypt.**
Cairo: Central Agency for Public Mobilisation and Statistics,
1960- . pocket-book ed. annual.
This is a small-format pocket-book edition of the statistical yearbook, exactly
reproduced and therefore having exactly the same title. The English edition was
originally called *Statistical pocket-book United Arab Republic*, then *Statistical
handbook* from 1964 to 1972, and then *Statistical yearbook* following the standard
edition.

868   **UNESCO statistical yearbook, Arab member states.**
Paris: Unesco, 1983-. annual.
An annual volume devoted to data drawn from Unesco surveys and publications,
this yearbook contains over 500 statistical charts which provide detailed data on
education, manpower and expenditure, book production, newspapers and
broadcasting, cinema and theatre. A standard reference tool which lists all its
sources.

869   **United Arab Republic statistical atlas 1952-1966.**
Cairo: Central Agency for Public Mobilisation and Statistics, 1968.
123p. maps.
A volume of charts and tables covering the following subjects: population,
employment and wages, the national economy, agriculture and agrarian reform,
industry, foreign trade, transport and communications, education, and services.
All data refer only to Egypt.

870   **Mufakirrat al-iḥṣā'āt al-ijtimā'īyah** (Annual of social statistics).
Cairo: Ministry of Social Affairs, 1966- . annual.
The material for 1974 and 1975 was published in 1978 in one volume (423p.). Part
1 covered administrative statistics about the Ministry's staff and social centres,
and the distribution of social services according to type of activity. Part 2 gives
statistics of social development, and also includes a brief census of the population
by governorates. Previously published as *Al-kitāb al-sanawī li'l-iḥṣā'āt al-
ijtimā'īya.*

Education

871 **The nationalization of Arabic and Islamic education in Egypt: Dar al-'Ulum and al-Azhar.**
Lois A. Aroian. Cairo: American University in Cairo Press, 1983. 80p. bibliog. (Cairo Papers in Social Science, Vol. 6, Monograph 4).

Describes the vital roles of Dar al-'Ulum, the first university-level Arabic teacher training institution, and of al-Azhar University, in the nationalization of Islamic and Arabic education in Egypt.

872 **The development and expansion of education in the United Arab Republic.**
Amir Boktor. Cairo: American University in Cairo Press, 1963. 182p.

A complete survey of the Egyptian educational system one decade after the revolution of 1952. The author includes enrolment statistics, curriculum requirements, regulations, fees, and pay scales for all levels from the primary to the postgraduate.

873 **Education in Egypt.**
Judith Cochran. London: Croom Helm, 1986. 161p.

This volume covers the roots of modern education in Egypt, education during the British occupation, 1882-1920, the nationalization of education, 1920-1952, the socialization of education, 1952-1970, the open door educational policy, 1970-1981, and the reorganization of mass education. The author also discusses foreign assistance from USAID and the World Bank for Egyptian education.

874 **Al-Azhar: a millennium of Muslim learning.**
Bayard Dodge. Washington, DC: Middle East Institute, 1961.
239p.
A detailed account of the history of the most prestigious and oldest Muslim
university in Cairo. The author examines the historic role of al-Azhar in
preserving Islamic culture from 970 AD to the present.

875 **Egypt.**
In: *Education in the Middle East.* Edited by Leslie C. Schmida,
with Deborah G. Keenum. Washington, DC: America-Mideast
Educational & Training Services, 1983, p. 23-32. bibliog.
Provides a description of the structure of the Egyptian educational system from
the primary to the university level.

876 **Egyptian higher education: retrospect and prospect.**
Mohamed Samir el-Sayed Hassanein. PhD thesis, University of
London Institute of Education, 1966. 2 vols. bibliog.
This study investigates the development of higher education in Egypt in the light
of socio-economic conditions, particularly manpower needs, throughout the
period under examination, which includes roughly the last two centuries.

877 **An introduction to the history of education in modern Egypt.**
J. Heyworth-Dunne. London: Frank Cass, 1968. New
impression. 442p. bibliog.
A chronological study, first published in 1939 by Luzac, of the development of the
educational system and educational practice in Egypt from the 18th century to the
end of the 19th. Covers Muslim as well as non-Muslim education, and examines
civil and religious education for both sexes. Includes statistics for schools and a
glossary.

878 **The future of culture in Egypt.**
Taha Hussein, translated from the Arabic by Sidney Glazer.
Washington, DC: American Council of Learned Societies, 1954.
164p. (American Council of Learned Societies Near Eastern
Translation Program, No. 9).
This book, written by a great Egyptian writer and former minister of education,
is an important source for the history of education in Egypt.

879 **Education in modern Egypt: ideals and realities.**
Georgie D.M. Hyde. London; Boston, Massachusetts:
Routledge & Kegan Paul, 1978. 225p. bibliog.
Discusses the current problems facing education in Egypt – especially modernization and an expanding population – and describes the structure of the system and
the administrative organization. This book covers all sectors of education,
ordinary, technical and higher education.

Education

880 **University expansion and student life in Egypt.**
M. Martin. In: *Islamic law and change in Arab society.* Beirut:
Dar El-Mashreq Publishers for the Centre for the Study of the
Modern Arab World, Saint Joseph University, 1978, p. 187-211.
(CEMAM Reports, Vol. 4).
In this essay the author sets out the dominant facets of student life in Egypt. The
democratization and expansion of secondary education and the increasing number
of university centres have brought in their wake structural changes in the youth
population which are most clearly manifested in the conditions of student life.
These changes highlight the pressing problems of administering an education
which is now more widely available than ever before, problems which include the
utilization of time and space, and eventual adaptation to future employment.

881 **Education in the Arab world.**
Byron G. Massialas, Samir Ahmed Jarrar. New York: Praeger,
1983. 373p. (Praeger Special Studies in Comparative Education).
The author's purpose in writing this book is to identify and analyse key
educational issues in the Arab world in the light of recent developments and
trends. Egypt is mentioned in every chapter and the study is supported by
statistics about every facet of educational activities in all the Arab countries.

882 **Cairo University and the orientalists.**
Donald Malcolm Reid. *International Journal of Middle East
Studies*, vol. 19, no. 1 (February 1987), p. 51-76.
This article shows the importance, in introducing Western techniques of critical
scholarship into Egypt, of European orientalists and their Egyptian successors at
the university, and sketches the involvement of different national schools of
European orientalism at the university. The case studies used demonstrate the
vehemence of the reaction that orientalist-influenced scholarship can stir up. Brief
attention is given to the views and actions of individual orientalists who taught at
Cairo, and other foci of Egyptian debate are mentioned in passing: religious
journals, such as *al-Manar*; the Arabic Language Academy; al-Azhar and its
affiliates; and massive books, such as Najib al-'Aqiqi's defence and Muhammad
al-Bahi's denunciation of orientalism.

883 **University education and the labour market in the Arab Republic of
Egypt.**
Bikas C. Sanyal, Abdel Aziz el-Koussy, Richard Noonan,
Mohamed Khairy Harby, Shafik Balbaa, Lahcène Yaici. Oxford,
England: Pergamon Press, 1982. 264p. bibliog. (UNESCO
International Institute for Educational Planning).
The rapid expansion of higher education in Egypt has created as many problems
as it has solved, especially in the context of the 'guaranteed employment' scheme
for university graduates initiated in 1961. This study examines Egypt's manpower
and labour force, its education system, and the worlds of higher education and
work.

884 **Education in Egypt.**
Abdel Aziz Soliman. In: *Education in Africa, a comparative survey.* A. Babs Fafunwa, J.U. Aisiku. London: Allen & Unwin, 1982, p. 49-61.

After providing a brief historical background, the author examines the organization and control of education, educational administration, finance, primary education, curriculum, the preparatory schools, secondary education, and teacher education.

885 **National education projects in Egypt before the British occupation.**
Fritz Steppat. In: *Beginnings of modernization in the Middle East. The nineteenth century.* Edited by William R. Polk, Richard L. Chambers. Chicago, Illinois; London: University of Chicago Press, 1968, p. 281-97.

A condensed review of the structure and function of the educational system in Egypt before the British occupation in 1882. National education in Egypt before the British occupation consisted of a variety of projects and some attempts to execute them – attempts that were undertaken with insufficient means and insufficient time. But small though the results were, the projects are significant to the student interested in how the peoples of the Middle East became conscious of the need to modernize, what problems were involved in this modernization, and how they set about solving them.

886 **Education and modernization in the Middle East.**
Joseph S. Szyliowicz. Ithaca, New York; London: Cornell University Press, 1973. 477p.

The case of Egypt is considered in chapter 3, 'The introduction of modern education'; chapter 4, 'The creation of national educational systems'; and chapter 5, 'Toward a modern educational system in a revolutionary society'.

Export of Egyptian schoolteachers to Saudi Arabia and Kuwait: a cost benefit analysis.
See item no. 859.

Arab education 1956-1978: a bibliography.
See item no. 983.

Selected bibliography of Arab educational materials, 1976- .
See item no. 993.

Science and Technology

887 **Current problems in science and technology policy: Arab Republic of Egypt; mission report.**
Paris: UNESCO, 1972. 22p. (UNESCO Doc. Code: 2753/RMO.RD/SP).

A report of a UNESCO mission (May-September 1972) on science policy in Egypt. It stresses the need for an estimation of scientific and technological potential, especially in human resources, refers to problems of science education and technical training, and advises on research policy and technology transfer.

888 **Egyptian national system for scientific and technical information.**
Dennis McDonald, and others. Rockville, Maryland: King Research, 1984. 44p. (US National Science Foundation Doc. No. PN-AAP-155).

A report on how to develop bibliographic information services in support of scientific and technical activities in Egypt.

889 **Images of development: Egyptian engineers in search of industry.**
Clement Henry Moore. Cambridge, Massachusetts: MIT Press, 1980. 386p. bibliog.

The major argument of this book is that the 'Nasserite Model', an authoritarian corporatist state following populist and *étatiste* policies, failed to lead Egypt to modernization. The author examines the role of engineers in Egyptian society under Nasser's regime in order to prove his theory.

890 **Education and science in the Arab world.**
Fahim I. Qubain.   New York: Arno Press, 1979. Reprint ed.
515p. bibliog.

This study, which was first published in 1966 (Baltimore, Maryland: Johns Hopkins Press), is divided into two main parts. Part I, consisting of four chapters, provides a very brief survey of elementary, secondary, and vocational education. Its chief purpose is to indicate the effects of lower education on college and science training and to provide, at least roughly, an appreciation of the present and future flow of students from lower to higher levels. Part II, constituting the bulk and main concern of the study, deals with higher education, science training, and scientific manpower. Here the treatment is by country. Science education in Egypt is discussed mainly in chapters 6, 7, and 8. Originally published in 1966.

891 **Egypt.**
Tagi Sagafi-Nejad.   *World Development*, vol. 12, no. 5 (May 1984), p. 567-73.

A study of Egypt's technology exports from 1970 to 1983. The author surveys 23 companies engaged in technology exports and establishes that most transfers involved person-embodied technology and that political-cultural motives took precedence over economic advantages. The recipients of Egypt's technology were mainly state-owned firms in Arab countries. Export of skilled manpower is a prime source of hard currency for Egypt.

892 **Science and technology in the Middle East: a guide to issues, organizations and institutions.**
Ziauddin Sardar.   London; New York: Longman, 1982. 324p. map.

The first part of this volume presents an overview, the second part describes regional organizations, and the third part gives country profiles. Egypt's scientific profile appears on p. 128-43. Includes an appendix providing a directory of major establishments in the Middle East arranged by country.

Cuisine

893   Egyptian cuisine.
Nagwa E. Khalil.   Washington, DC: Worldwide Graphics, 1980.
406p. bibliog.

The author aimed in choosing and preparing the material for this book to make it
truly representative of Egyptian cuisine; to present the recipes in a simple way
which can be followed easily by readers not familiar with Egyptian food; and to
put emphasis on modern cooking methods and techniques rather than the
traditional ones.

894   A book of Middle Eastern food.
Claudia Roden, illustrated by Alta Ann Parkins.   New York:
Alfred A. Knopf, 1972. bibliog.

An excellent cookery book written by a native Egyptian living in England. It
includes recipes from all Middle Eastern countries, but especially Egypt. First
published in 1968 (Harmondsworth, England: Penguin Books).

The Arts

895   **The Academy of Arts silver jubilee.**
    Prism: Quarterly of Egyptian Culture, vol. 10 (October-December
    1984), p. 23-5.
This academy is an umbrella organization which includes the Higher Institute for
Arabic Music, the Conservatoire, the Higher Institute of Ballet, the Higher
Cinema Institute, and other organizations.

896   **Jewels of the pharaohs: Egyptian jewelry of the dynastic period.**
    Cyril Aldred, special photography in Cairo by Albert Shoucair.
    New York: Ballantine Books, 1978. 128p.
One of the few books on this subject, written by a well-known Egyptologist and
art historian. The author studies the materials of which jewellery was made, the
craftsmen and their tools, the techniques and the forms. Includes 173 illustrations,
of which 109 are in colour.

897   **Mahmoud Said.**
    Mahmoud Alnabawi Alshal, translated by Ahmad Kamal.   Cairo:
    Ministry of Culture, 1982. unpaged. (Prism Art Series, 1).
Consists of a brief introduction about the life and work of this famous Egyptian
painter (1897-1964), followed by 33 plates of his works.

898   **A history of Egyptian architecture.**
    Alexander Badawy.   Cairo: the author, 1954 (Vol. I); Berkeley,
    California: University of California Press, 1966-68 (Vols. II-III). 3
    vols. bibliog.
This encyclopaedic and fully illustrated work was written by an Egyptian architect
and archaeologist who is an international authority on the subject. Volume I

217

covers the period from the earliest times to the end of the Old Kingdom; volume II covers the first intermediate period, the Middle Kingdom, and the second intermediate period; and volume III covers the Empire (the New Kingdom) from the 18th Dynasty to the end of the 20th Dynasty (1580-1085 BC).

899   **Abdel Wahab Marsi: visions of Egyptian contemporary art.**
Hussein Bikar.   *Prism: Quarterly of Egyptian Culture*, vol. 11 (Jan.-March 1985), p. 13-15.

The author, an artist himself, writes about an artist who has ingeniously found a means by which the ancient can be combined with the modern in his work.

900   **Muhammadan architecture in Egypt and Palestine.**
Martin S. Briggs.   New York: Da Capo Press, 1974. Reprint ed. 243p. bibliog.

A reprint of the work originally published in 1924 (Oxford: Clarendon Press). After a general discussion of the first mosques built by the Muslims, the next chapters discuss the historical background of the mosque of Ibn Tulun at Cairo (868-969), the Fatimids in Cairo (969-1171); the architecture of Saladin and the influence of the crusades (1171-1250); the buildings of the Turkish Mamlukes (1250-1382); the buildings of the Circassian Mamlukes (1382-1517); and architecture after the Turkish conquest in 1517. The later chapters deal with domestic architecture, Saracen ornament, and craftsmanship in stone, marble, stucco, woodwork, metalwork, glass and ceramics. There are many black-and-white illustrations and drawings.

901   **Art of Islam: language and meaning.**
Titus Burckhardt, with photographs by Roland Michaud, translated by J. Peter Hobson, foreword by Seyyed Hossein Nasr.
London: World of Islam Festival Publishing Company, 1976. 204p.

This fully illustrated book presents the reader with detailed documentation of every aspect of Islamic art. Some of Cairo's most famous Islamic monuments are illustrated and discussed, as are also examples from Egypt of Islamic architecture and the minor and decorative arts.

902   **The inspiration of Egypt: its influence on British artists, travellers, and designers, 1700-1900.**
Edited by Patrick Conner.   Brighton, England: Borough Council, 1983. 168p. bibliog.

The catalogue of an exhibition held at Brighton Museum, May-July 1983 and at Manchester City Art Gallery, August-September 1983. Includes 421 illustrations.

903 **The Egyptian revival: an introductory study of a recurring theme in the history of taste.**
James Stevens Curl. London: Allen and Unwin, 1982. 249p. bibliog.

Traces, with numerous unusual illustrations, the use of 'Egyptian' motifs, particularly in architecture, from the Graeco–Roman period down to the 20th century (cf. item no. 902).

904 **Arab art as seen through the monuments of Cairo from the 7th century to the 18th.**
Prisse D'Avennes, translated from the French by J.I. Erythraspis. Paris: Le Sycomore; London: Al Saqi Books, 1983. 265p.

The most comprehensive book on Islamic art and architecture in Egypt, this was the product of years of meticulous field research and nearly ten years of subsequent labour, and was first published in 1877 as *L'Art arabe d'après les monuments du Kaire depuis le VIIe siècle jusqu'à la fin du XVIIIe* (Paris: A. Morel). The author was one of the leading Egyptologists, orientalists and travellers of the 19th century. Illustrated with 200 colour and 34 black and white plates.

905 **The art of the Copts.**
Pierre M. DuBourquet, translated from the German by Caryll Hay-Shaw. New York: Crown Publishers; London: Methuen, 1971. 234p. bibliog.

A well-illustrated account of the history of Coptic art and architecture from the 1st to the 13th centuries AD, with reference to the influence of pre-Coptic art on the ornament, themes and techniques of the sculpture, painting, ivory work and architecture of the period.

906 **Egyptian students in Europe and the origins of Egyptian theatre (1834-1944).**
Prism: Quarterly of Egyptian Culture, vol. 8 (April-May 1984), p. 27-30; vol. 9 (July-September 1984), p. 27-29.

An account of Egyptian students who received their education in Europe and then developed Egyptian theatre on the basis of European techniques.

907 **Egyptian ornament.**
P. Fořtová-Šamalova, text by M. Vilimkova, graphic design by Vladimir Vácha, translated by Till Gottheiner. London: Allan Wingate, 1963. 162p.

A book published in the belief that Egyptian ornament must be given serious consideration by anyone who wishes to study ornament closely, be it historically or typologically, and that Egyptian ornament holds a unique position in the history of art.

The Arts

908 **The Egyptian cinema: industry and art in a changing society.**
Jane Gaffney. *Arab Studies Quarterly*, vol. 9, no. 1 (Winter 1987), p. 53-75.
An attempt to explore some aspects of the relationship between the cinema and social change in the Arab world. The class composition of the majority of the audience means that the emphasis has been on entertainment, and films have tended to ignore the problems of rural communities.

909 **Mālamiḥ miṣrīyah.** (Egyptian features.)
With an Arabic introduction by Badr Eddin Abū Ghazi. Cairo: General Organization of the Book [n.d.]. 5p. + 22 plates.
A collection of photographs of works by Egyptian artists which are representative of modern Egyptian art. Among the artists represented are Mahmud Said, Mohammed Naji, Margaret NaKhla, Hussein BiKar, Hamid Nada, Jazibiya Sirri and Mohammed Sabri.

910 **The carved masonry domes of mediaeval Cairo.**
Christel Kessler. Cairo: American University in Cairo Press; London: Art and Archaeology Research Papers, 1976. 40p.
An in-depth illustrated study of the art and architecture of the domes and minarets of the Mamluke era in late mediaeval Cairo.

911 **An interview with Faten Hamama.**
Khairiya Khairy. *Prism: Quarterly of Egyptian Culture*, vol. 10 (October-December 1984), p. 20-2. illus.
Faten Hamama is a leading Egyptian actress.

912 **The art of the Saracens in Egypt.**
Stanley Lane-Poole. London: Chapman & Hall, 1935. 260p.
An account of Islamic art and architecture, with reference to stone and plaster, mosaic, woodwork, ivory, metalwork, glass, heraldry on glass and metal, pottery, textile fabrics and illuminated manuscripts. Illustrated with 108 woodcuts.

913 **Egypt: architecture, sculpture, painting in three thousand years.**
Kurt Lange, Max Hirmer, with contributions by Eberhard Otto and Christiane Desroches-Noblecourt, and additional material in the 4th German ed. translated by Judith Filson, Barbara Taylor. London; New York: Phaidon, 1968. 4th ed. 559p. maps. bibliog.
A most important and profusely illustrated work. This greatly revised edition contains many new photographs of important works of art, and the text has been considerably enlarged.

914 **Mamluk costume: a survey.**
Louis A. Mayer. Geneva: Albert Kundig, 1952. 119p.
A descriptive text is accompanied by twenty illustrations of the dress of the Mamlukes of Egypt and Syria.

915   **Art of Ancient Egypt.**
Kazimierz Michalowski, conceived, designed and executed under
the supervision of Lucien Mazenod, translated and adapted from
the Polish and the French by Norbert Geterman.   New York:
Abrams, 1969. 600p. 3 maps. bibliog.
This work, which has over 800 illustrations, is an excellent documentary record of
Ancient Egyptian art. It is well documented and presents the art chronologically
through the various historical periods, including the Coptic period. An
introduction on each period is included.

916   **Great sculpture of ancient Egypt.**
Kazimierz Michalowski.   New York: Reynal & Co, 1978. 191p.
bibliog.
A superbly illustrated survey of the sculpture of all periods.

917   **Community, craft and lore: the tradition and technique of Egyptian
arabesque woodwork.**
Assad Nadim.   Cairo: American University in Cairo Press, 1979.
100p.
An examination and detailed description of the background and methods of
master craftsmen whose work is spread throughout the Islamic world, including a
discussion of Arabesque design, which is considered from the point of view of the
designer himself, rather than from that of the academic or religious mystic.

918   **The new Cairo opera house.**
Prism: Quarterly of Egyptian Culture, vol. 11 (January-March
1985), p. 2-4. illus.
Describes the new opera house being built in Cairo with the assistance of a
Japanese grant.

919   **Egyptian drawings.**
William H. Peck, photographs by John G. Ross, foreword by Cyril
Aldred.   New York: E.P. Dutton, 1978. 208p. bibliog.
A selection of Ancient Egyptian drawings covering the following topics: man,
woman, the royal image, music and dance, fable and humour, hunting and
combat, animal life, and architecture. Detailed comments on these drawings are
provided.

920   **Contemporary art in Egypt.**
Edited by Hamed Said, with photographs by D. Kazic.   Cairo:
Ministry of Culture and National Guidance in cooperation with the
Publishing House 'Jugoslavija', 1964. 6p. + 144 plates.
This book consists of an introduction of 6 pages on modern Egyptian art, 120
black-and-white plates, and 22 coloured plates. These 144 plates reproduce
examples of the work of 58 Egyptian artists.

The Arts

921 **European musical instruments reflect Egyptian influence.**
Fathy el-Sanafawi. *Prism: Quarterly of Egyptian Culture*, vol. 9
(July-September 1984), p. 21-23, 30.
An illustrated article on Ancient Egyptian musical instruments, with a comparison
between them and European examples.

922 **Principles of Egyptian art.**
Heinrich Schäfer, edited with an epilogue by Emma Brunner-
Traut, translated from the German and edited with an introduction
by John Baines. Oxford, England: Clarendon Press, 1974. 470p.
bibliog.
Schäfer's fundamental work on the way in which objects are represented in
Egyptian two- and three-dimensional art was first published in 1919, and enlarged
and revised by the author up to his death. Baines translates the posthumous
fourth German edition of 1963 with minor adjustments to the text, but the notes
and references are massively expanded and updated, and the illustrations
improved. Baines' edition was republished with corrections in 1986 (Warminster,
England: Aris & Phillips).

923 **The art and architecture of ancient Egypt.**
W. Stevenson Smith, revised with additions by William Kelly
Simpson. Harmondsworth, England: Penguin Books, 1981. 501p.
map. bibliog.
The first edition, published in 1958 (corrected reprint 1965), was the standard
survey of Egyptian art. The text of this new edition has been sensitively brought
up to date, chiefly by additions and revisions to the notes, and the number of
illustrations is increased.

924 **Egypt: paintings from tombs and temples.**
Introduction by Jacques Vandier. Greenwich, Connecticut: New
York Graphic Society, by arrangement with UNESCO, 1956. 10p.
+ 32 plates.
A four-page introduction is followed by 32 plates of paintings from Ancient
Egyptian tombs and temples.

925 **Cultural policy in Egypt.**
Magdi Wahba. Paris: UNESCO, 1972. 95p. (Studies and
Documents on Cultural Policies).
Describes Egyptian cultural policy from the following points of view: the
assessment of cultural needs, administrative and financial structures, the Ministry
of Culture, the conservation of the cultural heritage, state patronage, and the
training of cultural agents. Includes several organizational charts.

926   **Ancient Egyptian jewellery.**
       Alix Wilkinson. London: Methuen, 1971. 266p. bibliog.
A history of jewellery in Ancient Egypt from the pre-dynastic period to the late period.

927   **Ancient Egyptian designs.**
       Eva Wilson, designs by Roger Davies.   London: British Museum Publications, 1986. 175p.
A compendium of hundreds of selected designs which represent all periods of Ancient Egyptian history. The designs include motifs from paintings, jewellery, basketry, weaving, dress, pottery, glazed composition ware (faience) and scarab seals.

928   **Egypt: the art of the pharaohs.**
       Irmgard Woldering.   London: Methuen, 1965. 261p. 3 maps. bibliog.
A brief and well-illustrated survey of the essential facts and artistic monuments.

929   **Youssef Chahine.**
       Prism: Quarterly of Egyptian Culture, vol. 9 (July-September 1984), p. 24-6.
A portrait of a leading Egyptian film director.

Islamic Cairo: endangered legacy.
See item no. 62.

Mawsū'at al-masraḥ al-miṣrī: al-bībliyūjrāfīyah, 1900-1930.
(Encyclopedia of the Egyptian theatre: the bibliography, 1900-1930).
See item no. 958.

A bibliography of the architecture, arts and crafts of Islam to 1st Jan. 1960.
See item no. 960.

A bibliography of the architecture, arts and crafts of Islam. Supplement January 1960 to January 1972.
See item no. 961.

Mass Media

930 **A guide to bookshops in Cairo and the Cairo International Book Fair.**
Paul Auchterlonie. *British Society for Middle East Studies Bulletin*, vol. 8, no. 1 (1981), p. 51-9.
A listing and description of bookshops and publishing houses in Cairo. The al-Azhar Square area specializes in Islamic studies, while Ezbekiya Park sells second-hand books and Faggala Street bookshops deal in school and college textbooks. Appendices list additional publishers in Cairo and Alexandria and the participants in the Cairo International Book Fair.

931 **Problems of book development in the Arab world with special reference to Egypt.**
Salib Botros. *Library Trends*, vol. 26, no. 4 (Spring 1978), p. 567-73.
Explains how the publishing industry in the Arab world is faced with a number of challenges which have impeded rapid book development. The book is not understood as a special product and is often treated as an ordinary commodity; as a result, the process of production and distribution is often misunderstood and not handled efficiently. In essence, the lack of a publishing 'infrastructure' and of experts in the field able to produce and market books has hampered the establishment of an effective book industry.

932 **Broadcasting in the Arab world: a survey of radio and television in the Middle East.**
Douglas A. Boyd.   Philadelphia, Pennsylvania: Temple University Press, 1982. 278p. bibliog.
An excellent survey of radio and television systems in the Arab Middle Eastern and North African countries. The section on Egypt (p. 13-49) covers the following

topics: government broadcast administration; prerevolutionary broadcasting – Egyptianization; radio broadcasting after the revolution; radio studio facilities and services; domestic and regional broadcasts; foreign-language and beamed services; radio transmission facilities; Egyptian television; television from 1960-1967, 1967-1974, 1974-1980; set ownership and viewing patterns.

933 **Egypt's role as a major media producer, supplier and distributor to the Arab world: a historical descriptive study.**
Karen Finlon Dajani. PhD dissertation, Temple University, 1980. 282p. bibliog. (Available from University Microfilms International, Ann Arbor, Michigan, order no. NBK 80-14483).

The emphasis of this study is on the export of Egyptian media products to other Arab countries, and it includes a history and overview of the role of the Egyptian News Agency (Middle East News Agency), the Egyptian film industry, the Egyptian daily and periodical press, Egyptian radio and television programme exports, and Egyptian education and training programmes in communications. One of very few studies on this topic.

934 **Occupational status and mass media in rural Egypt.**
Kamal el Menoufi. *International Journal of Middle East Studies*, vol. 13, no. 3 (August 1981), p. 257-69.

This paper was based on empirical social research in six Egyptian villages, which examined the hypothesis that non-peasants, in general, surpass peasants in possession and general usage of mass media facilities. The results of the research support this hypothesis and also suggest that non-peasants are more affected by the forces of changes that seep down through the media from the national policy centre.

935 **Press, politics and power: Egypt's Heikal and *al-Ahram*.**
Munir K. Nasser. Ames, Iowa: Iowa State University Press, 1979. 175p. bibliog.

An account of Mohamed Hassanein Heikal, former editor of the influential newspaper *al-Ahram*, in the context of the Middle Eastern press and politics. The book is not a biography of Heikal, but rather an attempt to represent Heikal as thoroughly as possible as a unique phenomenon in Arab journalism and to discuss in depth his powerful role as the alter ego of President Nasser. Heikal's achievements, personality, thought and journalistic style are analysed in detail. His influence on Egyptian and Arab politics and press is emphasized. The book presents the story from Heikal's point of view, but the views of his opponents are given in a separate chapter.

936 **The book publishing industry in Egypt.**
Nadia A. Rizk. *Library Trends*, vol. 26, no. 4 (Spring 1978), p. 553-65.

The author focuses on three aspects of the Egyptian publishing industry: title selection processes, pricing methods, and channels of distribution. Since descriptive information on the industry is scarce, the orientation of this paper is towards exploration rather than definitive analysis. Egypt provides a particularly good case study of Arab publishing, since it is the country with the most extensive publishing operations in the Arab world and its influence is widespread.

937   **A book world directory of the Arab countries, Turkey and Iran.**
Compiled by Anthony Rudkin, Irene Butcher.   London: Mansell; Detroit: Gale, 1981. 143p.

The section on Egypt in this book (p. 8-23) includes names and addresses of libraries in the major Egyptian cities, names, addresses, telephone and telex numbers of newspapers and magazines, and names of major periodicals with addresses, telephone and telex numbers.

938   **A comparison of political persuasion on Radio Cairo in the eras of Nasser and Sadat.**
Mahmoud Ibrahim Shalabieh. PhD dissertation,   Ohio State University, 1985. 303p. bibliog. (Available from University Microfilms International, Ann Arbor, Michigan, order no. NBK 85-26247).

Explains and examines the role of Radio Cairo as a tool of persuasion and propaganda in the hands of the Nasser and Sadat governments. Whereas the Egyptian mass media, particularly radio, were employed by President Sadat to reconcile the masses to the peace with Israel, in the era of President Nasser Radio Cairo played a different role, that of influencing the masses in favour of revolution. An excellent study.

Libraries and Museums

939   **Introduction to Egyptian archaeology with special reference to the Egyptian Museum, Cairo.**
Edited by R. Engelbach.   Cairo: General Organization for Government Printing Offices, 1961. 392p. map. bibliog.
The aim of this volume is to give the visitor or student who visits the Cairo Museum a greater understanding of the objects.

940   **Catalogue of Egyptian revenue stamps, with Sudanese revenues and Egyptian cinderellas.**
Peter R. Feltus, with an historical note by Jon Manchip White.
Southfield, Michigan: Pastilion Publications, 1982. 209p.
This extremely comprehensive handbook and catalogue, which contains detailed listings and prices, covers all the various forms of revenue stamps from the first general issue in 1887 to the Writer's Union Tax stamps of 1979. The Egyptians have a multitude of revenue stamps issued to collect all the different types of tax that are required including salt tax, cigarette and match tax, and the taxes on such items and services as playing cards, airports, ID cards, legal witnessing fees, amusements, hospital treatment, and free clinic treatment.

941   **Guide to U.A.R. government publications at the A.U.C. Library.**
Cairo: American University in Cairo, Periodicals and Documents Department, 1965. 61p. In English and Arabic.
This guide comprises the holdings in 1965 of the AUC library of government publications and publications of the Arab League. Arranged alphabetically according to the various titles of the publishing agency.

227

Libraries and Museums

942 **Training Egyptian information specialists: a multi-faceted system approach, final report.**
Bahaa el-Hadidy. Washington, DC: Catholic University of America, School of Library and Information Science, 1982. 222p. (US National Science Foundation Doc. No. PN-AAP-016).
A report on methods of developing professional manpower to support information systems and services in Egypt.

943 **Introduction of machine-readable cataloguing at the National Information and Documentation Centre, Arab Republic of Egypt.**
Paris: UNESCO, 1977. 7p. (UNESCO Doc. Code: FMR/BER/PGI/77/144).
Report of a UNESCO mission which visited Egypt from December 1976 to 26 January 1977, and examined library automation with particular reference to the automation of cataloguing processes at the Egyptian National Information and Documentation Centre. The report recommends an information science training course in computerized cataloguing for the personnel of the Centre.

944 **The Coptic Museum in Old Cairo.**
Jill Kamil. *Archaeology*, vol. 40, no. 3 (May/June 1987), p. 39-45.
An informative, up-to-date and illustrated article about the Coptic Museum, undergoing renovation at the time of writing. Written by a specialist on ancient and mediaeval Egypt's tourist attractions.

945 **The Luxor Museum of Ancient Egyptian art: catalogue.**
Cairo: American Research Center in Egypt, 1979. 219p. maps. bibliog.
This catalogue lists, describes, and illustrates over one hundred sculptures, reliefs, paintings, and products of the minor arts chiefly from the Theban area and ranging in date from the pre-dynastic period to the Islamic period, a span of over four thousand years. The Luxor Museum has only recently been assembled, and includes pieces formerly in the Egyptian Museum, Cairo.

946 **Mechanization of the National Library catalogues: Egypt.**
A. E. Jeffreys. Paris: UNESCO, 1975. 23p. (UNESCO Doc. Code 3158/RMO.RD/DBA).
Report of a UNESCO mission (Oct.-Nov. 1974) on the development of the computerized catalogue at the National Library of Egypt. It considers a system of bibliographic control as a component of the system, describes the introduction of ISBN and ISBD into the system design and discusses the adaptation of computer software to local needs and the Arabic language.

947 **Al-Nashrah Al-Misriyah Lil Matbu'at.** (Accession List of
Publications.)
Cairo: Dar Al-Kutub wa Al-Watha'iq Al-Qawmiyah (National
Library and Archives), 1968- . annual.

The accession list of Arabic and Western-language books acquired by the
National Library of Egypt. Issued in two sections, one for Arabic books, the
other for Western-language books.

948 **Catalog of the Islamic coins, glass weights, dies and medals in the
Egyptian National Library, Cairo.**
Norman D. Nicol, Raafat el-Nabarawy, Jere L. Bacharach.
Malibu, California: Undena Publications, 1982. 314p. (American
Research Center in Egypt Catalogs, No. 3).

One of the richest collections of Islamic numismatic material in the world is
housed in the Egyptian National Library, Cairo. Until the publication of this
study, the 6,400 pieces, including 5,269 coins, 886 glass weights and their
imitations, 164 coin and metal dies, medals, amulets and paper money, were
virtually inaccessible to scholars. For this catalogue every piece has been carefully
identified, and in each case details are given of mint, date, size, weight, and any
unusual inscription, and, whenever possible, a reference to a similarly published
item is included. The approximately 2,200 coins published in the 1897 catalogue
of the Khedival library by Stanley Lane-Poole are cross-referenced. Indexes by
year, mint and dynasty are included, and over 450 pieces are illustrated on 28
plates. An introduction in Arabic is provided.

949 **Department of Librarianship and Archival Studies and University
of Cairo libraries: fact resource paper and evaluation and
recommendations.**
R.P. Palmer, U.E. Mahmoud, M.W. Albin.   Cairo: US Agency
for International Development, Bureau for Near East, 1978.
90p.(Doc. No. PN-AAG-438).

An evaluative report of library and archival education as offered by Cairo
University and the University library.

950 **Preservation of materials at the National Library, Cairo, Egypt.**
Paris: UNESCO, 1975. 13p. (UNESCO Doc. Code:
3154/RMO.RD/DBA).

This UNESCO mission report presents a plan for book preservation at the
National Library of Egypt, with reference to the organization of a laboratory for
conserving archives and books.

Libraries and Museums

951 **Official catalogue: the Egyptian Museum, Cairo.**
Mohamed Saleh, Hourig Sourouzian; photographs by Jürgen
Liepe. Munich, GFR: Prestel Verlag; Mainz, Austria: Verlag
Philipp von Zabern, 1987. 267p.

The English edition of the new, superbly illustrated catalogue, aimed at the
general public, dealing with a selection of the finest objects in the Cairo Museum.

952 **A teledocumentation system for the National Information and
Documentation Center, Arab Republic of Egypt.**
Paris: UNESCO, 1977. 40p. bibliog. map.

Report of a UNESCO mission of April 1977, describing how to develop and
upgrade the services of the National Information and Documentation Centre
through the connection of the Centre to the international information network,
i.e., the databases of the European Space Agency, which operates an online
management system. The report also suggests the creation of an information
storage and retrieval department responsible for all documentary analysis and
literature search activities. In addition, the report explains why a microfiche bank
and the adoption of the international ASV-CODAR system for data processing
activities in Arabic are needed.

953 **University instructional materials project: inputs on library
development, concepts paper.**
Washington, DC: US Agency for International Development,
Office of Development Information and Utilization, 1978. 23p.
(Doc. No. PN-AAG-436).

Contains suggestions for the development of library instruction materials for
university libraries in Egypt.

Bibliographies

954 **Bibliographie géographique de l'Egypte. Vol. 1: Géographie
physique et géographie humaine. Vol. 2: Géographie historique.**
(Geographical bibliography of Egypt. Vol. 1: Physical and human
geography. Vol. 2: Historical geography.)
Henriette Agrel, Henri Munier, edited by H. Lorin.   Cairo:
Institut Français d'Archéologie Orientale pour la Société Royale
de Géographie d'Egypte, 1928-29. 2 vols.
These two volumes contain 6,158 and 2,683 unannotated entries respectively.
They include books, periodical articles, papers, reports and pamphlets in Western
languages, including many in English. The entries are classified by subject and
cover the land and people of Egypt from ancient times to the first quarter of the
20th century.

955 **Suezkanal-bibliographie: eine Auswahl des europäisch-sprachigen
Schrifttums seit 1945.** (Bibliography on the Suez Canal: a selection
of literature in European languages since 1945.)
Munir D. Ahmed, Gesa Mertins.   Hamburg, GFR: Deutsches
Orient Institut, 1974. 59p. (Dokumentationsdienst moderner
Orient, Reihe A, 3).
In spite of the bi-lingual title, the explanatory text of this bibliography is entirely
in German. About 400 books and articles of representative literature on the
subject are listed, and there are good subject and author indexes. Many of the
items included are in English.

Bibliographies

956 **Fihrist wathā'iq al-Qāhirah ḥattā nihāyat 'asr salāṭīn al-mamālik 239-922 AH (853-1516 AD) ma'a nashr wa taḥqīq tis'ah namādhij.**
(Index of the documents in Cairo archives until the end of the Mamluke sultanate, 239-922 AH (853-1516 AD), with detailed study of nine documents.)
Compiled by Muḥammad Muḥammad Amīn. Cairo: Institut Français d'Archéologie Orientale, 1981. 564p. In Arabic. bibliog. (Textes Arabes et Islamiques, no. 16).

Index of the documents related to this period of Egyptian history available in the National Archives at the Citadel, the Ministry of Awqāf, the Coptic Patriarchate and the National Library of Egypt. Has a title-page, contents page and six-page introduction in French, and indexes of names and documents.

957 **Arabic collection: Aziz S. Atiyah Library for Middle East Studies.**
Salt Lake City, Utah: University of Utah Libraries and the Middle East Center, 1968-79. 3 vols.

Each volume is arranged topically according to the Library of Congress subject classification system. Most of the books included were published in Egypt.

958 **Mawsū'at al-masraḥ al-miṣrī: al-bībliyūjrāfīyah, 1900-1930.**
(Encyclopedia of the Egyptian theatre: the bibliography, 1900-1930.)
Ramsīs 'Awaḍ. Cairo: al-Hai'ah al-miṣrīyah al-'āmmah lil-kitāb, 1983. 902p.

This work contains 14,000 entries, and has a subject and name index. It also provides a list of periodicals referred to.

959 **An annotated research bibliography of studies in Arabic, English and French of the *fellah* of the Egyptian Nile, 1798-1955.**
Lyman H. Coult, Jr., with the assistance of Karim Durzi. Coral Gables, Florida: University of Miami Press, 1958. 144p. 2 maps.

This bibliography includes 831 annotated entries for books and journal articles covering the social, cultural, economic, political and religious life of the peasants of Egypt, the *fellaheen*.

960 **A bibliography of the architecture, arts and crafts of Islam to 1st Jan. 1960.**
Sir K. A. C. Creswell. Cairo: American University in Cairo Press, 1961. 1330p.

Creswell's monumental work covers all branches of Islamic architecture, arts and crafts except numismatics and records, and includes 16,000 bibliographic items and a table of periodicals. Many entries throughout the volume deal with Egypt.

961   **A bibliography of the architecture, arts and crafts of Islam.**
Supplement January 1960 to January 1972.
Sir K. A. C. Creswell.   Cairo: American University in Cairo
Press, 1973. 366p.
This supplement continues Creswell's previous work and includes over 4,000
listings.

962   **Dalil al-kitāb al-miṣrī**(Egyptian books in print.)
Cairo: al-Hai'ah al-miṣrīyah al-'āmmah lil-kitāb (Egyptian General
Organization of the Book), 1972-73-. annual.
An annual checklist of books published in Egypt, arranged by authors and titles.

963   **Egypt, North Africa and Sub-Saharan Africa: a dissertation**
bibliography.
Ann Arbor, Michigan: University Microfilms International, 1978.
53p.
Lists 2,633 doctoral dissertations, 88 master's theses and 5 advanced research
papers submitted to American and Canadian universities between 1969 and 1978.
Arranged by subject with author index. Includes many dissertations on Egypt.

964   **Egypt: subject catalogue.**
Cairo: Egyptian National Library Press, 1957-63. 3 vols.
A catalogue of books about Egypt in Western languages in the collection of the
National Library, classified by subject: general pure science, sociology, political
science, administration, economics, law, education, medicine, agriculture,
engineering, transport and communication, commerce, industries, fine arts,
recreation and geography. The third volume is an author index.

965   **Fihrist al-tashrī'āt al-miṣrīyah, 1864-1971.** (Index to Egyptian
legislation, 1864-1971.)
Cairo: al-Hay'ah al-'Ammah li-shu'un al-Mataba'a al-Amiriyah,
1972. 1234p.
An index to the statutes, decrees, ordinances, etc., issued by the heads of state
and official government bodies of Egypt.

966   **An analytical guide to the bibliographies on modern Egypt and the**
Sudan (1798-1972).
Charles L. Geddes.   Denver, Colorado: American Institute of
Islamic Studies, 1972. 78p. (Bibliographic Series, No. 2).
A listing of 135 bibliographies, arranged by author with detailed annotations. An
index of authors, titles, journals, institutions and subjects is included.

Bibliographies

967 **Arabic papyri in the Egyptian National Library.**
Adolf Grohmann.   Cairo: National Library, 1934-63. 6 vols.
These volumes present annotated English translations and photographic repro-
ductions of early Muslim Egyptian materials written on papyrus.

968 **Bibliographie critique de la Commission des Sciences et Arts de
l'Institut d'Egypte.** (A critical bibliography of the Commission of
Sciences and Arts of the Institut d'Egypte.)
Gabriel Guémard.   Cairo: Imprimerie Paul Barbey, 1936. 127p.
An historical and bibliographical study of Bonaparte's Commission of Sciences
and Arts and of the founding of the Institut d'Egypte by that Commission.

969 **Modern European imperialism: a bibliography of books and articles
1815-1972.**
Compiled by John P. Halstead.   Boston, Massachusetts: G. K.
Hall, 1974. 2 vols.
Includes documents, papers, books and articles in Western languages, arranged
by country.

970 **Select bibliography on modern Egypt.**
Gamal-Eddine Heyworth-Dunne.   Cairo: Renaissance Bookshop,
1952. 41p. (Muslim World Series, No. 2).
Contains 167 entries arranged in alphabetical order by author. Some annotations
are long enough to be seen as book reviews.

971 **A bibliography of the Anglo-Egyptian Sudan from the earliest times
to 1937.**
Richard L. Hill.   London: Oxford University Press, 1939. 213p.
A classified listing of books and articles in European languages.

972 **The Middle East in paperback.**
Compiled by Harry N. Howard.   *Middle East Journal*, vol. 18
(1964), p. 355-66; vol. 23 (1969), p. 383-91; vol. 28 (1974), p. 315-
26.
A list of paperbacks in English about the Middle Eastern countries. Many of the
titles are about Egypt.

973 **Islamic movements in Egypt, Pakistan and Iran: an annotated
bibliography.**
Asaf Hussain.   London: Mansell Publishing, 1983. 168p.
The section devoted to Egypt in this annotated bibliography consists of a 12-page
introduction on the Muslim Brothers movement in Egypt, and 108 entries
covering books and journal articles in English.

974 **Development in Egypt: bibliography and informative abstracts of selected research, 1970-1982.**
Frederick C. Huxley.   Berkeley, California: Development
Research Services, 1983. 123p.

This bibliography was compiled for the United States Agency for International
Development, and includes research reports in English, French and Arabic about
development in Egypt. The works were selected and evaluated on the basis of
four criteria: relevance to development, high quality, empirical base, and balance.
The 289 entries are arranged by author; 270 of them are in English.

975 **The literature of Egypt and the Soudan from the earliest times to the year 1885 inclusive.**
Ibrahim-Hilmy, Prince of Egypt.   Nendeln, Lichtenstein: Kraus
Reprint, 1966. Reprint ed. 2 vols.

A bibliography originally published in 1886-87 (London: Trübner) comprising
printed books, periodical writings, papers of learned societies, maps and charts,
ancient papyri, manuscripts, drawings, etc.

976 **Dalīl al-matbūʻāt al-miṣrīyah, 1940-1956.** (Egyptian books in
print, 1940-1956.)
Compiled by Aḥmad Muḥammad Manṣūr, and others.   Cairo:
American University in Cairo Press, 1975. 419p.

Contains 13,797 items, including dissertations, published during a period that
included the Second World War, the Palestine conflict, the 1952 revolution and
the establishment of free public education in Egypt.

977 **Bibliographie économique, juridique et sociale de l'Egypte moderne, 1798-1916.** (Economic, juridical and social bibliography
of modern Egypt, 1798–1916.)
René Maunier.   Cairo: Institut Français d'Archéologie Orientale,
1918. 372p. (Travaux Spéciaux de la Société Sultanier d'Economie
Politique, de Statistique et de Législation, No. 1).

A bibliography consisting of 6,695 entries in French, English and other European
languages with author and subject indexes. Reprinted in 1971 (New York: Burt
Franklin).

978 **The status of the Arab woman: a select bibliography.**
Compiled by Samira Rafidi Meghdessian, under the auspices of the
Institute for Women's Studies in the Arab World, Beirut
University College, Lebanon.   London: Mansell; Westport,
Connecticut: Greenwood Press, 1980. 176p.

This unannotated bibliography aims to provide a listing of research material on
the economic, legal, religious and social status of the Arab woman in the 20th
century. The section on the Egyptian woman contains 159 entries.

Bibliographies

979 **Mideast File, 1982-**
Oxford, England; Medford, New Jersey: Learned Information, 1982- . quarterly.
An index of books, articles, government publications and research projects on all the Middle Eastern countries, including Egypt. Issued by the Shiloah Center, Department of Middle Eastern and African History, Tel-Aviv University.

980 **The Middle East: abstracts and index.**
Pittsburgh, Pennsylvania: Library Information and Research Service, 1978- . quarterly. Author and subject indexes.
Offers citations, with abstracts, of English-language materials in the humanities and social sciences related to the Middle Eastern countries. Egypt is well covered.

981 **Al-Kutub al-'arabīyah allatī nushirat fī Miṣr bayn 1926-1940.** (A bibliography of Arabic books published in Egypt between 1926 and 1940.)
'Ā'ida Ibrāhīm Nusayr.   Cairo: American University in Cairo Press, 1980. 2nd ed. 315p.
Includes 4,538 titles, which the editor compiled from all the major libraries of Egypt, arranged by subject following the Dewey classification. The introduction is in English and Arabic. Now standard, this work replaces all previous sources.

982 **Al-Kutub al-'arabīyah allatī nushirat fī Miṣr bayn 1900-1925.** (A bibliography of Arabic books published in Egypt between 1900 and 1925.)
'Ā'ida Ibrāhīm Nusayr.   Cairo: American University in Cairo Press, 1983. 596p.
A companion volume to the author's *Bibliography of Arabic books published in Egypt between 1926 and 1940*, compiled from the holdings of more than thirty major libraries as well as from written sources, this work offers author and title indexes with reference numbers and will replace all previous bibliographies, including the Sarkis bio-bibliographical dictionary, which has been long regarded as standard for the period.

983 **Arab education 1956-1978: a bibliography.**
Compiled by Veronica S. Pantelidis.   London: Mansell Publishing, 1982. 552p.
A comprehensive bibliography in which Egypt is dealt with on pages 98-165. Articles, books and dissertations on education in Egypt are covered under such headings as: administration and supervision, adult education, agriculture, art, associations, cuisines, curricula, educational exchange, educational technology, elementary education, evaluation guidance and counselling, and health professions. A total of 835 entries on Egypt are included.

984   **The quarterly Index Islamicus: current books, articles and papers on Islamic studies.**
Edited by J. D. Pearson.   London: Mansell, 1977- .
An essential bibliography of books and articles covering all aspects of history, social sciences, culture, and literature. There is a section on Egypt in every issue. For earlier works, see *Index Islamicus 1906-1955* (Cambridge: Heffer, 1958), and the various supplements. Books are not included before 1976.

985   **Ancient Egypt: sources of information in the New York Public Library.**
Compiled by Ida A. Pratt, under the directorship of Richard Gottheil.   New York: New York Public Library, 1925. 486p.
A classified bibliography of books and articles in European languages on Ancient Egypt, covering all the aspects of Ancient Egyptian history, culture, civilization, language, religion, art and music. A supplement, *Ancient Egypt 1925-1941*, appeared in 1942.

986   **Modern Egypt: a list of references to materials in the New York Public Library.**
Compiled by Ida A. Pratt, under the direction of Richard Gottheil.   Nendeln, Lichtenstein: Kraus Reprint, 1969. Reprint ed. 320p.
Books and articles in Middle Eastern and European languages arranged by topic in a bibliography originally published in 1929 (New York: New York Public Library).

987   **Women in the Middle East and North Africa: an annotated bibliography.**
Ayad al-Qazzaz.   Austin, Texas: Center for Middle Eastern Studies, University of Texas at Austin, 1977. 178p. (Middle East Monographs, 2).
A total of thirty entries in this bibliography relate to Egyptian women.

988   **The modern Arab woman: a bibliography.**
Michelle Raccagni.   Metuchen, New Jersey; London: Scarecrow Press, 1978. 262p.
The section in this bibliography relating to Egypt covers 64 pages and includes 801 entries. The subjects include Islam, rural women, bedouin women, Coptic women, marriage and the family, education and sports, and literary works. Although unannotated, this is the most comprehensive bibliography on Egyptian women.

989   Recueil de firmans impériaux Ottomans adressés aux valis et aux
      Kedives d'Egypte, 1006-1322 H (1597 J.-C.-1904 J.-C.). Réunis sur
      l'ordre de Sa Majesté Fouad ler, Roi d'Egypte. (Catalogue of
      imperial Ottoman edicts addressed to the valis and Khedives of
      Egypt. Compiled at the order of His Majesty King Fuad I of
      Egypt.)
      Cairo: Institut Français d'Archéologie Orientale du Caire, 1934.
      366p.

Contains 1,064 such firmans or edicts. Includes a list of Turkish words with their
French equivalents.

990   The Dār al-wathā'iq in 'Ābdīn Palace at Cairo as a source for the
      study of the modernization of Egypt in the nineteenth century.
      Helen Anne B. Rivlin.   Leiden, The Netherlands: E. J. Brill,
      1970. 134p.

A list of the Arabic, Ottoman Turkish, and European-language documents and
registers in the archives of the royal palace. Has a ten-page introduction and nine
appendices which tabulate the collection.

991   Articles on the Middle East, 1947-1971: a cumulation of the
      bibliographies from the Middle East Journal.
      Edited by Peter N. Rossi, Wayne E. White.   Ann Arbor,
      Michigan: Pierian Press, 1980. 4 vols.

Covers Egypt among the other countries of the Muslim world. The emphasis is on
modern history, politics, social conditions, language and literature from the 19th
century to the present. Material in all European and Middle Eastern languages is
included. Volume I covers 1947-54, volume II 1955-65, volume III 1966-71.
Volume IV includes subject, author and title indexes and a list of periodicals.

992   Materials for a corpus of Arabic documents relating to the history
      of Syria under Mehmet Ali Pasha.
      Asad Rustum.   Beirut: American University Press, 1930-34. 5
      vols. in 4.

Original archival materials of court and public records preserved in private
collections.

993   Selected bibliography of Arab educational materials, 1976- .
      Compiled by the Documentation Center for Education.   Cairo:
      al-Ahram Center for Scientific Translations, 1978- . biannual.

This bibliography includes published literature in Arabic and English on
education in the Arab countries including Egypt. It covers topics such as abilities,
school administration, adult education, Arabic language teachers, art education,
civics, curricula, education and democracy, and educational planning.

994   **American doctoral dissertations on the Arab world, 1883-1974.**
       George Dimitri Selim.   Washington, DC: Library of Congress,
       1976. 2nd ed. 173p. Supplement, 1975-1981: Washington, DC:
       Library of Congress, 1983. 200p.

A list of United States and Canadian dissertations on all subjects related to the
Arab world accepted from 1883 to 1981, including dissertations on Egypt.

995   **Catalogue of the Coptic and Arabic manuscripts in the Coptic
       Museum, the Patriarchate, the principal churches of Cairo and
       Alexandria and the monasteries of Egypt.**
       Marcus Simaika, Yassa Abd al-Masih.   Cairo: Bulag
       Government Press, 1939-42. 2 vols.

Volume I includes 304 entries and 56 plates, volume II 1,105 entries and 57
plates. English and Arabic indexes are provided.

996   **Theses on Islam, the Middle East and North-West Africa (1880-
       1978) accepted by universities in the United Kingdom and Ireland.**
       Compiled by Peter Sluglett.   London: Mansell, 1983. 147p.

Includes over 3,000 titles. The section on Egypt (p. 55-67) covers the following
subjects: agriculture and agrarian reform, architecture, biology, economics,
education, geography, geology and palaeontology, history before 1798, history
after 1798, language and dialect, law, literature, medicine, politics and political
thought, religion and social studies. Has subject and author indexes and an
addenda section for titles accepted since 1978.

997   **A bibliography of the literature of the city of Cairo.**
       Abdel Rahman Zaki.   Cairo: Société de Géographie d'Egypte,
       1964. 40p.

Consists of two sections, dealing respectively with Arabic and with Western
languages. Includes books and periodical articles.

Bibliographies

998 **Annual Egyptological bibliography.** (Bibliographie égyptologique annuelle.)
Compiled by Jozef M. A. Janssen. Leiden, The Netherlands: E. J. Brill, 1948- . annual.
The first volume of this bibliography covered 1947. Subsequently, volumes have appeared at irregular intervals to cover each year's publications, with changes in editors and publishers. The latest volume, vol. 35, is for 1981, and is 'compiled by L. M. J. Zonhoven with the collaboration of W. Brunsch and I. Hofmann' (Warminster: Aris & Phillips for the International Association of Egyptologists, 1985). From 1979, the bibliography has been organized under subject headings. The gap between the supplement to Ida A. Pratt's bibliography (q.v.) and the first volume of the *Annual Egyptological bibliography* was filled by the 'Egyptian bibliography Jan. 1, 1939-Dec. 31, 1947' by Walter Federn published in *Orientalia*, vols. 17-19 (1948-50).

Middle East Journal.
See item no. 1017.

Periodicals

999 Annales du Service des Antiquités de l'Égypte.
Cairo: Service des Antiquités, 1900- . irregular.
In its earlier years this periodical published many important excavation reports and articles by scholars of many nationalities. In recent years, it has tended to confine itself to reports of many excavations undertaken by the Service itself. It includes some articles in English.

1000 Bulletin de l'Institut Français d'Archéologie Orientale.
Cairo: Institut Français d'Archéologie Orientale, 1900- . annual.
This institute was founded in 1880 and exists to carry out excavations and research, and to issue publications, with the intention of widening knowledge of Egyptian history from the pharaohs to the Islamic period. In addition to the *Bulletin*, the Institute publishes *Annales Islamologiques* (1900- . annual), and sometimes supplements to the *Annales* are issued (1946-).

1001 La chronique de'Égypte.
Brussels: Fondation Égyptologique Reine Élisabeth, 1925- . annual.
One of the major periodicals devoted to Ancient Egypt, consistently publishing work of high quality, with an equal commitment to pharaonic, Graeco-Roman, and Christian Egypt. Includes articles in English.

1002 Economic Bulletin.
Cairo: National Bank of Egypt, Research Department, 1947- . quarterly.
An important source of information on economic conditions and development in Egypt, published in Arabic and English. Each issue includes notes and comments, leading articles, a quarterly economic review of the Egyptian economy, information on the economic activities of other countries, and a statistical section.

Periodicals

1003 **Economic Indicators.**
Cairo: Central Agency for Mobilisation and Statistics, 1952- .
monthly.

1004 **Economic Review.**
Cairo: Central Bank of Egypt, 1960- . quarterly.
This review is issued in Arabic and English by the Research Department of the
Central Bank, and deals with economic developments in Egypt and abroad.

1005 **L'Egypte Contemporaine.** (Contemporary Egypt.)
Cairo: Society of Political Economy, Statistics and Legislation,
1910- . quarterly.
A journal which covers social, economic, political and cultural aspects of
Egyptian society. Articles are published in Arabic, French, and English.

1006 **Egyptian exports and industries.**
Cairo: Middle East Public Relations Co., 1969- . annual.
This directory aims at giving a general review of the varied aspects of Egypt's
industry, trade and agriculture. Listed for easy reference are the names, addresses
and main lines of activity of all public and private sector manufacturers,
producers, exporters and business concerns.

1007 **International Journal of Middle East Studies.**
New York: Middle East Studies Association of North America,
1970- . quarterly.
Contains many articles about Egypt, and covers all aspects of historical, political,
economic and social studies, as well as literature, culture and Islamic studies
generally, including contemporary affairs.

1008 **The Journal of Egyptian Archaeology.**
London: Egypt Exploration Society, 1914- . annual
Publishes articles, chiefly in English, on every aspect of Egyptology, including
Graeco-Roman and Coptic Egypt. Prints regular preliminary reports on the
Society's various excavations in Egypt and Nubia.

1009 **Journal of the American Research Center in Egypt.**
New York: American Research Center in Egypt, 1962- .
irregular.
Publishes scholarly articles and book reviews on Ancient Egypt. The Center also
publishes a *Newsletter*.

1010   **Al-Kitab al-Sanawi Li Ilm al-Ijtim'ā.** (Egyptian yearbook of
   sociology.)
   Edited by Mohammed al-Jawhari.   Cairo: Dar al-Maaref,
   1980- . annual. Mainly in Arabic.
An annual which publishes the contributions of Arab sociologists and aims to help
towards understanding and solving the problems of Arab society. English
summaries of papers in Arabic are included, and one quarter of the papers are
published in English.

1011   **List of current periodicals.**
   National Library Cataloguing Department.   Cairo: National
   Library Press, 1959. 86p.
A list of Western-language periodicals in the National Library of Egypt, classified
by subject. Includes an alphabetical index.

1012   **Al-Majallah al-Misriyah lil-Ulum al-Siyasiyah.** (Egyptian political
   science review.)
   Cairo: Egyptian Society of Political Science, 1963- . monthly.
An Arabic-language academic publication which contains articles on theoretical
and applied political, economic and social sciences. Each issue contains one
article in either French or English. Most articles are written by university
professors.

1013   **Majallat al-Iqtisad wa al-Siyasah wa al-Tijarah.** (Review of
   economics, politics and business studies.)
   Cairo: Cairo University Press, 1953- .
An Arabic-language journal containing academic articles on economics, political
economy, politics and related business topics. Each issue has one article either in
French or English.

1014   **MEN Economic Weekly.**
   Cairo: Middle East News Agency, 1962- . weekly.
Reports the news relating to economics, finance, business, government and
technology in Egypt and the Arab countries.

1015   **Middle Eastern Affairs.**
   New York: Council for Middle Eastern Affairs, 1950- . monthly.
This periodical is mainly concerned with current affairs in the Middle East, and
20th century history. Many issues contain articles about Egypt.

1016   **Middle Eastern Studies.**
   London: Cass, 1964- . quarterly.
This periodical is mostly concerned with the 19th and 20th centuries, and has a
strong historical bias, though it also includes articles on contemporary affairs.
Many issues contain articles about Egypt.

Periodicals

1017 **Middle East Journal.**
Washington, DC: Middle East Institute, 1947- . quarterly.
An English-language periodical which regularly publishes book reviews, bibliographies and chronologies of events in the Middle East, as well as academic articles.

1018 **Middle East Observer.**
Cairo: 8 Chawarby Street, 195?- . weekly.
An English-language weekly.

1019 **Middle East Review.**
Saffron Walden, England: Middle East Review, 1974- . annual.
Each volume includes a survey on Egypt which covers politics, foreign relations, social conditions, budget, development plans, foreign investment, etc.

1020 **Population Studies.**
Cairo: Population and Family Planning Board, Research Office, 1973- . quarterly.
A scientific journal specializing in the publication of studies and research reports in English and Arabic related to demographic concerns and issues.

1021 **Revue d'Egyptologie.** (Review of Egyptology.)
Paris: Société Française d'Egyptologie, 1933- . irregular.
A multi-lingual periodical which had issued 36 volumes up to 1985. Specializes in Egyptology and Ancient Egyptian culture, language, social life and history up to the Islamic period.

1022 **Zeitschrift für Ägyptische Sprache und Altertumskunde.** (Journal for the study of Egyptian language and antiquity.)
Leipzig: J. C. Hinrichs'sche Buchhandlung, 1863- . irregular.
The first major Egyptological periodical, still published (now by Akademie Verlag, Berlin). Includes articles in English.

Country report: Egypt.
See item no. 762.

Middle East Economic Digest.
See item no. 775.

Indexes

There follow three separate indexes: authors (personal and corporate); titles; and subjects. Title entries are italicized and refer either to the main titles, or to other works cited in the annotations. The numbers refer to bibliographic entry rather than page numbers. Individual index entries are arranged in alphabetical sequence.

Index of Authors

B

Bacharach, J. L. 948
Badawi, M. M. 488
Badawi, el-S. M. 449
Badawi, Z. 380
Badawy, A. 898
Badawy, S. Z. 420
Baddour, A. el-F. I. el-
S. 715
Badeau, J. S. 2, 333
Badeeb, S. M. 677
Badran, M. 584
El Badri, H. 347
Baer, G. 102-103, 110,
383, 695, 823, 850
Baer, K. 154
Bahig, A. F. 449
Baikie, J. 200
Baines, J. 127, 361, 922
Baker, A. 357
Baker, R. W. 302
Baker, Sir Samuel W.
264
Bakir, A. M. 461-462
Balbaa, S. 883
Ball, J. 27
al-Banna, Hasan
381-382
Bar-Siman-Tov, Y. 303
Barawy, R. al- 759
Barbour, K. M. 809
Bardenstein, C. 321
Barker, E. B. B. 231
Bartlett, S. C. 65
al-Barudi, M. S. 488,
521
Bassili, W. F. 369
Basta, M. 370
el-Batrik, A. H. 110
Bayyoumi, A. 424
el-Baz, F. 28
el-Beblawi, H. 771
Beeson, I. 316
Behn, W. H. 487
Behrens-Abouseif, D.
104
Beinin, J. 692
Bell, H. Idris 201, 427
Belon, Pierre 66
Ben-Dor, G. 616
Benedick, R. E. 29

Berg, W. 38
Berger, M. 384, 556,
650
Berque, J. 252
Beshai, A. A. 785
Beshara, A. 751
Bevan, Aneurin 722
Bevan, E. 202
Beyerli, J. 489
Bianchi, R. 851
Bierbrier, M. 128
Bikar, H. 899
Bindari, S. 490
Bindary, A. 420
Binder, L. 617-618
Birdi, I. T. 232
Birks, J. S. 839, 852
Blackman, A. M. 478
Blackman, W. S. 557
Blake, G. H. 30
Blaxland, G. 105
Bleser, P. 87
Blunt, W. S. 265
Boatner, H. L. 25
Boktar, A. 872
Booth, M. 341
Borthwick, B. M. 619
Bosworth, C. E. 492
Botman, S. 620
Botros, S. 931
Boutros-Ghali, B. 668
Boullata, I. J. 486
Boullata, K. 515
Boulos, L. 92
Bowman, A. K. 203
Boyd, D. A. 932
Brackman, A. C. 163
Brademeyer, B. 848
Bradford, E. 204
Bratton, F. G. 129
Bréant, M.-T. 68
Brejnik, A. 78
Brejnik, C. 78
Bremond, Gabriel 67
Briggs, M. S. 900
Brinton, J. Y. 651, 731
Broadhurst, R. J. C.
223
Broadley, A. M. 266
Brown, D. S. 732
Brown, K. 571
Browne, Edward 68

Brugman, J. 491
Brunner-Traut, E. 922
Brunsch, W. 998
Bruton, H. J. 693, 760
Budge, Sir E. A. Wallis
463-465, 477
Bull, D. 69
Bulloch, J. 304
Bullock, M. 183
Burckhardt, J. L. 492
Burckhardt, T. 901
Burden, S. K. 420
Burkhardt, R. 598
Burns, W. J. 733
Burri, C. 63, 87
Butcher, I. 937
Butler, A. J. 215
Buttery, A. 130

C

Cachia, P. 493
Calvocoressi, P. 331
Caneve, I. 375
Cantori, L. J. 621
Cappelletti, L. 785
Cappin, Jean 70
Carman, B. 71
Carpenter, F. G. 72
Carr, D. W. 761
Carre, O. 622
Carsten, A. 778
Carter, B. L. 428
Carter, Howard 131
Carter, M. 132
Castela, H. 63
Černý, J. 358
Cezzar Ahmed Pasha
245
Chambers, R. L. 102,
400, 591, 847, 885
Chapot, V. 109
Charles-Roux, F. 109,
253
Chirman, M. 571
Chirman, S. 571
Chitham, E. J. 429
Choucri, N. 810
Chown, J. 792
Churchill, R. S. 694
Churchill, W. S. 694

Index of Titles

255

257

261

the year 1885
inclusive 975
Lives of the pharaohs
167
Local politics and
development in the
Middle East 621
Lonely minority: the
modern story of
Egypt's Copts 448
Lost pharaohs: the
romance of
Egyptian
archaeology 135
Love songs of the New
Kingdom 481
La lutte de classe en
Egypte de 1945 à
1968 571
Luxor Museum of
Ancient Egyptian
art: catalogue 945

M

Magic and medical
science in ancient
Egypt 161
Mahkama! Studies in
the Egyptian legal
system. Courts and
crimes; law and
society 655
Mahmoud Said 897
Maiden of Dinshway
498
Al-Majallah al-Misriyah
lil-Ulum
al-Siyasiyah 1012
Majallat al-Iqtisad wa
al-Siyasah wa
al-Tijarah 1013
Making of a war: the
Middle East from
1967 to 1973 304
Malāmih miṣrīyah 909
Mameluke or slave
dynasty of Egypt:
1260-1577 A.D.
243

Mamluk costume: a
survey 914
Mamlūk military
society: collected
studies 230
Man of defiance: a
political biography
of Anwar Sadat
321
Man who did not see
the next day 548
Man who lost his
shadow 500
Man who loved Egypt:
Bimbashi
McPherson 71
Management
development in
Egypt 815
al-Manar 882
Manners and customs
of the modern
Egyptians 13
Manpower and
employment in
Arab countries:
some critical issues
860
Manuscript, society and
belief in early
Christian Egypt
377
Many sisters 577
Marital bliss 518
Materials for a corpus
of Arabic
documents relating
to the history of
Syria under
Mehmet Ali Pasha
992
Mawsū'at al-masraḥ al-
miṣrī:
al-bībliyūjrāfīyah,
1900-1930 958
Maze of justice 501
Al-Mazini's Egypt 534
Mechanization of the
National Library
catalogues: Egypt
946
Mediaeval Cairo and

the monasteries of
Wādi Natrūn: a
historical guide 56
Medical doctors: a
study of role
concept and job
satisfaction – the
Egyptian case 602
Memoirs from the
women's prison
341
Memoirs of Hasan al-
Banna Shaheed
(1906-1949) 382
MEN Economic
Weekly 1014
MERI Report: Egypt 18
Midaq Alley 527
Middle East: abstracts
and index 980
Middle East and North
Africa 16
Middle East and North
Africa: a political
geography 30
Middle East and the
Western Alliance
675
Middle East
contemporary
survey, 1976/77- 17
Middle East Economic
Digest 775
Middle East economies
in the 1970s: a
comparative
approach 757
Middle East in crisis: a
historical and
documentary
review 330
Middle East in
paperback 972
Middle East Journal
1017
Middle East mission:
the story of a major
bid for peace in the
time of Nasser and
Ben-Gurion 700
Middle East Observer
1018

273

275

Index of Subjects

277

Ancient Egypt *contd.*
bibliography 985
birds 94
civilization 155, 170, 196197
culture 115, 150, 185, 1021
customs 141
drawings 919
first nation-state 152, 164, 191
health 144
historical geography 155
history 122-199
jewellery 896, 926
law 8, 150, 168
literature 8, 476-485
manners and customs 141
medicine 161
monuments 75, 82, 84
see also Pyramids; Tombs
musical instruments 921
periodicals 1001
popular stories 484
rediscovered 73
religion 58, 356-367
science and technology 8
social life 150, 177, 1021
structure 163
women 160
Angiospermae 97
Anglo-Egyptian relations 283, 289, 296, 720
dispute 717
(1882-1956) 295
1899 agreements 715
(1914-51) 721
Anglo-Egyptian treaty (1936) 285, 297, 726
Animal products 161
Ankhesenamum 134
Annapolis 736
Anthropology 23, 398, 562

Anticolonialism 496
Anti-imperialism 571
Anti-peace movement 308
Apion family 205
Apollo Group 488
al-'Aqiqi, N. 882
Arab conquest (640 AD) 109, 114, 201, 203, 206, 215, 217, 220
see also Muslim conquest
Arab embargo 686
Arab International Insurance Company 803
Arab League 705, 709, 726
publications 941
Arab Socialist Union 641, 648
Arab solidarity 299
Arab states and Suez (1956) 295
Arab treaties 715
Arab world 579, 684
biographical dictionary 24
Cairene dialect 453
education 881
Egypt's role 687, 689
employment planning 860
influence of Muslim Brothers 622
publishing 936
role of lawyers 665
socialist movement 629
Arab-Israeli wars (1947-1974) 696
(1967) 25, 113, 704
see also Attrition; June War; October War
Arabesque design 917
Arabia 653
Arabic language 449-455
alphabet 451
Cairene 453, 455

dictionaries 449-451, 454
Egyptian 449-450
colloquial 451-452, 454
literary 497
Arabic Language Academy 882
Arabic sources 110, 220, 224, 239, 297, 376, 477
Arabism 274
Arabs 70
desert 63
Archaeologists 6
see also Egyptology; Excavators
Archaeology 32, 50, 75, 106, 182, 939
bibliography 939
Bronze Age 193
major sites list 359
oases 32
Old Kingdom 159
periodicals 1000, 1008
Upper Egypt 49
see also History; Pyramids; Tombs
Archaic period 122
Architecture 200, 923, 996
bibliographies 960-961
Bulaq 237
feudal Nubia 375
history 898
Islamic 47, 54, 904, 960
Mamluke 910
mosques 900
Old Kingdom 122
Archives 922
bibliographies 990, 992
British 110, 261, 624
Egyptian 261, 290, 624
European 990
French 261
National 956
preservation 950

Royal Palace 990
training at Cairo
University 949
Turkish 110, 990
Armenia
Egyptian conquest
227
Armenian Orthodox
Church 373
Armenian rite 373
Armenians 83
in modern Egypt 431
Army
Ancient Egypt 130,
168
Byzantine 210
(1870s) 734-736
Mamluke 227, 229
political role 646
see also Military
Art 5, 8, 15, 19, 21,
189, 200, 361, 871
Ancient Egyptian
189, 915, 945
birds 94
contemporary 899,
920
Coptic 371, 905, 915
education 983, 993
Islamic 901, 904, 912,
960
Mamluke 910
modern 909, 920
Old Kingdom 122
Artefacts
Ancient Egyptian 181
stealing 6
Arts 447, 895-929
ballet 895
bibliographies
960-961, 964
jewellery 896,
926-927
painting 897, 909,
920
pottery 161, 912, 927
sculpture 905
asala (traditionalism)
406
Ashmolean Museum,
Oxford
Egyptian Galleries 170

Assassination of Sadat
(1981) 314, 324,
393, 399, 567, 613,
668
Asset ownership 836
Assyūt 117
ASU see Arab Socialist
Union
ASV-CODAR system 952
Aswān 5, 49, 84
governorate 117
immigrants 419
see also High Dam
Aton worship 195
Attrition, war of (1969-
70) 303, 337
AUC
see American
University in Cairo
Authoritarianism 633,
776, 889
Authority
men over women 576
Autobiographies 503
Amīn, Ahmad 486
Hegab, Sayed 506
Hussein, Taha
510-512
Mūsā, Salāma 538
El Saadawi, Nawal
543
Sadat, Anwar 343
Awlad Ali tribe 576
awqaf deeds 237, 244
Ayyūbids 230
Azbakiyya 104
al-Azhar, S. 379
al-Azhar Square 930
al-Azhar University,
Cairo 119, 402,
511, 871, 874
centre of Muslim
learning 388
fear of modernization
400
al-Aziz, caliph 218

B

Baghdad 229, 586
al-Bahi, M. 882

Bahrain 221
Bahri Mamlukes (1250-
1390) 235, 241
Bahriya oasis 32
Bahriya regiment 229
Baibars I 241, 243
Balance of payments
765
Ballas 106
Ballet 895
Bani Suwayf 117
Banishment
Mamluke period 230
Bank Misr 693, 805,
814
Banking 18, 447, 805
directory 794
al-Banna, Hasan 395
Barrier Method Study
413
Bartlett, E. J. 65
Başbakanlik Arşivi,
Istanbul 110
Basic needs 560, 585,
836, 855
Basilica 38
Basketry 802, 927
Battles
(3200 BC-621 BC)
130
Megiddo 173
BBC see British
Broadcasting
Corporation
Beads 161
Bedouin
economy 116
settlement 103
Bedouin revolts
(1309-1341) 236
Begin, Menachem 308,
702
Beheira Province 630
Beirut 860
Beirut University
College, Lebanon
978
Beliefs 90
Ancient Egyptian 359
and contraception 413
Nubian 398
shaped by Islam 262

Davies, N. M. 481
da'wa (propaganda)
226
De Lesseps, F. 275
Dealers in antiquities
138
Death
Ancient Egyptian
hopes 360
life after 362
Debt 18
Decipherment
of hieroglyphs 464,
474
Rosetta Stone 465
Decision-making 817,
839
Decrees 965
Defeat by Israel 350
Defence 18
Ancient Egypt 177
Byzantine Egypt 206,
210
pact with Syria 681
Deir el-Medina 128
Deities 148, 361, 364,
367
Delta see Nile Delta
Demigods 148
Democracy 496, 660,
776
liberal 633
symposium (1976)
625
Demography 18, 772,
855, 866-867
periodicals 864, 869,
1020
profiles 420
resettlement areas
423
Tahir Province 424
see also Population
Demotic texts 474, 477
Dendur temple 124
Department of
Egyptian
Antiquities, British
Museum 149
Dervishes 80
Deserts 67, 77, 90, 99
development 843

see also Eastern
Desert; Negev;
Western Desert
Developing nations 770
Development 578
bibliography 974
desert 843
economic 17, 420,
585, 749-790, 808,
847, 862
influence of politics
621
natural resources 826
role of women 597,
607
rural 821, 829
(1952-67) 828
social
(1800-1914) 847
statistics 870
Development planning
1019
(1946-72) 763
Dialects 996
Cairene (Arabic)
453, 455
Sahidic (Coptic) 457-
458, 460
Dictionaries
Arabic 454
bio-bibliography 982
Coptic 456
of hieroglyphs 463
of politics 648
al-Din, K. M. 379
Diocletian 206
Diplomatic history
(1798-1812) 256
19th century 731
20th century 295
Directories 16
book world 937
business 794, 804
personnel 4
science and
technology 892
social scientists 23
Disability
social security 608
Disease 144
and overpopulation
412

see also Illness
Dissertations
bibliographies 963,
976, 994, 996
Divinities 362
Diwan Group 488
Domes 910
Domestic economy
Ancient Egypt 150
Domestic politics 298,
308
Domestic trade 25
Dominican monks 76
Dongola expedition
(1896) 714
Drama
Ancient Egyptian 478
Arabic 502, 518, 532,
548, 552
of al-Hakim 502,
504-505, 518, 525
development 522
Drawings
Ancient Egyptian 919
bibliography 975
Drugs 66
Dutch mission to Nubia
370
Dynasties
Ancient Egyptian
143, 175
Ayyubid (1169-1242)
223
Fatimid (909-1171)
221, 224
Shi'ite 224
21st-25th 156
see also Ancient
Egypt; History

E

Early Christian period
Upper Egypt 49
East Africa 735
East Canal 844
Eastern Desert 38
Ecclesiastical history
427
Ecology 29, 99
Economic assistance
programmes

Biblical times 169
see also Arab-Israeli
war
Israeli-Egyptian wars
303-304
Israelites 65, 169, 174
Istanbul 10
Italians 431
Ivory work 905, 912

J

Jaffa 78
Japan
grant for opera house
918
relations with Egypt
675
Jerusalem 63, 76-78
visit of Sadat 305,
323, 343, 699
Jesus 530
see also Christ
Jewellery 927
Ancient Egyptian
896, 926
Jewish antiquities 427
Jewish influence
on early Christian
Church 377
Jews 438, 442, 446, 471
attitude of Muslims
405
campaign against in
Palestine 279
in Roman Egypt 427
19th-century Egypt
110
jihad (holy war) 226,
393, 402
Jirjā 117
Jordan 621
Palestine problem
706
Journalism 447, 935
Judges
(640-860 AD) 219
Judicial authority 651
Judiciary 244
June War (1967) 304-
306, 317, 406, 747

Justice 574
Ancient Egypt 150,
168
Ottoman empire 244
under Turks 63

K

Kahun 137
Project 137
Kamil, F. 518
Karnak 20, 945
recent research 363
kashf (apocalypse) 226
Kaulla Incident (1893)
10
Kenya 72
Khaemwese 9
Khalsa settlement 586
Khedives 264, 272
library 948
see also Ismail
Killearn, Lord 276
King list 463
Kingship
and mythology 181
Kitchener, Lord 288,
726
Knesset 343
Kom Ombo 565
Koran *see* Quran
Kurds 230
al-Kuzbari, Mamum
691

L

Labour 18, 857
agricultural 822
migration 830, 839
constraints 590
expatriate 771, 852,
858
law 802, 853
market 825, 836, 856
movements 686, 851,
853
supply 760
Lactation
and contraception
420

Lakes 27
Land 822
constraints 590
distribution 823, 828,
833, 841
laws 666
ownership 103
tenure 840
Land reclamation 423,
843844
statistics 866-867
Land reform 820-821,
827
before 1952 823
(1850-1950) 110
law (1954) 832
under Nasser 581,
772
Land taxes
Ottoman period 110
revenues 225
Landholding
Ottoman period 110
Landowners 403, 823,
832
Language and writing
Ancient Egyptian
143, 461475, 985,
1021
see also Hieroglyphs
Languages 449-475,
991, 996
Arabic 449-455
Cairene 453, 455
Egyptian 449-452,
454
Coptic 456-460, 474
Egyptian (ancient)
461-475
Late Egyptian
literature 485
Latin rite 373
Law 23, 244, 996
Ancient Egyptian 8
and social change 662
bibliographies
964-965, 977
business 652, 795,
802
Fatimid 226
Islamization 765
labour 802, 853

291

Law *contd.*
land reform (1954)
832
Muslim family 653
shari'a 661-663
Law reform 577, 653
(1850-1950) 110
Lawyers 667
Lear, Edward 133
Lebanon 621
invaded by Israel
(1982) 692
relations with Egypt
238
Left, political 611, 614,
631, 637
Legal reform
see Law reform
Legal status
women 576, 978
Legends
Holy Family in Egypt
369, 372-373
Legitimacy
British army in Egypt
285
Léon, Jean 67
Lexicons
Arabic-English
449-451, 454
Coptic 459
English-Arabic 449,
451
Liberal
Constitutionalist
Party 110
Liberalism 634
Liberalization
economic 305
political 623, 643
Libraries 937, 981-982
automation 943, 946
Khedival 948
National 946-948,
950, 956, 964, 1011
statistics 864
university 949, 953
Library of Congress 957
Libya
union with Egypt 579
Libyan wars
pharaonic period 173

Life after death 362
Linguistic reform 497
Literary criticism 491,
494, 535, 546
bibliography
(Hussein) 519
Literary history 535
Literary renaissance
493
Literary trends
since 1952 352
Literature 8, 15, 360,
636, 991, 996
Ancient Egyptian 8,
476-485
Arabic 486-552
bibliographies 981-
982
bibliographies 975,
984, 997
Byzantine Egypt 206
periodical 1007
Livestock production
826, 839
Local government
Byzantine Egypt 205
London University 780
School of Oriental
and African
Studies
Centre of Middle
Eastern Studies
352
Love 481, 514, 542
Lower Egypt 20, 36,
831
immigrants 419
Lungfish 375
Luxor 3, 5, 20, 172, 363
Museum 945
Lyons 80
Lyric poetry
Ancient Egypt 481

M

Magic 169, 471
mahdi 226
Mahdists *see* Dervishes
Maḥfūẓ, Najīb 539

Mahmud, S. A. al-H.
379
al-Mahzūmī 217
Maize
production 831
el-Malakh, Kamal 151
Malnutrition 598
Mamluke and Turkish
rule (1250-1798)
227-251
architecture 900
see also Ottoman
Empire
Mamluke sultanate 230
Mamlukes 109
art and architecture
910
costume 914
Management 23, 815,
817
foreign companies 4
health care 598
of countryside 821
worker participation
816
Manchester City Art
Gallery 902
Manchester University
137
Manpower 757, 849-863
and education 876
export 852
scientific 890
shortages 858
statistics 868
Manufacturing industry
812
Manufiyah 117
Manuscripts
bibliographies 975,
995
illuminated 912
Ottoman 237
Mariette 9
Marine scientists 28
Mariout 843
Market economy 776
Maronite rite 373, 444
Marriage 77
advertisements 553
Marsi, Abdel Wahab
899

391, 395-396, 401,
622, 627, 973
founded 1928 394
Muslim conquest 112
see also Arab
conquest
Muslim leaders
in boycott movement
280
Muslim radicalism
(1954-66) 399
Muslim religious
institutions
al-Azhar 388
Muslim world 2, 864
Muslim writers 379
Muslims 76, 444, 711
attitude to Christians
405, 533
to Jews 405
relations with Copts
445, 448
rituals 91
sympathy 76
Syrian 447
al-Mustaali, caliph 218
Mustafa Fahmi crisis
269
al-Mustansir, caliph 218
al-Muwailihi 10
Mystical dances
Dervishes 80
Mythology
Ancient Egyptian
357, 362, 364, 366
and kingship 181

N

Nada, H. 909
Naji 488
Naji, M. 909
Nakhla, M. 909
Napoléon 73, 109, 253
artists accompanying
133
Commission of
Sciences and Arts
968
French expedition to
Egypt 474

military aims 259
political aims 259
invasion (1798) 260
Nasser, Gamal Abdul
2, 14, 107, 121,
298, 302, 308, 311,
314, 329, 342, 353-
355, 610, 620, 678,
691, 700-701, 716,
733, 743-744, 758
and Heikal 935
and Islamic
fundamentalism
394, 622
as author 332-334
biography 322, 326,
345, 349
charismatic leader
325
death (1970) 305-306,
317
ideology 339, 611, 636
land reform 581, 832
mass media 938
military regime 355
nationalization of
Suez Canal 317,
327
overthrow of Farouk
317
personal
relationships 312
position of Copts 443
régime analysed 611
revolution (1952) 7,
279, 329, 615
Charter 334
goals 332
philosophy 333-334
rural development
829
secular ideas 301,
396, 614
speeches against
Islamic Pact 671
Nasser revolution
see Coup (1952);
Nasser, Gamal
Abdul; Revolution
(1952)
Nasserism 311, 571,
617, 637

decline 406
political economy 750
'Nasserite Model' 889
National Bank of Egypt
782, 805
National Charter (1962)
659
National Export Bank
796
National income
statistics 864, 869
National independence
487
National Information
and
Documentation
Centre 943, 952
National integration 10
National Library of
Egypt 946-948,
950, 956, 964, 1011
National movement 12,
14
(1870s) 270
(1919) 252
National Progressive
Unionist Grouping
631
National security 22
National Spinning
Company 814
National
transformation
254, 558
Nationalism 291, 293,
612, 637
and Jews 438
development 296
Egyptian-Arab 617
in modern Egypt 271,
274, 280
(1919-39) 624
Islamic 296
liberal 644
Syrian 437
Nationalization 772
education 873
Suez Canal 317, 327,
346
textile industry 814
'Native son' concept
575

295

Natroon Valley 843
Natural resources
  see Resources
Naval power 229
Near East 10, 647
  culture 503
Nefertari, Queen 134
Nefertiti, Queen 134
  biography 192
Negev desert 65
Neutralism 739
Neutrality 617
New Arab economic
  order 771
New Arab political
  order 771
New Arab social order
  262, 771
New Kingdom
  (1554-1080 BC)
  150, 158
  architecture 898
  literature 483
  ships 158
  tombs 128, 153
New Testament
  historical setting 176
New Valley 843
New York
  Metropolitan
    Museum 123-124,
    146-147
  University 371
Newspapers 686
  directory 937
  statistics 868
Nile Delta 20, 825
  cities
    16th century 87
  fairs and fêtes 71
  morphology 35
Nile expedition (1897-
  98) 714
Nile River 27, 34, 37,
  63, 113, 133
  control 29, 36
  flooding 83
  hydro-politics 788
  see also Nilometer
Nile Valley 27, 35, 67,
  87, 155, 191, 375,
  716

ancient societies 191
British rule
  (1882-1956) 720
land reclamation 843
maps 38
morphology 35
river terraces 27
16th century 87
17th century 67
silts 27
unification 715
Nilometer
  Cairo 39
nisbas 230
Nobles
  guide to underworld
    482
Non-alignment 298, 668
Non-Muslim subjects
  (1309-1341) 236
North Africa 16, 30,
  676
  mass media 932
  (909-1171) 224
  political geography
    30
North America 675
  universities 963, 994
Novels 490-491,
  498-500, 503, 507,
  523, 526-530, 533,
  536, 540, 542, 547
  development 520
  (1913-52) 545
  (1914-70) 537
  of Taha Hussein 493,
  513-514
Nubar ministry 269
Nubia 72, 185
  architecture 200, 375
  Christian 375
  excavation reports
    1008
  8th-century church
    370
  history 106
  Old 398, 565
  religious beliefs and
    practices 398
  16th century 87
Nubians
  ancestral records 144

in Cairo 566
relocation for High
  Dam 36, 432, 434,
  562
Nuclear power 807
Numismatic material
  948
Nur al-Din 216
Nutrition 607

O

Oases 5, 32
  see also Bahriya;
  Faiyūm; Farafra;
  Siwa
Obstetrics 607
Oceanographers 28
October War (1973)
  299, 304, 313-315,
  338, 347, 712
ODA see Overseas
  Development
  Administration
Offering stands 123
Oil 771, 801
  Arab strategy 338
  as political weapon
    299
  foreign exchange
    revenue 760
  production 810
  reserves 779
  surplus revenues 753
Oils and waxes 161
Old age
  social security 608
Old Cairo 63, 215, 944
Old Dongola 375
Old Kingdom 122
  archaeology 159
  architecture 898
  cylinder seals 123
  governmental reform
    154
  literature 483
  ships 151
Old Nubia 398, 565
Old Testament 176
Open-door policy
  (1974) 301, 581,

723, 758, 760, 766,
771, 776, 786
re-assessed 789
Opera house 918
Opportunism
Sadat's 396
Oranges 806
Ordinances 965
Orientalists 882
Ornament 907
Ornithology see Birds
Orthodox Churches 80,
373, 439
Orthodox Greeks 80
Osiris 364-365
cult 362
Ostraca 207
Ottoman conquest
(1517) 217
Ottoman Empire 70,
109-110, 118, 220,
229, 233, 238, 388,
695
administration 249
and Sufism 405
bibliography of edicts
989
family life 593
guilds 850
justice 244
land taxes 110
law of protection and
nationality 666
partition (1886-97)
295
see also Mamluke;
Turkish
Ottoman firearms 228
Ottomanism 499
Overpopulation 412
Cairo 580
Overseas Development
Administration 781
Oxford
Ashmolean Museum
170
University 83

P

Paganism 371
Painters 909, 920
Said, Mahmoud 897,
909
Painting materials 161
Paintings 905, 924, 927,
945
Pakistan 653, 739
Palestine 372, 740
campaign against
Jews 279
conflict 976
history 78
relations with Egypt
668, 692-713
response to
Egyptian-Israeli
treaty 698
South 65
Palestine Liberation
Organization 430
Palestinian identity 430
Pan-Arabism 301, 626,
705
and Jewish
integration 446
Paperbacks 972
Papyri 201, 206-207
bibliographies 967,
975
Byzantine period 206
Greek 427
Roman period 207
Papyrology 201, 377
Papyrus 166
Paris 503
Parliament
Cabinet 623
(1952-77) 625
Pashas 109
Payment system
Mamluke military
society 229
Peace agreement with
Israel 22
see also Camp David
Peace moves 308, 668,
699, 709, 938
see also Camp David;
Sadat

Peace treaty 22
Egyptian-Israeli 697,
710-711, 713
text 702, 710
Peasants 557, 563, 586,
630
and land reform 581,
820
and mass media 934
bibliography 959
migration and
peasant wives 590
social conditions 294,
556
in literature 551
today 3
under the pharaohs 3
see also fellaheen
Pennsylvania
University
Museum 144
Pensions 604
People 5, 15, 21, 81,
801
and development 31
Byzantine Egypt 206
Roman Egypt 207
16th century 63
17th century 67-68,
70, 77
People's Assembly 635
People's revolution 571
Perfumes 161
Periodicals 958, 960,
999-1022
archaeology 1000,
1008
business 1013
culture 1007
current 1011
current affairs 1015-
1016
demography 1020
economics 1002-1005,
1007, 1012-1014
Egyptology 1001,
1008, 1021-1022
history 1007
industry 1005
Islamic studies 1007
literature 1007
Middle East studies

297

299

Women *contd.*.
  (322-30 BC) 213
  in Ancient Egypt 160
  in boycott movement
    280
  in Islamic law 653,
    988
  in Ottoman Egypt
    405
  legal status 978
  literary works 988
  marriage 988
  peasant 590, 592, 988
  public role 588
  religious status 978
  role in development
    597, 607
  social status 978
  sports 988
  status among Awlad
    Ali 576
  status and role 569
  (1980s) 568
  urban lower class 592
  welfare 605
Women's associations
  570
Women's rights 569,
  577
Women's studies
  bibliographies 978,
  987-988

Wood 161
Woodworking 858
Workers 419
  and politics 730
  management
    participation 816
  social insurance 604
World Bank 781, 873
World leaders
  and Nasser 312
World War I 238, 295,
  437-438, 512, 567,
  624, 721
World War II 252, 285,
  295, 620, 624, 717,
  730, 812, 814, 846,
  861, 976
Writing materials 161

X

X-ray studies
  pyramids 142
  royal mummies 144

Y

Yale University 193
Ya'qub Sanu' 270

Yemen 32, 685, 740
  coup d'état (1962)
    677
  North 621
  relations with Egypt
    (1819-40) 110
    (1962-70) 677, 679,
    689
  Yemeni civil war (1961-
    67) 317, 677, 679,
    689
Yildiz Collection 110
Yom Kippur War
  see October War
York 83
Young Egypt Society
  638
Young people 502, 529,
  561, 597

Z

al Zafir, caliph 218
al-Zahir, caliph 218
el-Zakyab 375
Zanzibar 735
Zayden, J. 535
Zionism 438
Zoser, King 148

Map of Egypt

This maps show the more important towns and other features.

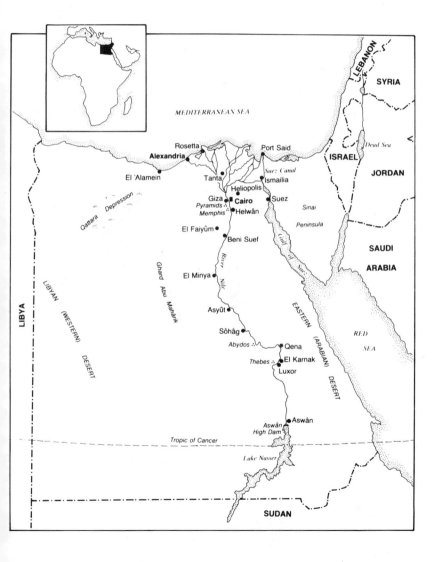